The Lean Accounting Guidebook

How to Create a World-Class Accounting Department

Third Edition

Steven M. Bragg

For more information about AccountingTools® products, visit our Web site at www.accountingtools.com.

ISBN-13: 978-1-938910-80-7

Printed in the United States of America

Table of Contents

Preface

The accounting department is the back office heart of a business. It takes in information from throughout the company and uses it to bring in cash from customers and pay out cash to suppliers and employees. Though it is an essential organ of a business, it tends to attract little notice from an operational perspective. Nonetheless, there are massive differences between the efficiency and effectiveness of average accounting departments and those that operate at a world-class level. The key difference is having a lean focus on how the operation is constructed and operated. *The Lean Accounting Guidebook* reveals how to restructure the department to take advantage of lean principles and catapult it into the realm of world-class organizations.

In Chapter 1, we give an overview of lean concepts and tools. In Chapters 2 through 6, we cover specific improvements to those accounting areas most likely to contain repetitive processes – billings, cash receipts, accounts payable, payroll, and financial reporting. Next, in Chapters 7 through 14, we make dozens of additional recommendations to improve other areas of accounting that involve less repetitive processes, ranging from cost accounting to the general ledger. The presentation in Chapters 2 through 14 includes key terms, tips, podcast references, and flowcharts. We also note in Chapter 15 the need for controls and procedures in a lean environment.

You can find the answers to many questions about lean accounting in the following chapters, including:

- Can a revised invoice layout improve the speed of collections?
- What impact does a bank lockbox have on my cash controls?
- How does a reduction in the number of suppliers impact accounts payable?
- Can I completely automate the collection of timekeeping information?
- Which actions should I take to compress the time needed to issue financial statements?
- Which behavioral triggers by a customer should initiate a credit review?
- What approval level should be used for smaller account write-offs?
- What types of variance reports should the accounting department issue?
- How can adjusting the capitalization limit impact fixed asset record keeping?

The Lean Accounting Guidebook is designed for both professionals and students. Professionals can use it as a reference tool for upgrading their accounting systems, while it provides students with an overview of how the accounting department should operate. Given its complete coverage of lean accounting, *The Lean Accounting Guidebook* may earn a permanent place on your book shelf.

Centennial, Colorado
February 2017

About the Author

Steven Bragg, CPA, has been the chief financial officer or controller of four companies, as well as a consulting manager at Ernst & Young. He received a master's degree in finance from Bentley College, an MBA from Babson College, and a Bachelor's degree in Economics from the University of Maine. He has been a two-time president of the Colorado Mountain Club, and is an avid alpine skier, mountain biker, and certified master diver. Mr. Bragg resides in Centennial, Colorado. He has written the following books and courses:

7 Habits of Effective CFOs
7 Habits of Effective Controllers
Accountant Ethics [for multiple states]
Accountants' Guidebook
Accounting Changes and Error Corrections
Accounting Controls Guidebook
Accounting for Casinos and Gaming
Accounting for Derivatives and Hedges
Accounting for Earnings per Share
Accounting for Inventory
Accounting for Investments
Accounting for Intangible Assets
Accounting for Leases
Accounting for Managers
Accounting for Stock-Based Compensation
Accounting Procedures Guidebook
Agricultural Accounting
Behavioral Ethics
Bookkeeping Guidebook
Budgeting
Business Combinations and Consolidations
Business Insurance Fundamentals
Business Ratios
Business Valuation
Capital Budgeting
CFO Guidebook
Change Management
Closing the Books
Coaching and Mentoring
Constraint Management
Construction Accounting
Corporate Cash Management
Corporate Finance
Cost Accounting (college textbook)
Cost Accounting Fundamentals
Cost Management Guidebook
Credit & Collection Guidebook
Developing and Managing Teams
Employee Onboarding

Enterprise Risk Management
Fair Value Accounting
Financial Analysis
Financial Forecasting and Modeling
Fixed Asset Accounting
Foreign Currency Accounting
Fraud Examination
GAAP Guidebook
Hospitality Accounting
How to Run a Meeting
Human Resources Guidebook
IFRS Guidebook
Interpretation of Financial Statements
Inventory Management
Investor Relations Guidebook
Lean Accounting Guidebook
Mergers & Acquisitions
Negotiation
New Controller Guidebook
Nonprofit Accounting
Partnership Accounting
Payables Management
Payroll Management
Project Accounting
Project Management
Public Company Accounting
Purchasing Guidebook
Real Estate Accounting
Records Management
Recruiting and Hiring
Revenue Recognition
Sales and Use Tax Accounting
The MBA Guidebook
The Soft Close
The Statement of Cash Flows
The Year-End Close
Treasurer's Guidebook
Working Capital Management

On-Line Resources by Steven Bragg

Steven maintains the accountingtools.com web site, which contains continuing professional education courses, the Accounting Best Practices podcast, and hundreds of articles on accounting subjects.

The Lean Accounting Guidebook is also available as a continuing professional education (CPE) course. You can purchase the course (and many other courses) and take an on-line exam at:

www.accountingtools.com/cpe

Chapter 1
Overview of Lean Accounting

Introduction

There is always room for improvement in any accounting department. However, few controllers know which processes are inefficient, which improvements to make, or even what kinds of outcomes they should be targeting. The overall goal of a lean accounting environment is to create a department that operates in a frugal manner, while still retaining the capability to meet a specific set of goals on a consistent basis. By engaging in improvements designed to reach this goal, a controller can contribute to the operations of a business in a cost-effective manner.

In this chapter, we define a lean accounting department, while also explaining the concepts that interfere with the creation of such a department. We also make note of several tools that can be used to spot areas of potential improvement, as well as to evaluate changes that have been made. The topics addressed in this chapter are only general conceptual issues; in the following chapters, we define faulty accounting processes and then show exactly how they can be changed to achieve lean results.

> **Related Podcast Episode:** Episodes 59 and 228 of the Accounting Best Practices Podcast discuss lean accounting in general and the best practices trap, respectively. The episodes are available at: **accountingtools.com/podcasts** or **iTunes**

The Definition of Lean

The simplest definition of lean from the perspective of the accounting department is to maintain the function while spending as little as possible. However, the department must meet certain objectives that are time sensitive, such as preparing financial statements, paying employees, and issuing customer invoices. These tasks must be handled within certain time constraints, which introduce bottlenecks into a department that might be operating with minimal staffing. Consequently, we need a looser definition of the lean concept when applying it to the accounting department. Thus, we propose the following mix of characteristics for lean accounting:

- *Minimize resource usage.* There is certainly an overall goal of being cost-effective, but this goal is subject to the following limitations.
- *Maximize cash flow.* The effective management of customer billings, cash receipts, credit, and collections can have a strongly positive impact on cash flows from customers, but doing so may require additional expenditures.
- *Minimize transaction errors.* A major problem in many accounting departments is the amount of time spent tracking down and correcting transaction

errors. It usually requires far more time to find and fix an error than it would have taken to process the transaction correctly in the first place. Thus, eradicating errors is a key target when trying to minimize resource usage. Error eradication requires enhanced levels of employee training, so training costs can be expected to increase.

- *Enhanced financial analysis.* As noted later in the Lean Cost Accounting chapter, the department can generate very specific financial analyses that, if acted upon, can increase company profits. Doing so calls for an investment in the cost accounting area.
- *Rapid reporting.* A company needs feedback on its results, and this calls for a rapid-turnaround financial reporting system, which will only be effective if it is adequately supported.

In short, the controller needs to understand that the accounting department is primarily a cost center for which cost minimization is expected, but only within the goals of maximizing inbound cash flows, providing excellent financial analysis, and issuing financial reports as rapidly as possible.

Now that we have an understanding of lean as it applies to accounting, we turn to a discussion of several issues that impact the creation of a lean system of accounting.

Issues that Interfere with a Lean Department

There are a number of issues that can interfere with the realization of a lean department. Problems can arise in many areas due to unnecessary costs, slow processing flows, additional work that is not needed, and inherent inefficiencies. All of these issues are excellent starting points for improvement projects. Examples are:

- *Bottlenecks.* A visual review of any accounting process can easily spot the bottleneck – the place where work piles up, while anyone downstream from that spot is starved for work. By knowing where the bottlenecks are, it is possible to adjust staffing levels and work flows to reduce or even eliminate the bottlenecks.
- *Controls.* A prudent controller wants to have a number of overlapping controls placed throughout the accounting processes, to ensure that mistakes are avoided and fraud prevented. However, controls introduce additional costs, and also slow down processes. Consequently, it is useful to determine which controls are interfering with the proper functions of the department, and find ways to rework the controls to be less intrusive.
- *Distance.* When the accounting department relies on paperwork coming from outlying locations, this introduces a delay in accounting for transactions. There is also an increased risk of losing documents entirely, because of the prolonged time in transit. Converting to electronic transmissions is usually the answer to this issue.

- *Errors.* Accounting errors require a considerable amount of time to uncover and rectify – and usually take up a disproportionate amount of the time of the senior accounting staff. Consequently, there should be an error collection system in place that aggregates error information. The resulting report can be used to target those error types that arise the most frequently and are the most trouble to correct. A common result is the mistake-proofing of processes to keep errors from ever occurring.

- *Inappropriate technology.* It is possible to have *too much* technology. A truly lean accounting department is one that operates with minimal resource usage. Since some types of technology can be quite expensive, a controller may find that an efficient manual process is more cost-effective than a fancy technology solution. For example, document imaging is probably not necessary in a small accounting department where source documents are readily accessible.

- *Measurements.* The metrics used to monitor the performance of the accounting department and the company at large says a good deal about what is considered to be important. Usually, the focus is on a standard set of ratios that have been in use for years, do not change much, and provide no insight into the underlying issues that create the results shown by the ratios. In short, the time spent creating these measurements is a waste of time. Instead, they should be replaced by lists of specific problems that have arisen, which is a more actionable approach to dealing with measurements. We have provided a list of actionable measurements as part of the discussion in most of the following chapters.

- *Reports.* The reports that the accounting department issues tend to drive some aspects of how the department is structured. The principal example of this is the financial statements, for which a well-organized controller will have a detailed closing procedure that spans several days of intensive work. This type of effort may be applied on a smaller scale to other reports, such as a daily or weekly status or "flash" report. Thus, examining reports in terms of the underlying amount of work can lead to changes in the contents of reports, or the elimination of reports, which in turn can reduce the work load of the department.

- *Wait times.* Whenever a process step moves from one person to another, a wait time occurs before the recipient of the transaction begins work. This wait time can be startlingly long, depending on the size of the work queue already built up in front of the recipient. Further, if there is a really long interval between process steps, the recipient is more likely to require a learning period in which to reacquaint himself with the background of the transaction, and the thought process that brought the item to the recipient's attention. This tends to be a particular problem for general ledger transactions, where the more complex entries may require review by multiple people. Wait times should be of great interest if the controller wants to accelerate the processing of transactions.

- *Work flows.* Some efficiency can be unlocked by examining the physical flow of work through the accounting area. This is driven by many factors, such as:

    o The clustering of employees by functional area
    o Where document storage is positioned in relation to where people are located
    o The positioning of office equipment, such as copiers and printers, in relation to where the staff is located
    o The impact of walls and other obstacles on traffic flows
    o The height of cubicle walls and their impact on communications

    Even a seemingly ideal office configuration should be revisited from time to time, as changes in the work load of the department, its staffing, and the available technology alter the work flow.

Related Podcast Episode: Episode 72 of the Accounting Best Practices Podcast discusses office work flow. The episode is available at: **accounting-tools.com/podcasts** or **iTunes**

In short, the accounting function can safely be considered a target-rich environment. Any reasonably diligent controller will find many opportunities for improvement that will eventually lead to the creation of a lean department.

Lean Tools

This book relies almost exclusively on the application of specific improvement suggestions to enhance the operations of the accounting department. To delve even deeper into the bricks and mortar of an accounting operation to find other improvement opportunities, we list in this section several tools that may be of use. Value stream mapping is used to document a variety of information in each step of a process. Flowcharts are used to provide an at-a-glance visual representation of a process. Accounting run charts are useful for spotting changes in long-term trends that can indicate an out-of-control process. Check sheets are a simple technique for collecting information, usually about error rates. Traffic analysis is used to reduce travel time by the accounting staff by reconfiguring the department. Root cause analysis is used to find the reasons why a problem is occurring. These tools can be used individually or as a group to accumulate the information needed to overhaul the accounting department.

Value Stream Mapping

A value stream map (VSM) reveals a large amount of information about the activities that we engage in to create value. Depending upon the format used, it can point out such information as:

- The work time and wait time required for each step in a process
- The amount of labor needed for a work step, including the identification of overtime
- The error rate by work step
- Downtime by work step

VSM can be applied to the various accounting processes. The resulting charts can be used to pinpoint areas needing improvement, such as reductions in errors, automation to eliminate staff time, and altered controls to shorten process flows.

The VSM concept is best explained with an example. In the following sample of the timekeeping process, we see that the accounting staff requires only a small amount of staffing and time to process two steps, which are issuing reminders to employees and verifying supervisory approval of time cards. However, the VSM indicates that the controller must allocate more staff to the tasks of reviewing received time cards and summarizing hours worked. These latter two tasks are so time-sensitive that they routinely require the use of overtime to be completed on time. The map also shows a high error rate. Further, the VSM reveals that a total of 25.5 hours are needed to complete this step, which is the lengthiest part of the payroll process.

Sample Value Stream Map - Timekeeping

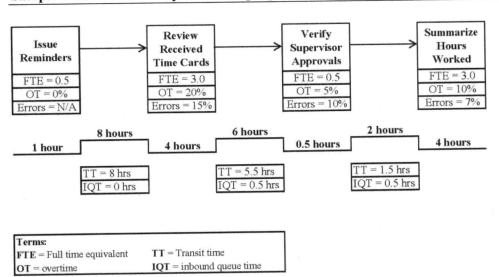

Given the issues shown in the map, it would be reasonable for a controller to implement a more automated method of time tracking, such as a computerized time clock. By doing so, the two bottlenecks in the process can be eliminated, along with overtime and the high error rate. Automation will also likely reduce the total processing time by a substantial amount. The controller might not have realized the severity of the problems with timekeeping without a VSM to clarify the issues.

> **Related Podcast Episode:** Episode 67 of the Accounting Best Practices Podcast discusses value stream mapping. The episode is available at: **accounting-tools.com/podcasts** or **iTunes**

Value stream mapping is an especially effective tool when used to break down the elements of high-volume processes; these processes are completed many times in a typical year, so even small changes can yield large cumulative benefits. Conversely, there is little point in using VSM to analyze tasks that require little time and are only rarely completed, since there is only a modest opportunity for improvement.

Flowcharts

A flowchart is extremely useful for creating a visual representation of how a process operates. It usually incorporates references to any forms and reports used, making it easier to see the complete scope of a process at a glance. Flowcharts are particularly useful for before-and-after views of a process, to see what will happen once a proposed improvement has been installed. For example, the following flowchart reveals what happens to the payroll timekeeping process flow that we just analyzed with a value stream map, after several improvements (noted in bold) are made to the process.

Sample Timekeeping Flowchart

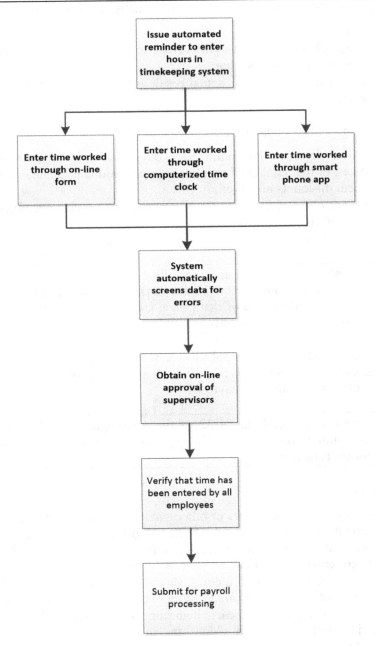

Accounting Run Charts

A run chart shows the performance of a process on a trend line. It is used to highlight spikes or dips in process results that could indicate the presence of problems in the underlying system. This information would then serve as the trigger for a more in-depth investigation. The chart usually incorporates two trend lines, which are:

- *Average.* This is the short-term average results of the process, and should be a straight line across the chart.
- *Actual results.* This is the actual results of the most immediate set of time periods.

Examples of accounting applications for run charts are:

- *Accounts payable.* The number of days to obtain approval of supplier invoices, or the number of supplier invoices paid late, or the number of early payment discounts not taken.
- *Customer billings.* The number of hours to issue a customer invoice, or the number of invoicing errors found by customers.
- *Payroll.* The number of payment errors found per payroll.

Tip: There is always some natural variability around the average results of a process. The accountant should establish the normal amount of variability and then focus on results that fall outside of that range, especially if they remain outside the normal range for a series of consecutive measurements.

Run charts are most useful in applications where there are a large number of transactions, so they are most applicable to such areas as accounts payable, customer billings, inventory valuation, and payroll.

Related Podcast Episode: Episode 32 of the Accounting Best Practices Podcast discusses accounting run charts. The episode is available at: **accounting-tools.com/podcasts** or **iTunes**

Check Sheets

When tallying the number of errors or other events in a process, it is useful to use a structured format, known as a check sheet, to collect the information. This is a simple grid on which is listed down the left side the errors or events that are to be tracked, with columns for each day of the measurement period, and a totals column on the far right side. The intent of a check sheet is to allow someone to easily mark down the number of observed instances of an event within a certain period of time, so that the relative frequency of each item can be determined. Management will likely authorize further action to reduce the instances of whichever items have proven to be the most common.

In the following sample, we show a check sheet that the accounting staff has constructed to compile different types of errors that they are finding while observing a series of cycle counts in the warehouse.

Sample Check Sheet for Cycle Counting Issues Found

	Day					
	Mon.	Tue.	Wed.	Thu.	Fri.	Total
Incorrect unit of measure	II	IIII		I	IIIII	12
Incorrect quantity		II	IIII	I	III	10
Incorrect part number	III	I		IIIII		9
Incorrect bin location	I	I	III		II	7
Total	6	8	7	7	10	38

The sample check sheet reveals that incorrect units of measure have the largest number of observed errors, and so might be worth the most immediate corrective action.

Traffic Analysis

Traffic analysis involves observing the movements of employees through the accounting department, as well as to and from other parts of the company. Write down the tasks which are required within or outside of the department, and the distances traveled while engaged in each one. These observations will likely highlight the need for several changes in the layout of the department, because of the following issues:

- Filing cabinets are clustered at one end of the department, requiring a long walk by those clerks located at the other end of the department.
- Office equipment is clustered at one end of the department, or is located outside of the department, which calls for more travel time by everyone.
- Employees are not clustered together by job function, so they must travel within the department to confer on certain issues.
- Those employees that regularly interact with other departments are not located as close to those departments as possible.

A likely outcome of traffic analysis is the reconfiguration of the department into production cells. A production cell is a work area that is specifically configured to achieve a certain task with a high level of efficiency. The concept has been used for many years in the manufacturing area, where a set of machines may be clustered together to most easily create a particular component. The same concept can be used in the accounting area, which can be configured to most efficiently complete specific tasks. For example:

- *Billing.* A work area can include a computer terminal, all files relating to sales orders and bills of lading, ready access to customer folders, and a printer that is pre-loaded with a supply of the company's invoice form.
- *Cash receipts.* A work area can include a computer terminal, check scanning equipment, a small photocopier, and a safe in which checks may be stored.
- *Payroll.* A work area can include a locked cabinet containing payroll reports and confidential employee information, a computer terminal giving access to computerized time clocks, a printer that is pre-configured for paycheck printing, a safe for the storage of paychecks, and a supply of overnight delivery packages for the issuance of payments to outlying company locations.

The production cell concept may still work even when there are only a few people in the accounting department. A small number of cubicles can be set up in this manner, and employees simply move to a different location when they need to complete a different task.

Root Cause Analysis

Root cause analysis is the task of looking underneath the symptoms of a problem to find the reasons why the problem is occurring. By correcting the underlying root causes of problems, the incidence of the problems can be greatly reduced or eliminated. This approach can be used to uncover issues related to the failure of a system, an error by a person, or an organizational issue (such as an incorrect work instruction). The basic process steps to follow in a root cause analysis are as follows:

1. *Define the problem.* State the issue that requires correction, including a specification of the nature, magnitude, timing, and location of events. A high degree of specificity makes it easier to find a root cause.
2. *Obtain evidence.* Collect data pertaining to the problem. The information obtained should relate to every behavior, condition, action, or inaction relating to the problem.
3. *Ask why.* In going through the collected data, inquire into the factors that directly resulted in an effect. This may involve drilling down through a series of "why" questions.
4. *Eliminate causal factors.* A causal factor is an action or inaction that caused an incident or exacerbated an incident. These are simply triggering events and not root causes, and so no action is taken. For example, an employee turns on a laptop computer, which then explodes. Turning on the laptop was not the root cause, but rather something within the device. In short, we must sort through the data and eliminate causal factors, which leave root causes in the data.
5. *Identify corrective actions.* Note those actions that will likely prevent a recurrence of the defined problem.
6. *Identify usable actions.* From the initial set of corrective actions, identify those that are within the control of the business, are cost-effective, and will probably not introduce a new set of problems. When there are several possi-

ble actions that meet these criteria, pick the simplest one, since it is easier to implement and maintain.

7. *Implement usable actions.* Obtain the required resources and implement those actions considered usable.
8. *Examine outcome.* Review the process to see if the changes are having a positive impact on the identified problem.
9. *Repeat.* If the problem has not been entirely corrected or at least reduced below a threshold level, repeat the process to identify and implement other usable actions.

It is quite possible that finding and correcting a single root cause will not completely eliminate a particular problem. If so, root cause analysis can be conducted on a recurring basis, to gradually locate and eliminate a series of issues. Eventually, the number of times the triggering problem arises may decline to the point where additional effort is considered unnecessary, though there may be additional root causes still causing problems; the remaining issues are simply considered too immaterial to pursue, or their correction is not cost-effective.

Root cause analysis may require a considerable amount of detailed investigation, not only to find a root cause, but also to generate several possible solutions that will correct the root cause. The solution selected will usually be the simplest or least expensive alternative available, and one that does not trigger a new root cause that leads to a new problem or reinforces an old problem.

Root cause analysis suffers from several problems. A key concern is that project teams tend to find problems that they already suspect. Thus, they tend to select and interpret data that supports their existing opinions, which means that new and unique root causes may not be found. Also, this type of analysis does not identify the severity of a root cause, only the existence of the root cause. When there are several possible root causes, this means that management may choose to spend time and resources eliminating an issue that may prove to have a relatively minor impact on a problem. Finally, root cause analysis can be quite time-consuming, since it may involve a large amount of data gathering and investigatory work.

The Lean Culture

We have so far discussed some of the concepts and tools that can be used to build a lean environment, but not the most important factor of all – culture. The entire accounting department must be involved in the gradual evolution to lean concepts. This means that commands are not issued from on high by the controller. Instead, the controller should be working mostly behind the scenes, setting up a system where errors and inefficiencies are readily brought to light, mutually investigated, and corrected.

Creating this environment may come naturally to some controllers, but can represent a complete 180-degree change from the top down, command-and-control style that some are accustomed to. The "new" approach needed to create a lean environment is typified by three management characteristics:

- *Focus on the problem.* All too many managers fundamentally believe that the source of all problems lies with other employees. If they persist in this belief by blaming their subordinates for errors and other process failures, they will receive no cooperation, and will likely see unusually high staff turnover. Instead, they should focus on the system itself as being the cause of most issues. If the entire team can focus on the problem, rather than each other, it is much easier to cooperatively find solutions.

- *Delegate.* There are dozens, if not hundreds, of minor changes that will eventually lead to a lean accounting department. There is no way that the controller can personally initiate or administer all of them. Instead, the controller must be willing to hand off responsibility for many projects to his or her subordinates. Not only does this make it easier to engage in many improvements at once, it also yields better buy-in to projects by those responsible for the projects.

- *Management by walking around.* As we explain in the Lean Cost Accounting chapter, many of the reports issued by the accounting department are not useful, and should be replaced by white boards on which status updates are noted throughout the day. This same approach can be used in the accounting department. The controller should be seen walking around in the accounting area, discussing status issues with the staff, coming to mutual decisions, and supporting them as needed. Otherwise, the accounting staff will consider all the talk about lean concepts to be just another management fad, and will pay little attention to it.

A Note of Caution

We must introduce a note of caution in this discussion of lean concepts. The controller should not attempt to arrive at a lean department by enforcing a tsunami of change. Instead, we strongly recommend an experiment-and-test model. This approach involves the following steps:

1. Measure an unaltered process, so there is quantitative information about its performance.
2. Alter the process on a pilot basis with a new concept, and run the pilot for a sufficiently long time to be reasonably sure that the revised process has settled down and is producing consistent results.
3. Measure the altered process.
4. If the altered process yields improved results, expand or fully roll out the concept. However, if the alteration does not yield a verifiable improvement, either continue altering the process within the existing pilot project or cancel the change.

This type of carefully delineated testing makes it much more likely that the accountant will be able to arrive at a lean operating environment, though the necessary amount of testing will probably delay the end result.

Another consideration when constructing and evaluating a lean system is to only introduce those changes that make sense from a cost-effectiveness perspective. All too frequently, we see controllers embrace advanced technological solutions when their accounting operations are simply too small to make the investments worthwhile. For example, it is absolutely unnecessary to invest in a document imaging system when accounting records are already stored adjacent to the accounting staff, and the incidence of record searches is relatively low. Similarly, a small company that operates from a single location probably does not need to invest several million dollars in an advanced enterprise resources planning system that ties together the operations of every department. Instead, there are simple and inexpensive alternatives to many of these technology solutions that may not be quite as efficient, but which are vastly more cost-effective.

A final consideration is driving down costs *too much*. A controller who is in love with the idea of cost reduction may pursue every possible technological and procedural improvement, usually with the goal of shrinking the headcount within the department. The outcome might appear laudable from the perspective of improving the profitability of the business, since the accounting department is usually perceived to be a cost center. A cost center is any grouping within an organization that incurs costs but does not generate revenue. But is this really the case? The accounting department can also be utilized as an in-house consulting group, offering advice and issuing relevant reports to other parts of the company. If the department's headcount is slashed, this can eliminate any prospect of being able to provide more value to the firm. Consequently, it can make more sense to selectively cut costs through lean practices, while preserving a core group of experienced personnel.

The Failure of Lean Initiatives

A lean accounting system requires that the department engage in a long series of improvement projects. There are a number of reasons why these lean initiatives fail, which can be grouped into a small number of core issues. These issues are noted in the following bullet points, along with suggested methods for avoiding them:

- *Minimal funding.* A lean initiative may require a significant up-front investment of cash. If a controller attempts to initiate a project without a clear source of funds, it is likely that the initiative will die in short order. The result will be a bad reputation for the controller, who is therefore even less likely to receive funding for his next proposed project. Here are several ways to deal with funding issues:

  - When developing a funding proposal, consider all possible expenditures, such as for training, software maintenance fees, and employee overtime. Be pessimistic when deriving these sums, so that the amount of funding proposed is very likely to be sufficient.
  - Have a portfolio of possible lean initiatives, along with the approximate amount of cash needed to fund each one. Then match the amount of available funding to the portfolio, to see which prospec-

tive project is the best match. This approach may not result in the most needed project being addressed first, but it will ensure that whatever is chosen will receive adequate funding.

- *Minimal planning.* If the controller does not create a sufficiently detailed plan for a lean initiative, the project is likely to suffer from a variety of problems, such as excessively short deadlines, too much overtime, not enough staffing, and inadequate funding. A controller who gains a reputation for poor planning is very likely to receive no support from senior management for future projects. To avoid this issue, compile a standard planning template to be used for every subsequent project. This template is likely to be custom-designed, based on the department's record of results from previous projects. The intent of the template is to ask a series of questions to ensure that the necessary level of planning has been addressed, such as:

  - Have the following list of expenses [include a checklist] been included in the budget for the project?
  - Is it necessary to convert data from the old system? Does this include consideration of the complexity of the underlying records that must be converted?
  - Which specific skill sets are needed to ensure that the project is successfully completed? Do these people have prior commitments? Will any scheduled vacation time for these people interfere with the project?
  - Will the project impact the operations of other departments or business partners? If so, has the project been discussed with them? Do they need to have representatives on the project team?
  - Will it be necessary to schedule a pilot phase to test the change? If so, which subset of transactions will be included in the pilot phase, and how will the results be tested?

- *Excessive change.* A really massive lean initiative or an unending series of smaller ones can cause the organization to react negatively, simply because that level of change is unsettling. This reaction may increase over time, to the point where it is impossible to continue making alterations. To mitigate this effect, schedule breaks between lean initiatives, so that the organization can settle down again. Alternatively, move each new lean initiative to a different part of the organization that has been allowed to lie fallow for some time, and which will therefore be less likely to react poorly to the new project. In addition, launch a detailed communications campaign for each project, so that anyone impacted by it is aware of the nature of the change, and how it will alter how they work.

- *Custom programming.* A major cause of failure is when a project requires that the existing software be customized to accommodate a prospective change. When this happens, the customization is likely to take longer than expected, be more expensive than planned, and more likely to fail. In addition, if the customization involves a custom interface to a commercially available software package, expect that the next version of the software will have been sufficiently altered that the custom interface no longer works. Generally, the solution is to completely avoid software customization. It is better to work on other lean initiatives and wait for the next version of the relevant software to be released by the vendor, to see if the needed feature is now available within the standard package.

- *Minimal testing.* Many lean initiatives require some amount of testing to ensure that they work properly. Otherwise, a new project may be foisted upon the organization by an excessively enthusiastic project team, only to crash and bring down some key part of company operations. To avoid this very public failure, it is better to budget for an extended testing period. Also, do not publicize an expected project rollout date, since this can put too much pressure on the testing team to give a passing grade to a lean initiative that is not ready for release.

- *Individual intransigence.* An organization is likely to harbor a few individuals who are entirely comfortable with how their jobs are currently structured, and who do not want to change anything. If a project impacts them, their response may range from passivity to active sabotage. If these actions threaten the project, it will be necessary to shunt these employees aside, and possibly even terminate their employment.

- *Management intransigence.* The probability of success for a project drops markedly when the cooperation of other departments is needed, and drops even more when *many* departments must assist in the effort. This is because other department managers may not see the project as a high priority for them, or do not have the available funding or staff resources, or simply have some level of animosity towards the controller. Given these issues, it is better to initially target projects that can be completed entirely within the accounting department, and then work on projects for which cooperation from other departments is relatively minimal.

- *Multiple accounting locations.* It can be quite difficult to replicate lean practices across multiple locations. There are a number of problems that can arise, including the following:
  - Project teams are given an inadequate amount of time and staff to make changes at each location.
  - Inadequate attention is given to providing sufficient training to employees at each new location.
  - There is an inadequate travel budget, making it more difficult for employees to travel to sites where lean practices are already functioning. This issue also keeps experienced personnel from temporarily relocating to other company facilities to assist with installations.
  - The executive team does not provide sufficient oversite, so that the work becomes bogged down without a senior manager to push it along.

- o Inexperienced personnel are tasked with installing lean practices, usually because they are the only ones currently available to take on the work.
- o Cultural and language differences are not taken into account, so that employees at some locations reject proposed changes.
- o Employees are not required to implement new practices exactly as they were originally formulated, resulting in a large number of modified lean practices across the organization.
- o There can be turf wars between the managers of different locations, where new lean practices are seen as being an attempt to take over certain accounting operations.

- *Missing controls.* A lean initiative may require that certain controls be modified or dismantled (that may even be the point of the project). However, if the revised system of controls is not properly examined, it is possible that a control weakness will be created by the project, which will eventually result in a control breach that could be substantial. To mitigate this risk, have the company's internal or external auditors review lean initiatives before they are implemented, to spot control weaknesses and recommend alternatives.

The preceding points highlight a number of areas in which lean initiatives can certainly fail, or at least be slowed down. One should be highly cognizant of these failure points and guard against them when designing a new project. In general, we recommend that the lean process begin with the simplest, lowest-budget projects that are most likely to succeed. The accounting department can become comfortable with these easier implementations and gain confidence from their success; this mindset can then be used to address more difficult projects. As the organization becomes accustomed to success with its lean projects, senior management will be more likely to assign funding to new projects, while other department managers will be more likely to cooperate with initiatives impacting them. In short, start small and gradually build toward larger lean projects, keeping in mind the pitfalls noted in this section.

The Structure of this Book

In developing this book, we found that lean concepts could be addressed by using two different chapter formats. If a chapter was primarily concerned with a specific process flow, then we began by stating the typical process sequence, pointing out its flaws, and then resolving the issues with a variety of recommendations that then resulted in a more streamlined process flow. During this discussion, we also made note of four issues that can impact a lean process:

- *Bottlenecks.* A bottleneck in a process flow is one in which there are snags or hitches in the process where transactions can pile up. The controller should be cognizant of the areas in which these bottlenecks can arise, and work on removing or mitigating them.

- *Distance.* The physical distance between the members of the accounting department, or between the accounting and other departments can introduce delays in the transfer of documents, and therefore the processing of transactions. Inter-departmental transfers also increase the risk that documents will be lost entirely.
- *Controls.* Some controls can build significant delays into accounting processes. It may be possible to replace obstructive controls with others that do not interfere with a lean operating environment.
- *Error rates.* Some transactions have high natural error rates, which require either prevention controls or additional clerical work to correct. It is sometimes possible to reconfigure transaction flows to reduce these error rates.

In chapters where recommendations were not focused on specific process flows, we instead opted for a more general discussion that did not focus on bottlenecks, distance, controls, or error rates.

In all chapters, tips are provided in highlighted blocks wherever there are possible enhancements to the basic improvement suggestions. In addition, we make note of episodes in the author's Accounting Best Practices podcast that are relevant to the discussion. The indicated episodes can be accessed on iTunes or by finding them on the accountingtools.com website.

Summary

This chapter has covered general conceptual issues for how to review the accounting function and establish a lean culture. The indicated analysis tools are useful for making changes to the accounting department, since it probably contains a number of unique features that must be reviewed, evaluated, and corrected.

However, the vast majority of accounting functions are very similar in *all* companies, and so do not require specialized analysis. For these latter situations, we have provided in the following chapters an extremely detailed itemization of more than 150 improvements that can be applied to a variety of accounting processes, from accounts payable to the production of financial statements. The recommendations should be applicable to most companies, and can put the accountant well on the way to the goal of having a lean accounting department.

Chapter 2
Lean Customer Billing

Introduction

Customer billing is the process of converting shipping information into a standard billing format from which customers will pay the seller. When examining how to arrive at a lean billing function, it is important to understand the key goal of billing – to be paid. This means that the billing process may possibly require *more* effort than has historically been the case to ensure that invoices arrive quickly and are free of errors.

In this chapter, we describe the standard billing system and its characteristics, and then show the impact of improvement concepts. The text includes flowcharts of the billing process after lean concepts have been applied as well as those measurements that are most effective in achieving a lean customer billing process.

> **Related Podcast Episode:** Episode 73 of the Accounting Best Practices Podcast discusses billing best practices. The episode is available at: **accounting-tools.com/podcasts** or **iTunes**

Improvement Concepts

The application of lean concepts in this chapter involves the following improvements to existing systems:

- *Evaluated receipts system.* Being paid by customers based on quantities delivered, rather than from invoices. Customers using evaluated receipts do not need invoices from their suppliers.
- *Payments in advance.* Encouraging customers to pay in advance by using discounts, thereby eliminating most of the problems associated with creating an invoice.
- *Systems integration.* Using integrated computer systems to automatically transfer information to the billing clerk, thereby increasing billing efficiency and reducing errors.
- *Buffer staff.* Having trained accounting personnel on hand to assist with billing during high-volume invoicing periods, which reduces invoice turnaround time.
- *Invoice layout improvement.* Altering the invoice structure to present only the key information needed for customers to pay invoices on time. The intent is to reduce the confusion caused by adding extraneous information.

- *Complex invoice separation.* Splitting complex invoices into several smaller ones to increase the odds of having most of the invoice line items paid on time.
- *Invoice proofreading.* Having a second person review the details of the more complex invoices before they are issued to customers, to reduce the risk of issuing incorrect invoices.
- *On-line invoice entry.* Entering invoices into customer accounting systems with on-line forms, thereby ensuring that invoices are received.
- *Invoice creation at delivery point.* Creating invoices on the customer premises to incorporate issues that might otherwise prevent the customer from paying.
- *Invoice creation at shipping dock.* Creating invoices at the shipping dock and including them with shipments, to ensure that invoices are always created and delivered.
- *Pricing simplification.* Reducing the number of pricing errors on invoices by simplifying the corporate pricing structure and/or number of product configurations.

Billing Processing

The processing of customer billings can be fairly automated or require a large amount of accounting staff time to construct. In this section, we present the outlines of a billing system that requires the manual creation of an invoice, which is still the predominant approach in most businesses. We then follow the outline with a discussion of the problems with such a system.

Billing Processing

The following steps show the basic transaction flow for the creation of a customer invoice. The steps are:

1. *Access shipping documents.* This is a document sent from the shipping department that states what has been shipped to a customer. It is frequently a copy of the bill of lading or packing slip.
2. *Access customer order.* Locate the sales order, of which a copy should have been sent from the customer service department to the accounting department when the customer originally placed an order.
3. *Verify prices (optional).* Compare the prices listed on the sales order to the standard price list, and flag any items that vary from the standard rates for additional review.
4. *Calculate shipping.* Determine the shipping charge to add to the invoice.
5. *Charge sales tax.* Charge the sales tax rate for the government entity in which the customer is receiving the goods.
6. *Print invoice.* If a pre-printed invoice form is used, make sure that it is positioned properly in the printer, conduct a test print if necessary, and print

the invoice. Otherwise, simply print all invoices and verify that they have printed correctly.

7. *Mail invoice.* Stuff the completed invoices into envelopes and mail them.

8. *Retain extra sales order copy (optional).* If the sales order has not been entirely fulfilled, make a copy of it, circle the remaining items that have not yet been shipped, and store it in a pending file. This is eventually matched to the shipping documents for the backordered items when they are shipped.

9. *File documents.* File an invoice copy in the customer's file, along with the sales order and proof of shipment.

10. *Adjust with credit memo (optional).* After the customer receives the invoice, it may take issue with some items and request that adjustments be made. If so, it may be necessary to create a credit memo to alter the net amount of the issued invoice.

The billing process is approximately the same if the company is providing services, rather than delivering products. There are two possible process flows for service billings:

- *Service order.* Employees may be called upon to complete a specific one-time service, after which they indicate the number of hours worked and other charges on a service order, which they submit to the billing clerk. The service order is treated as a notification to invoice the customer.

- *Project based.* Employees may be working for a customer on an hourly or fixed-fee basis, in which case their efforts are usually compiled at the end of each month and converted into an invoice.

Analysis of Billing Processing

The billing process flow requires that information be successfully transmitted from the order entry and shipping departments to the billing clerk, transformed into an accurate invoice, and forwarded to the customer. The timing and nature of these information flows can result in a billing process that is most decidedly not lean. The following bullet points explain these issues:

- *Bottlenecks.* In many businesses, there is a surge of shipping at month-end. Since the billing function is not typically staffed to handle this jump in transaction volume, it may require several days to complete all invoicing for the month, which can delay payment by customers.

- *Distance.* The customer order must be transferred to the billing clerk from the order entry staff, while the shipping notification must be delivered from the shipping department. The inter-departmental transfer of these documents can occasionally result in the delay or loss of documents.

- *Controls.* There is a risk that the billing clerk will not always be notified that an order has shipped, which means that no invoice is sent to the customer.

- *Error rates.* One of the key problem areas with billings is issuing incorrect invoices, since customers then hold up payment until a correction can be made. This also typically calls for the issuance of a credit memo to cancel or adjust the original invoice, which creates additional work for the accounting staff.

In short, the billing function relies upon the accurate and timely flow of information from two other departments in order to initiate an invoice, after which the billing staff may have trouble issuing an accurate invoice in a timely manner. These issues can cause problems with the ultimate goal of customer billing, which is to be paid. In the next section, we will examine a number of improvement options that can increase the ability of a business to be paid on time.

Lean Billing Processing

There are two ways to essentially sidestep all of the invoicing problems noted in the last section, which are to either participate in the evaluated receipts systems used by customers, or to obtain payment in advance from customers. Neither scenario is likely to be the case for most customers, so the typical business must instead use a number of incremental billing improvements. In this section, we first present the two options for sidestepping the billing function, and then proceed to the more likely improvement alternatives.

Evaluated Receipts System

If a customer has an evaluated receipts system, it will pay the company based on the quantities the company delivers, not on an invoice. In fact, such customers do not want to receive invoices. Thus, an evaluated receipts system is the ideal solution for the billing function, since no invoices are issued. However, very few companies use evaluated receipts, so most businesses will find that they must still issue invoices to the vast majority of their customers.

See the Accounts Payable Processing chapter for more information about evaluated receipts systems.

Payment in Advance

The key issues for a billing system are to ensure that there are no invoicing errors, and that the customer's accounts payable staff receives the invoice, with the eventual goal of being paid in full and on time. What if we can eliminate both problems by obtaining payment in advance from customers? This can be accomplished by offering a small discount for payment in advance, and may also be encouraged by offering a somewhat higher commission to the sales staff if they can obtain these kinds of sales. Once the cash is in hand, the billing staff can create an invoice at its leisure, stamp it "paid," and forward a copy to the customer. The only problem with this approach is that the accounting staff must initially spend the time to record the payment as a liability, and then shift the liability into a sale transaction once the goods have shipped or services have been provided.

Systems Integration

A significant problem with the billing function is that the billing clerk must assemble information from multiple departments in order to generate an invoice — the sales order from the order entry staff, and the shipping notification from the shipping department. Given the need to transfer documents across the company, sometimes over long distances, there is a strong likelihood that some of this information will be lost in transit, resulting in no invoices being generated.

The issue can be rectified by installing a computer system where the transactions generated by the order entry, shipping, and accounting departments are fully integrated. Under such a system, the billing clerk is notified by the system as soon as a shipment has been made, and can generate an invoice from an on-line copy of the sales order. An integrated system mitigates the risk of not issuing invoices, while also requiring minimal re-typing of information for each billing — which reduces the incidence of invoice errors.

The downside of having integrated systems is the cost of installing and maintaining them. In particular, the shipping department in some heavy industries can be considered a hostile environment for computer equipment, so that the manual transfer of shipping information may still be needed when the computer system is not functioning.

Buffer Staff

If the billing staff is overwhelmed at month-end by the volume of deliveries that must be invoiced, consider training additional staff to shift into the billing function during this time period. The solution is not without risk, since part-time billing clerks are less practiced in issuing invoices, and so will probably generate more errors. However, it may be possible to use these extra staff in a supporting role, where they increase the overall capacity of the function without causing more errors.

> **Tip:** Installing an integrated billing system eliminates much of the billing bottleneck, since the system allows the billing staff to generate invoices much more quickly than would be the case if invoices were being individually prepared by hand.

Invoice Layout Improvement

It may be possible to make several modifications to the invoice template to reduce the time required to receive payments from customers, as well as to reduce the number of customer payment errors. Consider implementing the adjustments noted in the following table:

Invoice Format Changes

Credit card contact information	If customers want to pay with a credit card, include a telephone number to call to pay by this means.
Early payment discount	State the exact amount of the early payment discount and the exact date by which the customer must pay in order to qualify for the discount.
General contact information	If customers have a question about an invoice, there should be a contact information block that states the telephone number and e-mail address they can contact.
Payment due date	Rather than entering payment terms on the invoice (such as "net 30"), state the exact date on which payment is due. This should be stated prominently.

The goal in creating an invoice format is to present the minimum amount of information to the customer in order to prevent confusion, while presenting the required information as clearly as possible. The following sample invoice template incorporates the invoice format changes that we just addressed.

Sample Enhanced Invoice Template

Complex Invoice Separation

When a company issues a complex, multi-line invoice, there is an increased risk that the customer will find issue with some portion of the invoice and refuse to pay it. The billing staff can mitigate this risk by separating the invoice into a larger number of invoices, each containing one or just a few line items. This approach involves more work by the billing staff, but increases the odds of immediate payment for the bulk of the line items being billed.

This recommendation should only be used for those customers that have a history of arguing over the details of invoices. Splitting apart invoices is not productive when there is a low risk of customer non-payment.

> **Tip:** Be aware that some customers can be quite annoyed when they receive a large number of invoices, so be prepared to abandon this practice if customers complain.

Invoice Proofreading

Some billings are extremely complicated. The billing clerk must assemble many line items of information, as well as account for an array of adjustments and discounts. These invoices will also be reviewed intensively by the customer's accounts payable staff, especially if the company has a reputation for issuing incorrect invoices. There is a strong likelihood that these invoices will be rejected due to errors, which means that even more time must then be spent to create a revised invoice.

The possible payment delay associated with invoice errors makes it nearly mandatory to have an experienced person review these more complex invoices before they are sent to the customer. The best reviewer is usually the person in charge of the business relationship with a specific customer, since they are deeply involved in the work being done for the customer. In addition, it may make sense to have an experienced clerk review these invoices for clerical-level errors that might also lead to invoice rejection.

> **Tip:** The key issue with proofreading invoices is deciding which invoices to proofread, since the process is time-consuming. Possible options are to require an invoice review for all invoices issued to the more picky customers, or to only require reviews when the number of invoice line items exceeds a certain amount, or when only a certain amount of funding remains available for a customer project.

On-line Invoice Entry

Whenever a customer creates an on-line form for the entry of invoices by suppliers into its accounts payable system, the billing department should embrace the form with enthusiasm. There are two reasons why on-line forms are useful:

- *On-line error checking.* Most on-line forms contain error-checking routines that ensure that all required fields are completed, that an authorizing purchase order number (if any) is referenced, and that sufficient funding has been reserved to pay the invoice. Some of these routines are so comprehensive that customer accounting staffs conduct no further invoice reviews. Thus, if the system accepts an invoice, it is more likely to be paid without further examination by the customer.
- *Delivery confirmation.* Once an invoice has been entered in the system, an acceptance message should be issued. This gives the billing staff confirmation that its invoice has been delivered. The company no longer has to worry that an invoice might be lost in transit to the customer.

The downside of on-line invoice entry is that these forms are not known for being quick and efficient methods of data entry. Instead, each form has its own quirks that make it time-consuming to enter invoices.

> **Tip:** Since there is no standard format for the layout of on-line forms, consider creating a standard data entry procedure for each customer's on-line form. The billing staff will likely be more efficient in entering information using these procedures.

Invoice Creation at Delivery Point

One of the ways in which an invoice can be considered in error is when the customer disputes the quantity delivered or the nature of the services provided. In these cases, it may be possible to sidestep the error by having the delivery person or service provider generate the invoice on the customer's premises. This can be done with a simple handwritten form, or through a tablet or smartphone app that creates and e-mails the invoice to the customer.

Once created, the delivery person sends a copy of each invoice to the billing clerk, who enters it into the accounting system. Since the invoice has already been delivered to the customer, there is no rush to input these invoices into the accounting system, which eliminates any bottleneck in the billing function.

There are three issues with creating invoices at the delivery point that may limit its effectiveness:

- *Employee only.* This option is not available when deliveries are made by a third-party freight carrier. Only an employee can generate invoices on-site.
- *Sales taxes.* The person creating the invoice must have access to the correct sales tax percentages to compile the invoice.
- *Training.* Employees must be well-trained in the creation of invoices, since there would otherwise be a significant risk that they might create incorrect invoices.

Invoice Creation at Shipping Dock

A variation on invoice creation at the delivery point is to do so at the shipping point. In essence, the invoice is automatically printed at the same time as the packing slip, and is included on the outside of the shipment. This approach eliminates the risk of not having the billing clerk create an invoice. However, it requires some customization of the accounting software to ensure that an invoice is automatically generated when the packing slip is printed. Another issue is that the customer's receiving staff may not forward the invoice to their own accounting department. Also, this method is limited to physical deliveries; it is useless for the billing of services. In summary, this approach eliminates the risk of not issuing an invoice, but introduces the risk that the invoice will not be sent to the appropriate party within the customer's organization.

General: Pricing Simplification

There is an increased risk of pricing errors on invoices if the system used to derive prices is extremely complex. Pricing complexity can arise not only from an overly enthusiastic sales manager, but also from selling products and services in an enormous number of configurations. If management can be persuaded to simplify the pricing and/or product structure, there will be a reduced risk of invoicing errors. This concept requires the cooperation of people outside of the accounting department, and over whom the controller and CFO have no control, so it is a difficult practice to implement.

Practices to Avoid

From the perspective of having a truly lean accounting system, we advise against the use of any practices that complicate the billing process flow. For example, there may be a temptation to provide an overwhelming amount of evidence to customers that the goods they ordered have arrived, in which case a company could wait several days to obtain proof of delivery from its freight carrier, and attach this information to its invoices. However, doing so delays the invoicing process by multiple days (especially if a customer elects to pay for the slowest form of delivery), and so may also delay customer payment.

Analysis of Lean Billing Processing

For the purposes of reviewing the impact of recommended improvements on the billing function, we will assume that evaluated receipts and customer prepayments are unlikely to arise. Of the remaining improvements, the one having the most profound improvement on the process is the use of systems integration. It eliminates all billing bottlenecks, eliminates all distance considerations between the various departments, and reduces the risk that an invoice will not be issued. The other improvement recommendations reduce the risk of issuing invoices that contain errors.

The use of an integrated system creates a billing function that is considerably more lean than a manual billing system, since there is less paperwork and invoices can be created much more easily. However, the remaining recommendations in this section were largely targeted at the goal of obtaining payments from customers, and so generally added to the work load of the billing department, so that the payment goal could be achieved.

The following flowchart reveals the altered process flow for the customer billing function, assuming the use of systems integration, occasional invoice proofreading, and the on-line entry of invoices into customer systems. To improve the clarity of the flowchart, minor recommendations and alternative forms of invoice preparation are not included. Process improvements are noted in bold.

Lean Billing Process Flow

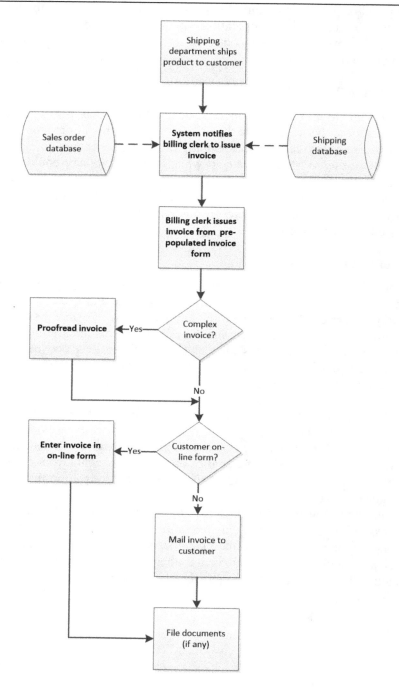

Additional Improvement Concepts

There are a number of additional concepts that can be applied to the customer billing process to enhance its performance or reduce costs. These concepts did not fit into any of the process flows noted previously or were considered minor elements, and so are noted here instead:

- *Issue consolidated invoice.* There are cases where the company sells a large number of low-value items to a customer. This may result in the issuance of a large, detailed invoice at regular intervals. To reduce the total amount of paperwork, consider waiting until the end of the month and issuing a single massive invoice. However, since this also delays the receipt of payment, shorten the allowed payment days for the invoice.
- *Issue invoices early.* If customers are on recurring payment plans, send them invoices a few days early. This is easy for the seller, since it already knows the amount that will be billed. Doing so may slightly accelerate the receipt of payments from customers. Better yet, debit their bank accounts or charge their credit cards for these pre-arranged amounts on predetermined dates.
- *Reduce number of copies.* If the company stores multiple copies of each invoice, question why this is needed. It may be possible to only archive one copy of each invoice. Better yet, see if the controller is comfortable with simply storing invoice records in the computer, and printing them out as needed.
- *Request address correction.* It can be useful to stamp "address correction requested" on the outside of any envelopes mailed to customers. The postal service will notify the company if the customer's address has changed, which is useful for updating company mailing records.
- *Review address.* The sales staff has the best knowledge of who should be receiving company invoices, which could be important if there will otherwise be a risk that the invoices will be shuffled around the customer, looking for an official approver. Consequently, it can make sense to first consult with the sales staff before issuing invoices, especially when the invoices are for large amounts.
- *Review contract terms.* Some customer contracts are quite detailed, and require that the seller issue invoices in a very particular format. If the seller does not adhere to the contract terms, the invoice will be rejected. To avoid this issue, institute a full review of all contracts prior to engaging in the construction of invoices, including an examination of the amount of funding remaining on each contract.

Billing Measurements

The following billing-related measurements should be compiled regularly and trigger immediate corrective action by the accounting staff:

- *Billing variances from shipping log.* The billing clerk relies on a notification by the shipping department in order to issue a customer billing. It can be difficult to ensure that this notification is made every time, resulting in some deliveries never being billed. A good measurement is to compare the shipping log (maintained by the shipping department) with the invoice register (resulting from billings). The accounting staff should investigate *all* differences between the two, since these variances are unbilled shipments.
- *Invoice errors.* Whenever the billing staff creates a credit memo to correct an invoice, flag the memo with a reason code that states the invoice error. Then periodically compile a report that shows the various invoicing problems. This is useful information for investigating why errors arose, and how to keep them from happening in the future.

Note that none of these measurements involve ratio analysis. Instead, they require that the accounting staff investigate individual transactions in detail, with the objective of locating and correcting the reasons for billing errors.

Summary

When creating a lean customer billing function, a key issue is to consider the billing function in concert with the collections function. Billings must be of a sufficiently high quality that the job of the collections staff is reduced. It is possible that higher billing quality will actually *increase* the workload of the billing staff, but when considered in conjunction with the workload of the collections staff, the overall efficiency of the combined groups should improve.

Of the improvement suggestions described in this chapter, the installation of an integrated computer system for the order entry, shipping, and billing functions has by far the greatest impact on achieving a more lean process flow. The other recommendations in the chapter either applied to rare circumstances or only impacted the accuracy of invoices.

Chapter 3
Lean Cash Receipts

Introduction

Cash receipts is an area that requires a great deal of manual labor, both to deposit and record cash. The process suffers from the additional risk of cash theft, which requires more controls than for other accounting processes, and which in turn makes the process less efficient.

In this chapter, we describe standard cash receipt systems and their characteristics, and then show the impact of improvement concepts. We provide separate analyses for:

- Check receipts
- Cash receipts
- Credit card receipts

The analysis for check receipts is listed first, because it presents the greatest opportunity for implementing lean concepts. The analysis of cash receipts is listed second, so that a process can be seen for which few improvements are possible, and which should generally be avoided. Credit card receipts are noted last, as being a reasonable alternative to the processing of cash. The text includes flowcharts of processes after lean concepts have been applied, as well as those measurements that are most effective in achieving a lean cash receipts process.

> **Related Podcast Episode:** Episode 137 of the Accounting Best Practices Podcast discusses a lean system for cash receipts. The episode is available at: **accountingtools.com/podcasts** or **iTunes**

Improvement Concepts

The application of lean concepts in this chapter involves the following improvements to existing systems:

- *Bank lockbox.* Shifting the receipt of checks to a third party, thereby eliminating a number of internal check-handling steps and controls.
- *Automatic cash application.* Using the automated application of cash to accounts receivable to reduce manual labor in the same area.
- *Cash application from check copies.* Applying cash from check copies, so that checks can be deposited more quickly.
- *Remote deposit capture.* Scanning check information on-site and submitting it to the bank, to avoid using a courier to deliver checks to the bank.

- *Daily bank reconciliations.* Continually comparing bank to book balances to spot errors.
- *Discounts for credit card purchases.* Offering discounts if customers use credit cards, thereby eliminating the handling of cash.
- *Discounts on company credit card.* Offering discounts to buy with a company credit card, thereby eliminating the handling of cash.
- *Credit card information immediately entered into on-line form.* Processing credit card payments while still in contact with customers, so that errors can be corrected at once.
- *On-line payment apps.* Using payment apps to enter sales transactions, process payment, and issue e-mail receipts at the same time.

Check Receipts Processing, Basic Process

The basic process flow for the handling of received checks has been settled for many years. It involves the receipt, recordation, and depositing of checks by different people, where there are controls in place to monitor the checks at each transfer from one person to the next. This process is designed to mitigate the risk of loss, but does so at the price of being extremely inefficient, as the following discussion will make apparent.

Check Receipts Process

The processing of check receipts involves the transfer of incoming payments from the mailroom to the cashier, then to a bank courier, and finally to a person who reconciles received to deposited cash. The following steps show the basic transaction flow.

1. *Record incoming checks.* The mailroom staff opens incoming mail, records all checks received, and stamps checks "for deposit only," before forwarding payments to the cashier. This step is a control point, designed to keep a second record of check receipts in case the cashier attempts to abscond with any funds.
2. *Transfer checks.* The mailroom uses a locked pouch to transfer checks to the cashier, along with a copy of their record of checks received.
3. *Apply checks.* The cashier records the received checks, either directly to sales or as reductions of specific accounts receivable. The amount of the checks recorded by the cashier should match the amount of the checks recorded by the mailroom staff.
4. *Deposit checks.* The cashier creates a deposit slip for the checks. A courier takes the deposit to the bank, where a bank teller tallies the deposit and issues a receipt.
5. *Match to bank receipt.* The cashier matches the company's record of checks transferred to the bank to the bank's record of the amount received. This step is a control point that can detect checks removed from the deposit by

the courier, or a recordation difference between the cashier and the bank teller.

6. *Conduct bank reconciliation.* At month-end, reconcile the bank's record of check and cash transactions to the company's record. This is not part of the daily check receipts process flow, but is closely related to it.

Analysis of Check Receipts Process

The check receipts process flow is extremely inefficient, given the number of people involved, distances traveled, and inordinate number of controls. The following bullet points expand upon these issues:

- *Bottlenecks.* There are two key bottlenecks in check receipts processing. The first resides in the mailroom, where the mail may not arrive until late in the day, and the mailroom staff may not assign much priority to tabulating check receipts. The cashier is another bottleneck, since this person may have difficulty ascertaining how some payments are to be applied. Further, the company has no control over bank teller availability, which can extend the time period required to deposit funds. The net result is a possible overnight delay before payments can be forwarded to the bank and accepted for deposit.

- *Distance.* Check receipts involves one of the longer physical transfers in any company process. Not only must check payments be sent internally from the mailroom to the accounting department, but they must then be driven to the bank for deposit, which can delay recordation activities.

- *Controls.* The check receipts process is laced with controls, since a business wants to ensure that no payments are lost or stolen. This means that payments are recorded at each step of the process and reconciled to the information recorded in the preceding step, which slows down the entire transaction.

- *Error rates.* Errors are most likely to arise because check totals were incorrectly recorded during one processing step, requiring a reconciliation at the next processing step. Thus, the system of controls is itself causing errors that must be reviewed and corrected.

The preceding issues should make it clear that check receipts processing is one of the least lean tasks in the accounting department. In the next section, we will explore two alternatives that use different enhancements to arrive at more lean solutions.

Lean Check Receipts Processing (with Lockbox)

The best way to create a lean check receipts process is to add a bank lockbox to the front end of the process. In addition, we will cover the use of automatic cash application, since it is frequently initiated from a data feed from the bank that operates the lockbox. However, the key element is the bank lockbox, which is addressed next.

Bank Lockbox

Much of the preceding discussion of check receipts processing relates to the controls over the handling of checks. The process can be made much more lean by having customers send their payments to a bank lockbox. Under this approach, the bank manages the mailbox address to which payments are sent, so that the company is taken out of the business of handling checks. Instead, the bank deposits all checks received, and posts scanned images of all receipts on its website. The cashier then accesses the check images on this secure site, which are then used to record the payments. This approach has the added advantage of posting cash to the company's bank account somewhat sooner, so that the company can take advantage of additional interest income on its invested funds.

The downside of the bank lockbox is a combination of fixed monthly fees and per-receipt fees charged by the bank, which makes this alternative cost-effective only for medium to larger-size companies. If this method does not appear to be cost-effective, then consider the later discussion of remote deposit capture, which may be available for free, and which can accelerate the speed with which cash becomes available to earn interest.

Tip: The bank lockbox concept is especially useful if a company has customers spread over a large region, since it can create a network of lockboxes that are situated close to groups of customers. This network reduces the amount of mail float, and so increases the speed with which cash is deposited.

Tip: If customers persist in sending their payments to the company, rather than to the lockbox, consider having the mailroom staff re-mail these payments to the lockbox, rather than processing them in-house. Doing so eliminates all in-house check handling controls and procedure steps.

Automatic Cash Application

When a company receives a large number of customer payments every day, it can be quite difficult for the cashier to apply the receipts against open accounts receivable in a timely manner. If so, deposits may be delayed. The cash application process can be substantially reduced through the use of automatic cash application.

Automatic cash application requires that the lockbox operator use a data feed to forward to the company the magnetic ink character recognition (MICR) information from each check received at the lockbox, as well as the total payment amount. The cash application software uses a decision table to decide how to apply these payments to open accounts receivable. The automated decision process generally follows these steps:

1. Match the bank account number shown in each check's MICR information to the correct customer. This accesses the correct customer record of open accounts receivable.

2. Only match payments to invoices where the payment amount exactly matches the invoice amount.
3. Of the remaining payments, only match cash to invoices where the cash amount matches the exact amount of several invoices that have just come due for payment.
4. Kick out all remaining payments for manual review.

The decision table can contain more sophisticated rules, such as applying cash if payment amounts do not include the freight and/or sales tax elements of an invoice. As a company examines the payments kicked out by the system, it can gradually adjust the decision table to increase the number of automatic cash applications. However, the variety of deductions taken makes it unlikely that it will ever be possible to completely automate the cash application process. Nonetheless, automatic cash application can greatly improve the speed with which cash is applied.

Analysis of Lean Check Receipts Process (with Lockbox)

The key process improvement for check receipts is the use of a bank lockbox. We have also mentioned automatic cash application in conjunction with the lockbox, because a data feed from the lockbox typically triggers the automatic cash application module. The use of a lockbox has several positive impacts on the check receipts process flow, which are:

- *Bottlenecks.* The only person directly involved in check receipts is now the cashier, so the bottlenecks related to the mailroom staff, courier, and bank teller are eliminated.
- *Distance.* Transaction flows are entirely electronic, so all physical transfers are eliminated.
- *Controls.* Most of the controls in this process relate to the physical handling of checks. Thus, with no checks on hand, most controls are eliminated.
- *Error rates.* There is still a risk of misapplication of cash, but all errors related to incorrect recordation as checks move from one person to the next are eliminated.

The following flowchart reveals the drastically reduced process flow when funds flow through a bank lockbox. Process improvements are noted in bold.

Check Receipts Lean Process Flow (with Lockbox)

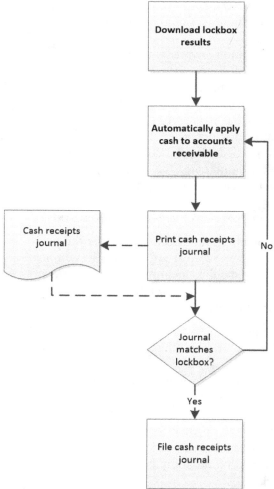

Lean Check Receipts Processing (without Lockbox)

It is not always cost-effective to operate a bank lockbox. If so, this section contains several possibilities for creating a more lean process flow for the in-house processing of checks. In total, these alternatives do not result in as clean a process flow as a system using a bank lockbox, but there is still an improvement over the traditional check processing system.

Apply from Check Copies

The cashier may sometimes receive check payments from customers for which there is no information about the invoice being paid. If so, the cashier may be tempted to hold onto the check until the uncertainty is resolved and the payment can be applied properly. However, doing so means that cash is not available to earn interest, presents the risk that the check could be stolen or mislaid while it is on-site, and creates a difference between the amount of checks recorded by the mailroom staff and the amount deposited each day.

A simple technique for eliminating these issues is for the cashier to photocopy all payments received and to apply cash from the copies, rather than from the payments. Doing so means that the full amount of daily receipts can be deposited at once.

> **Tip:** Having check photocopies available might result in some laziness in applying cash, since the cashier knows this task can now be deferred. To guard against late applications, assign a senior clerk to review all remaining unapplied check payments every day.

Remote Deposit Capture

A remote deposit capture system involves the use of a check scanner and bank-provided scanning software that creates an electronic image of each check to be deposited. The accounting staff then sends the scanned check information in an electronic message to the bank, rather than making a physical deposit. The bank accepts the deposit information directly into its database, posts the related funds to the company's account, and assigns funds availability based on a predetermined schedule.

Remote deposit capture requires slightly more time by the accounting staff to prepare a deposit (by scanning checks) than by the traditional approach of preparing a deposit slip. However, it completely eliminates the time required to make a physical deposit at the bank, as well as the control point of matching the bank's receipt to the deposit slip.

> **Tip:** Remote deposit capture has the side benefit of allowing a company to do business with a bank that is not located nearby. Thus, a business can search among a larger group of banks for the best pricing deal.

> **Tip:** Some banks require a monthly scanner rental fee. Consider shifting to a bank that offers the scanning equipment for free, or attempt to negotiate a lower rental charge.

Remote deposit capture will require the inclusion of new steps in the check processing work flow, which are:

1. Derive the batch total for all checks to be scanned.
2. Scan all checks in the batch.
3. Match the scanned total to the batch total and adjust as necessary.
4. Transmit the batch to the bank.

5. Print and retain a deposit slip.

There may also need to be an additional step to retain the scanned checks for a short time to ensure that they have been accepted by the bank, after which they should be shredded or perforated with a "deposited" stamp.

Conduct Daily Bank Reconciliation

The trouble with the typical month-end bank reconciliation is that recordation problems are only uncovered at long intervals. If the cashier wants to maintain more accurate cash records, it usually makes more sense to access the bank's on-line account records every day, and use this information to maintain a daily bank reconciliation.

A daily reconciliation almost certainly requires more accounting staff time to complete than a single month-end reconciliation, and does not therefore contribute to having a lean accounting function. However, it is quite effective from the perspective of finding and correcting recordation problems immediately, and also ensures that the company's cash records are correct at all times.

Analysis of Lean Check Receipts Process (No Lockbox)

Applying cash from check copies and using remote deposit capture eliminates some of the traditional check processing steps, and has several positive impacts on the process flow, which are:

- *Bottlenecks*. The courier and bank teller are eliminated, making it more likely that checks can be applied and deposited within one day.
- *Distance*. The funds transfer to the bank is now electronic, though the physical transfer of checks from the mailroom to the cashier remains.
- *Controls*. Cash remains on-site, so most controls are retained, with the exception of those involving the courier.
- *Error rates*. Error rates may decline slightly, since the cashier now has more time in which to apply payments to accounts receivable.

The following flowchart reveals the altered process flow when no bank lockbox is used, but where other alternatives are employed to streamline the process flow. Process improvements are noted in bold.

Check Receipts Lean Process Flow (No Lockbox)

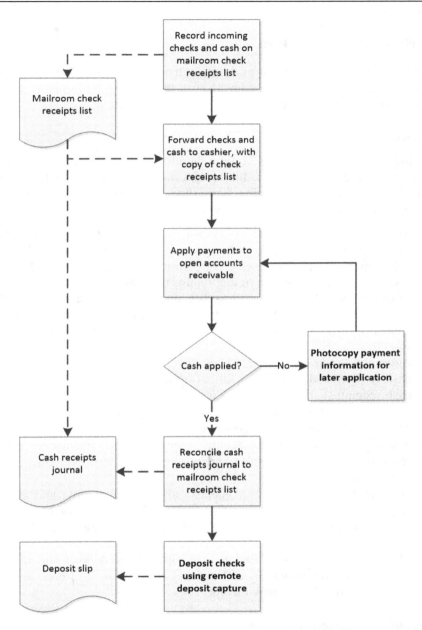

Clearly, the most lean alternative is to move checks completely off-site with a bank lockbox. Retaining *any* check processing on-site immediately expands the process flow, controls, and error rate by an order of magnitude. Thus, the key point with implementing a lean check receipts processing function is to *completely* eliminate the in-house receipt of checks. Otherwise, the process flow remains excessively complicated.

Cash Receipts Processing

The cash receipts process is about as far away from the lean concept as it is possible to go. In this section, we will document how the process traditionally flows, and move on to possible process improvements in the next section.

Cash Receipts Process

Cash is the most fungible of all assets, and therefore the one most likely to be stolen. Because of the high risk of theft, the receipt and subsequent handling of cash is choked with controls. The following steps show only the most basic cash receipts processing steps, but should convey the point that cash receipts is *not* a lean process.

1. *Accept and record cash.* If a customer pays in cash, record the payment in a cash register. If there is no cash register (as may be the case in a low-volume sales environment), the sales clerk instead fills out a two-part sales receipt, gives a copy to the customer, and retains the other copy.
2. *Match receipts to cash.* Compare the amount of cash received to either the cash register receipt total or the total of all sales receipt copies, and investigate any differences. Complete a reconciliation form for any differences found.
3. *Aggregate and post receipt information.* Summarize the information in the cash register and post this information to the general ledger as a sale and cash receipt. If the cash register is linked to the company's accounting system and is tracking individual sales, then sales are being recorded automatically, as is the reduction of goods in the inventory records. If sales clerks are manually completing sales receipts, summarize the information in the sales receipts and record the sales and any related inventory reductions in the general ledger.
4. *Deposit cash.* Prepare a bank deposit slip, retain a copy, and enclose the original slip along with all cash in a locked container for transport to the bank. After counting the cash, the bank issues a receipt stating the amount it has received.
5. *Match to deposit slip.* Compare the copy of the deposit slip to the bank receipt, and investigate any differences. A variation is to compare the cash receipts journal to the bank receipt.

Analysis of Cash Receipts Process

The cash receipts process involves multiple participants and many controls, and so can certainly be considered inefficient. The most critical points of inefficiency are:

- *Bottlenecks.* There are two bottlenecks in cash receipts processing. The first is the sales clerk, who piles up cash receipts in batch mode until someone counts and removes the cash. This delay is not the fault of the sales clerk – the nature of the process mandates that cash will be transferred to accounting in batches. The second bottleneck is the cashier, since the relatively paltry volume of cash (in most businesses) will tend to push cash recordation down in the cashier's list of work activities, below processing checks and credit card receipts.

- *Distance*. There can be a considerable distance between store locations where cash is received and the cashier, who may be located at corporate headquarters. One solution is to assign cashier tasks to a local clerk at each store, though doing so increases the time during which cash is held on-site.
- *Controls*. The amount of cash on hand is counted and reconciled every time it shifts to another person in the cash receipts process flow. Counting and reconciling cash balances can comprise most of the time spent dealing with cash.
- *Error rates*. As was the case with handling check payments, errors are most likely to arise when cash is counted before being passed to the next person in the process flow. Again, this means that the control system itself is causing errors.

Lean Cash Receipts Processing

The preceding description of cash receipts processing makes it depressingly clear that the process contains few redeeming features. It is slow and inefficient. The only redeeming feature, and one which suggests a solution, is that cash comprises quite a small part of sales in many businesses (other than retail operations and casinos). If a business only deals with cash on an incidental basis, the primary solution is to completely eliminate the use of cash. There are two alternatives available:

- *Offer discounts for credit card purchases*. This alternative may seem counter-intuitive, since every business is charged a fee by its credit card processor when a payment is made by credit card. However, the complete elimination of cash payments may reduce paperwork to such an extent that the extra credit card fee still represents a cost-effective solution. Also, the discount can be more precisely targeted at the holders of debit cards, since purchases made with debit cards involve smaller processing fees for a business.
- *Offer discounts on company credit card*. As has been the case for many years, larger businesses offer their own credit card to customers, usually with an up-front cash savings. This approach immediately changes an impending cash payment to a credit card payment, while also placing the customer on the company's mailing list for future marketing activities.

In short, we can only suggest the complete elimination of cash from a company's list of accepted payments – there is no lean practice that can make a noticeable dent in this overwhelmingly inefficient procedure.

Credit Card Receipts Processing

The basic process for credit card receipts has been in place for a long time, but a combination of new hardware and software apps are now available that can improve the process flow. This section describes the current credit card receipts process, and the next section addresses enhancements to it.

Credit Card Receipts Process

The following steps assume the most complex version of credit card payments, where card information is written down and then manually entered into an on-line form. This more complex approach is used to illustrate the opportunities available with a lean system.

1. *Collect information.* Record not only the information needed for the credit card payment, but also the contact information for the customer, in case it is necessary to verify or replace credit card information.
2. *Enter card information.* Access the credit card processing site on the Internet and enter the credit card information through an on-line form. When the information is accepted, print a receipt and staple it to the sales receipt. If the payment is not accepted, contact the customer to verify or replace the card information.
3. *Record the sale.* Enter the sales receipt into the accounting system as a sale. Then stamp the sales receipt as having been recorded.
4. *Issue receipt to customer.* If customers pay by phone or e-mail, send them a receipt, which they may need when they reconcile their company credit card statements at the end of the month.
5. *Verify the transaction.* Before filing sales receipts for credit card transactions, verify that the cash related to them has been posted to the company's bank account, and that they were posted to the accounting system.
6. *File documents.* File the company's copy of the sales receipt, as well as the attached credit card processing receipt, in the accounting records by customer name. If an invoice was printed as part of the sale, then file all three documents together.

Analysis of Credit Card Receipts Process

In the following analysis of credit card receipts, take particular note of the feedback loop required to contact the customer if a card payment is not accepted. This loop introduces significant delays into the process.

- *Bottlenecks.* The time required to record credit card information, enter it into an on-line form, and then send a receipt back to the customer is so time-consuming that the clerk handling these transactions could become a bottleneck.

- *Distance.* If the customer is not physically positioned at the store location, and so is calling in with a credit card number, the more difficult credit card processing transaction just described is required.
- *Error rates.* When credit card information is being manually entered, the error rate is extremely high. The problem is caused by a combination of taking down credit card information incorrectly, and/or incorrectly inputting the information into the on-line form. The error rate is much lower when a credit card is swiped to obtain card information.

Lean Credit Card Receipts Processing

Though credit card processing involves a well-established procedure, the approach involving the manual entry of card information can be enhanced with either of the following improvements.

Enter Information in On-line Form Immediately

The largest flaw in the preceding description of credit card transactions is that the order taker is separating the collection of credit card information from the entry of this information in the on-line form provided by the company's credit card processor. This separation of tasks requires that information be written down and *then* entered, possibly also requiring a call back to the customer if the information was incorrect or the credit card was not accepted.

The lean approach is to call up the on-line form while still in contact with the customer, and enter the information immediately. Doing so eliminates the need to write down the customer's information, since it is going straight into the on-line form. Also, there is no need for a time-consuming feedback loop to obtain additional information from the customer, since the customer is still on the phone with the order taker if any problems arise.

This approach requires that the on-line form be available when customers call with orders, which may be a problem if the form is configured to automatically close after a certain amount of time has passed. However, it is still fairly efficient to log back into the form for every customer order, since logging in is much less time-consuming than the full process described earlier.

On-line Payment Apps

The full process flow described for the on-line entry of credit card information can be reduced with any of the on-line apps now available for smart phones and tablet computers. These apps allow the accountant to create a sale transaction on a portable computing device by typing in or swiping credit card information, processing payment with an integrated on-line form, and sending an e-mail receipt to the customer.

This combination of a fully integrated payment processing and receipt issuance platform allows for the elimination of many steps in the traditional credit card processing transaction. In essence, payment information is both collected and confirmed in one step, leaving only a final step to record the sale transaction.

The main problem with these apps is that they do not also relieve inventory when a sale is made, so this approach works best when a company is not using a perpetual inventory system.

Analysis of Lean Credit Card Receipts Process

The following bullets point out that the use of payment apps can increase the front-end bottleneck, though the overall process flow is much more lean and subject to fewer errors:

- *Bottlenecks.* There can be an increased bottleneck when on-line forms or on-line apps are used, rather than the delayed credit card processing noted for a traditional system. This can increase the wait time for those customers waiting in queue to be served.
- *Distance.* An integrated payment app allows a company to process any credit card transaction while still in communication with customers, so there is no longer a distance consideration.
- *Error rates.* Error rates related to payment should be nonexistent, since the approval of a credit card payment can be confirmed at once. It is still possible to have errors related to which items are sold, since a sales clerk could easily enter the wrong sale information in the app.

The following flowchart reveals the altered process flow when an on-line payment app is used to process credit card payments. Process improvements are noted in bold.

Credit Card Receipts Lean Process Flow

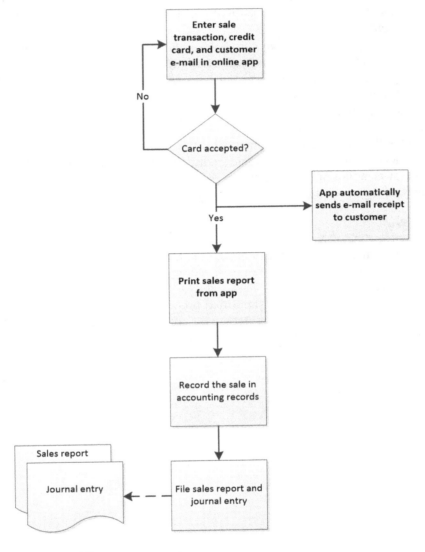

Cash Receipts Measurements

There are a minimal number of measurements for the cash receipts area that will have any great impact on the function's operations. The following two measurements are intended to be reviewed daily, and to trigger immediate corrective action by the accounting staff:

- *Unapplied cash.* Keep continual track of the amount of cash received that has not been applied to accounts receivable or some other account. This cash is most likely associated with open accounts receivable, and so is keeping the collections staff from having a complete view of the amount of accounts receivable requiring collection calls. The amount of unapplied cash can be tracked by reviewing the amount listed in a suspense account in the general ledger.

- *Cash rejected by automatic cash application system.* Whenever payments are rejected by a company's automatic cash application system, the accounting staff should investigate the reasons for the rejections and modify the system's decision table to increase the automatic application rate for future cash receipts.

Note that neither of these measurements involves ratio analysis. Instead, both require that the accounting staff investigate individual transactions in detail, with the objective of cleaning up the accounting records (in the first case) and enhancing the efficiency of the process (in the second case).

Summary

The primary lean concept for the cash receipts function is to completely remove cash and checks from the company premises. Doing so eliminates a number of control points, bottlenecks, and delays. This reduces cash receipts from a cumbersome, multi-person process to a vastly simplified procedure. Key to this effort are the use of a bank lockbox and a variety of credit card processing devices to route all types of payments directly to a company's bank account.

Chapter 4
Lean Accounts Payable

Introduction

Accounts payable is a clerically intensive process that verifies whether payments should be made to suppliers, and then issues the payments. A particular problem is the use of three-way matching to ensure that only the correct unit quantities are paid for, and that only authorized prices are paid. The result is a convoluted process that produces a large number of errors, may not result in timely payments, and which requires an inordinate amount of clerical time.

In this chapter, we describe the standard accounts payable system and its characteristics, and then show the impact of improvement concepts. We provide separate analyses for:

- Supplier invoice processing
- Supplier payment processing

There are two very different sets of solutions that can be applied to supplier invoice processing, so there are separate sections to describe each group of solutions. The text includes flowcharts of processes after lean concepts have been applied, as well as those measurements that are most effective in achieving a lean accounts payable process.

> **Related Podcast Episode:** Episode 138 of the Accounting Best Practices Podcast discusses a lean system for accounts payable. The episode is available at: **accountingtools.com/podcasts** or **iTunes**

Improvement Concepts

The application of lean concepts in this chapter involves the following improvements to existing systems, of which the first three are the most important:

- *Evaluated receipts processing*. Paying suppliers for items included in the cost of goods sold, based on the amount of finished goods produced. This eliminates the three-way match.
- *Pay from receipt*. Paying suppliers for all items passing through the receiving dock, based on authorizing purchase orders. This eliminates the three-way match.
- *Procurement cards*. Aggregating small purchases with procurement cards to arrive at a small number of large payments.

- *Supplier entry of invoices.* Having suppliers enter their invoices into the company's accounting system through an on-line form, thereby avoiding the manual data entry that would otherwise be associated with those invoices.
- *Direct invoice delivery.* Having suppliers send their invoices directly to the accounts payable department, to avoid having invoices linger in other parts of the company.
- *Invoice numbering convention.* Using a standard procedure to number those invoices that do not already have an identifying number, to reduce the risk of entering an invoice twice.
- *Incoming invoice scans.* Scanning invoices into the accounts payable system, to avoid the manual labor associated with invoice data entry.
- *Request aggregated invoice.* Having suppliers send a single invoice for all of a month's sales activity, to reduce the number of invoices processed.
- *Approval minimization.* Reducing the number of invoice approvals to the absolute minimum.
- *Expense report auditing.* Only reviewing a sample of all expense reports for errors and improper reimbursement requests.
- *Expense report outsourcing.* Having a third party process employee expense reports, to shift the reviewing work elsewhere.
- *Form W-9 requirement.* Requiring suppliers to submit a Form W-9 before being paid, so that less time is spent at year-end to issue the Form 1099 to qualifying suppliers.
- *Centralize accounts payable.* Shifting all accounts payable activities to a single location to achieve greater efficiencies.
- *Supplier reduction.* Shrinking the supplier base, thereby reducing the total amount of supplier record maintenance.
- *Vendor master file examination.* Reviewing the vendor master file for duplicate supplier records.
- *Supplier naming convention.* Using a standard procedure to create supplier names for the vendor master file, thereby avoiding the creation of duplicate records.

Supplier Invoice Processing

The processing of supplier invoices for payment can be found in a number of variations, depending upon whether invoices are handled on a distributed basis or out of a central location, the level of computer integration with other departments of a company and its suppliers, and the number of controls imposed on the process. In this section, we present the outlines of a simple, manual process that does not involve the use of an integrated computer system, followed by a discussion of the numerous problems with such a system.

Supplier Invoice Processing

The following steps show the basic transaction flow for the handling of supplier invoices, assuming the presence of a relatively strong control point called a *three-way match*. We also note the possible once-a-year requirement for issuing a Form 1099, which is not used outside of the United States. The steps are:

1. *Store purchase order*. When the purchasing department creates a purchase order to authorize the purchase of goods or services, they send a copy of the purchase order to the accounts payable staff. Upon receipt, the accounts payable staff stores the copy in an unmatched purchase orders file.

2. *Store receiving report*. When a supplier delivers goods to the receiving dock, the receiving staff completes a receiving report and sends a copy to the accounts payable staff. Upon receipt, the accounts payable staff stores the copy in an unmatched receiving reports file.

3. *Obtain invoice*. Supplier invoices may arrive in the mail or by e-mail. The most troubling route is when they arrive from company employees; this occurs when suppliers send invoices directly to the person who ordered goods or services from them. In many cases, the receiving employees lose the invoices or take many days to forward the invoices to the accounts payable staff.

4. *Conduct three-way match (optional)*. Match the invoice with the receiving report and purchase order. The invoiced price should match the purchase order price, and the invoiced quantities should match the received quantities. Any significant variances are investigated before the invoice is paid.

5. *Obtain approval (optional)*. If there is no purchase order for a supplier invoice, or if the invoice is an expense report from an employee, or if the invoice is for services (and therefore there is no receiving report), send the invoice to the person whose budget will be impacted by it and ask for an approval signature.

6. *Review invoice in detail (optional)*. If the invoice is an expense report, review it in detail to verify that all reimbursements claimed are in compliance with the company's travel and entertainment policy.

7. *Enter invoice*. Enter the invoice into the accounting system for payment. A check request form may be substituted for an invoice, if the request for payment comes from within the company.

8. *Issue Form 1099 (optional)*. Following year-end, the business must issue a Form 1099 to each qualifying supplier and the government, detailing the total amount of payments made during the year.

Analysis of Supplier Invoice Processing

The supplier invoice process flow is extremely inefficient, given the number of people involved, distances traveled, and inordinate number of controls. The following bullet points explain these issues:

- *Bottlenecks*. Whenever suppliers send invoices to their contacts at the company, rather than the accounts payable staff, there is a bottleneck when the recipient delays forwarding the invoice. Another potential bottleneck is waiting to obtain invoice approvals; some managers are terrible at returning invoices, which can delay payment. Yet another bottleneck is the amount of time required to review employee expense reports. Worst of all, the three-way match can create an enormous bottleneck, since there are frequent differences between supplier invoices, purchase orders, and receiving reports, many of which must be investigated.
- *Distance*. There is a significant problem with sending invoices out for approval, because they are then distributed all over a company, and can be hard to retrieve.
- *Controls*. The overriding issue with accounts payable is the concern that the business will pay for something that was never authorized; this concern leads to the pervasive use of invoice approvals, which can require a startling amount of staff time to issue invoices to managers for approval, and to eventually collect them.
- *Error rates*. A common error is that invoices containing no invoice number (such as expense reports and utility bills) are accidentally entered in the computer system multiple times, and therefore paid multiple times.

Accounts payable is a high-volume process for any larger company. Given the issues stated here, it typically calls for quite a large clerical staff to ensure that all bills are paid in a timely manner. In the next two sections, we will explore a number of ways to turn accounts payable into a significantly more lean operation.

Lean Supplier Invoice Processing – Complete Replacement

The most completely lean approach to accounts payable is evaluated receipts processing, which sidesteps all accounts payable functions by paying suppliers based on what they have shipped to the company, as inferred from the company's production records. There is no purchase order or supplier invoice, and electronic payments are made automatically. A variation on this concept is to pay based on the receipt of goods, where the receiving department calls up a purchase order in the computer system and authorizes payment as soon as an item arrives at the receiving dock. This latter approach requires the creation of a purchase order, and so is not as efficient a process as evaluated receipts. Both options are discussed in this section.

While both systems represent a massive step forward in creating a lean accounts payable function, the unique system requirements and highly accurate records needed are rarely found in practice. Also, a large number of payables do not involve items that come through the receiving dock (such as recurring payments, taxes, and services), and so require alternative processing, which we will cover in the next section.

Evaluated Receipts Processing

The evaluated receipts system involves sourcing all cost of goods sold items through a small number of suppliers, who are then authorized to deliver their raw materials on a just-in-time basis directly to the company's production lines, usually using kanban notifications for which prices have been specified under a master purchase order. Once manufacturing has been completed, the company uses its bills of material to determine what must have been delivered to the company, and pays based on this information and the price listed in its authorizing master purchase order. The supplier does not have to send an invoice, and may even be discouraged from doing so.

Evaluated receipts may seem like an awesome improvement that can yield an extremely lean accounts payable department. However, it only functions properly if a business has sole-sourced each of its raw materials, has very accurate bills of material, and has high-grade systems in place for tracking its scrap and finished goods production. Since all of these pre-conditions are located outside of the accounting department and therefore are not under the control of the controller or CFO, evaluated receipts is not encountered very frequently.

> **Tip:** The most efficient version of the evaluated receipts system is when suppliers bypass the receiving department and deliver directly to the production area. This calls for prior certification of the quality of suppliers, so that the company can rely on its suppliers to deliver the correct amounts of materials at the designated dates and times.

> **Note:** The evaluated receipts system is only designed for items that are eventually included in the cost of goods sold. There are a number of items that go through the receiving dock, such as fixed assets, that are not part of the cost of goods sold; evaluated receipts cannot be applied to them. The following pay from receipt option can include these additional items.

Pay from Receipt

Give the receiving department on-line access to purchase orders at the receiving dock, from which they can check off items on each purchase order as having been received. The system can then use the price stated in the purchase order and the quantity received to issue a payment to the supplier. No supplier invoice is needed. No invoice processing is required by the accounts payable staff at all.

This brief description hides a number of issues that make payment from receipt a fairly difficult proposition for most businesses. The issues are:

- *Purchase orders.* There must be near-total use of purchase orders for all purchases going through the receiving dock, which means that the issuance of purchase orders must be made hyper-efficient in order to achieve an all-around cost-effective solution.

- *Payment software.* The accounting software is designed to pay from invoices, not from the receipt of goods. This option is available on high-end software packages, but not on less-expensive systems.
- *Other payments.* The regular accounts payable system must still be maintained for all other payments that do not involve received goods, such as for services, taxes, and procurement cards.
- *Sales taxes.* The system must maintain a table of the sales taxes that should be paid to suppliers as part of each payment.

In short, paying from receipt initially appears to be an excellent solution, but it does not completely eliminate the base-level invoice processing system. Thus, it can reduce the volume of activity in the accounts payable area, but does not eliminate it.

Tip: The improvement suggestions made in this book are generally related to *new* concepts that can replace or upgrade an existing system. However, we must point out that a truly lean accounts payable function is much easier to attain with an *elimination* – of the inefficient three-way matching process. An evaluated receipts or pay from receipt system can circumvent the three-way match for some transactions. All remaining transactions should be investigated to see if they, too, can avoid the three-way match.

Analysis of Lean Supplier Invoice Processing

The following bullets point out that the evaluated receipts system and paying from receipts are extraordinary improvements over the traditional accounts payable process, though different types of errors are now more likely to occur. However, these major system improvements are only available for transactions involving received goods; the old system must still be used for all other payables transactions.

- *Bottlenecks.* All bottlenecks are completely eliminated.
- *Distance.* There are no invoices to be sent out for approval, so all distance considerations are eliminated.
- *Controls.* The evaluated receipts system is only used to pay for items that were included in the cost of goods sold, so there should be no issue with authorization. Similarly, purchase orders are an integral part of paying from receipt, and purchase orders are a strong form of authorization. Thus, control considerations are greatly reduced for these two systems.
- *Error rates.* Evaluated receipts payment errors can arise if the bills of material, production totals, or scrap information are incorrect. Errors can also arise when paying from receipts if the information on purchase orders is incorrect, or if received goods are incorrectly noted in the system.

The following flowchart reveals the altered process flow for accounts payable situations where suppliers are either issuing materials into a company's production process or sending goods through its receiving dock. The left side of the flowchart shows the process for an evaluated receipts system, while the right side shows the process for a pay from receipt system. The "other options" listed in the flowchart refers to all other forms of obligations due to suppliers, which are addressed in the next section.

Lean Supplier Invoice Processing – Complete Replacement

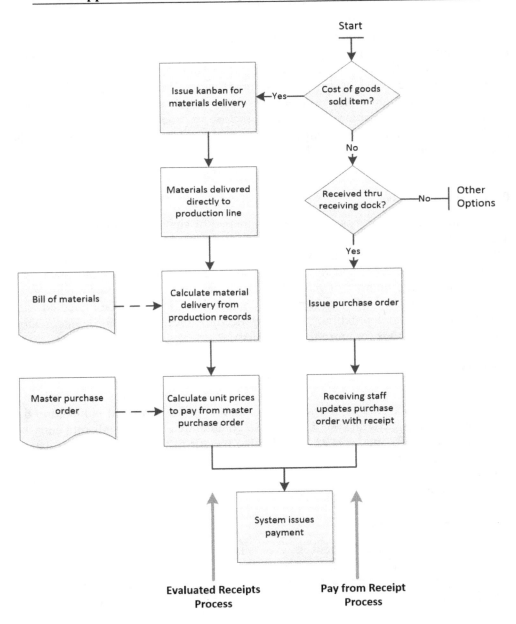

This section has shown that there are alternatives available that can completely eliminate the accounts payable function for certain types of purchases. A controller who is intent upon implementing the lean concept should force as many payments as possible through either or both of these systems.

Lean Supplier Invoice Processing – Incremental Improvement

In the last section, we pointed out a pair of options that generate a massive lean improvement by essentially avoiding the entire accounts payable process. However, those options only apply to physical items received by a company. All other payments must still be handled by the traditional accounts payable process. However, the traditional process can be made more lean, so that the remaining payments do not require quite so much effort. Of the possible improvements noted in this section, we particularly recommend the use of procurement cards, since they aggregate a large number of small purchases into a small number of payments. The other improvements have a smaller incremental impact on the accounts payable process.

Procurement Cards

A large amount of the transaction volume handled by the accounts payable function involves invoices for very small amounts. Many of these purchases can be eliminated by paying for them with company procurement cards. The result is a small number of card statements to be paid at the end of the month, each one aggregating a large number of individual purchases. Excessive use of procurement cards can lead to a lack of oversight of purchases, though that can be remedied with a properly configured procurement card procedure (see the author's *Accounting Procedures Guidebook* for more information).

Supplier Entry of Invoices

If the company is large enough, it may be able to impose on its suppliers a requirement to enter their invoices directly into an on-line form that is linked to the corporate accounts payable system. Doing so completely eliminates all data entry by the accounting staff, and so is of considerable benefit to the company. However, it requires extra labor by suppliers, which makes it a difficult concept to implement. Still, this practice will reduce accounting staff time even if only a small number of suppliers use it, and so should be pursued.

Direct Invoice Delivery

There is a large potential bottleneck when suppliers send invoices directly to their contacts at the company, since those contacts may not forward the invoices to the accounts payable staff in an overly brisk manner. Instead, the accounts payable staff should contact the billing departments of all suppliers that persist in sending invoices to their contacts, and request that the billing contact be changed to the accounts payable department. This may require multiple conversations with the more recalcitrant suppliers.

> **Tip:** An alternative to badgering suppliers after-the-fact is to do so in advance, by sending them a welcome packet when they first start doing business with the company. The welcome packet states the information to be included on each invoice, including the mailing address and references to authorizing purchase order numbers.

Invoice Numbering Convention

Adopt a standard procedure for creating invoice numbers for any invoices that do not already have an invoice number. By doing so, anyone entering an invoice should derive exactly the same invoice number from the information on the invoice, thereby mitigating the risk that such an invoice will be entered into the computer system more than once (the computer should reject any invoice number that already resides in the system). Examples of an invoice numbering convention are:

- Use the invoice date as the invoice number
- Use the packing slip number as the invoice number
- Never enter the leading zeros in an invoice number
- Never enter any dashes or other punctuation in an invoice number

Incoming Invoice Scans

It is possible to scan supplier invoices into the computer system. The scanning software is preconfigured to know where key information is located on each supplier's invoice, which the software then extracts and stores. This method is time-consuming to set up, and is likely to reject the invoices of suppliers whose invoice characteristics have not been entered into the system. Still, it can automate significant portions of the total volume of invoice data entry work. This solution is expensive, and so is only applicable to high-volume payables environments.

Request Aggregated Invoice

An interesting variation on paying from invoices is to negotiate with suppliers to send a single invoice each month, containing all goods and services provided to the company for the past month. Doing so can considerably reduce the amount of invoicing volume that the accounts payable staff must deal with.

The issuance of a single invoice departs from the standard invoicing procedure for most suppliers, where the shipment of goods automatically triggers the creation of an invoice. Also, there may be cash flow concerns when a supplier provides goods or services near the beginning of a month, but is not allowed to send an invoice until the end of the month. These concerns can be reduced by offering faster payment terms, or perhaps by offering to sole source with the supplier.

Approval Minimization

Approvals should be avoided as much as possible in the accounts payable process. There is a significant bottleneck involved in waiting for a manager to approve an invoice, so use as many other alternatives as possible. For example:

- *Use purchase order as approval.* If the purchasing department has already issued a purchase order, then the purchase order itself should be sufficient evidence that an invoice can be paid.
- *Eliminate approvals for small amounts.* Establish a threshold invoice amount, below which there is no need for an approval. If using this option, conduct an occasional examination of small invoices to see if anyone is engaging in fraudulent purchasing behavior.
- *Use negative approvals.* Send an invoice copy to an approver, with instructions to only respond if there is a problem with the invoice. The accounts payable staff will assume that all other invoices have been approved by default.
- *Obtain approvals in person.* If it is absolutely necessary to obtain an approval, have an accounting person hand-deliver the invoice, answer any questions posed by the approver, and bring back the signed invoice. Doing so is time-consuming, but ensures that invoices will be returned in a timely manner. This approach is most effective when a manager has a history of rarely approving invoices in a timely manner.

Expense Report Auditing

It is very time-consuming to review every reimbursement request on an employee expense report, as well as all attached receipts. The work is not cost-effective, since most employees are always in compliance with a company's expenditure policies. Therefore, an excellent alternative is to review expense reports on a random basis, while requiring a more intensive level of review for the expense reports submitted by those employees who have had compliance problems in the past.

Expense Report Outsourcing

An alternative to expense reporting auditing is to shift the entire expense report data entry and analysis function to a third party. There are several organizations that maintain on-line systems into which employees can enter their expense reports. The system compares all submissions to the company's travel and entertainment policies, and automatically flags any items that are not in compliance. This approach is comparatively expensive, and so is only effective for larger companies.

Form W-9 Requirement

The Form W-9 is the source document for the tax identification number used in the Form 1099 that is sent to qualifying suppliers at year-end. A company is in the best position to obtain this document when it can withhold payments from suppliers, so be sure to tell suppliers that no payment will be forthcoming until a completed form is received.

General: Centralize Accounts Payable

A larger organization likely has a number of divisions, and may have allowed each one to process its own accounts payable. Doing so results in the duplication of management staff, facilities, and accounting software licenses. It may be possible to achieve a reduction in the overall amount of resources assigned to accounts payable by centralizing accounts payable operations in a single location. This can eliminate several types of expenses, while the increased transaction volume may justify the acquisition of more expensive improvements, such as invoice scanning systems. It may also be possible to hire specialists, such as clerks experienced in processing deductions or reviewing expense reports. However, a central payables organization may call for the purchase of a more robust payables software package, which can be expensive.

General: Supplier Reduction

In general, the difficulty of running the accounts payable function is increased when there are many suppliers. Each supplier requires a separate vendor master file in the accounting system, and presents additional monitoring issues involving where invoices are sent, early payment discounts, and any other clerical minutiae required of the accounts payable staff. Consequently, if the purchasing department can limit its purchases to a select group of prime suppliers, this can reduce the workload of the accounting department.

General: Vendor Master File Examination

It is quite common to have multiple records in the vendor master file for a single supplier. This occurs when a supplier uses different company names or addresses on its invoices, possibly because it is shipping from different subsidiaries or locations. This causes errors that the accounts payable staff must resolve, such as paying to the wrong supplier location or paying the same invoice more than once to multiple supplier locations.

The accounts payable error rate can be reduced by conducting a periodic examination of the vendor master file, looking for duplicate names, addresses, and taxpayer identification numbers. If any are found, decide which one the company will use, and close down the other duplicate records.

General: Supplier Naming Convention

One way to keep multiple records from appearing in the vendor master file for a supplier is to adopt a standard naming convention. Such a convention requires the accounts payable staff to follow a set of rules when creating a unique supplier name. If the rules are always followed, there is a good chance that a clerk will find that a "new" supplier is already listed in the vendor master file.

For example, a set of naming rules could require that all punctuation, spaces and dashes first be removed from the name of a supplier, as well as all business designations, such as "Incorporated." Then use the first eight characters in the name, plus a three-digit sequential number. For example, Radford Designs would be coded as RADFORDD001.

Practices to Avoid

From the perspective of having a truly lean accounting system, we advise against the use of any practices that complicate the accounts payable process flow. For example:

- *Faster processing of invoices with early payment discounts.* The accounts payable staff could route all incoming invoices through an accelerated approval process if they have an early payment discount, to ensure that the business takes the discount in a timely manner. However, doing so results in an additional sub-routine. Instead, the entire invoice processing procedure should be designed to be sufficiently fast that all invoices will be ready for payment well within the time frame required for an early payment discount.
- *Automated three-way matching.* More expensive accounting software includes a feature that automates the three-way matching process. However, it also requires that the accounts payable staff enter each line item on every supplier invoice that is to be matched, so that the system can conduct the automated matching. Spending extra time entering these line items reduces the efficiency of the overall process. Thus, it is better to find ways to circumvent the entire three-way matching process than to spend more time and money automating it.

Analysis of Lean Supplier Invoice Processing

The following bullets point out that the preceding list of improvements has a favorable impact on the accounts payable process:

- *Bottlenecks.* Sending invoices directly to the payable department, using negative approvals, and auditing expense reports all reduce or eliminate bottlenecks. Three-way matching may still be in use, however, and that can be the worst bottleneck of all.
- *Distance.* Distance issues are eliminated if invoices are no longer sent out for approval.
- *Controls.* The suggestions noted in this section can weaken the authorization control, but the control weakness is primarily where low-cost invoices are being processed.
- *Error rates.* The procedures for deriving unique invoice and supplier numbers make it less likely that the same invoices will be paid more than once.

The following flowchart reveals the altered process flow when several lesser improvements are made to the accounts payable process. To increase the clarity of the exhibit, we have not included all of the possible changes noted in this section, focusing instead on the key items – using procurement cards, automating or eliminating data entry, and using negative approvals. Process improvements are noted in bold.

Lean Supplier Invoice Processing – Incremental Improvement

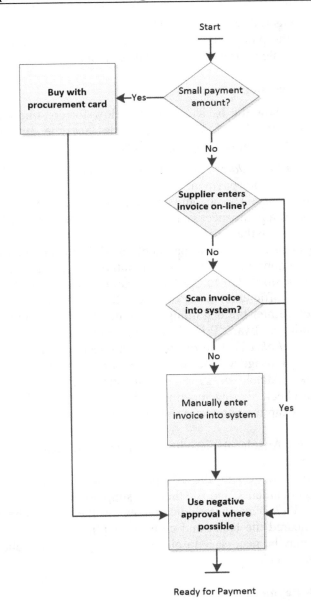

Note the absence of three-way matching from the flowchart. Since it is the most time-consuming of all accounts payable functions, the accounting staff should attempt to avoid matching at all times, mostly by using the replacement systems described in the preceding section.

Check Payment Processing

The issuance of checks follows a process that has not changed in years. We state the key components of the process flow in this section, as well as a number of issues with the system. Possible improvements are noted in the following section.

Check Payment Processing

The following steps show the basic transaction flow for creating check payments, though it does not include all possible controls. See the author's *Accounting Controls Guidebook* for complete coverage of these controls.

1. *Print payment due dates report.* Print the standard report that itemizes all invoices now due for payment.
2. *Approve payments.* The accounts payable manager or controller reviews the report to see if any prospective payments should be delayed. If so, they cross out these items on the report.
3. *Select payments.* Access the payments module in the accounting software and select all approved invoices listed on the payment due dates report.
4. *Obtain check stock.* Go to the locked cabinet where check stock is stored, and extract a sufficient number of checks for the check run.
5. *Print checks.* Enter the beginning check number for the unused checks into the accounting software. Print the checks and a check register.
6. *Return unused checks.* Return all unused checks to the locked cabinet and note in a check usage log the check number range that was used.
7. *Sign checks.* Attach all supporting documentation to each check. Then schedule a check signing meeting with an authorized check signer, where the signer examines the supporting materials and signs all acceptable checks.
8. *Issue checks.* Attach any required remittance advices to checks, and mail them to recipients.
9. *File documents.* Attach the company's copy of remittance advices to supporting documents, and file them by supplier name.
10. *Verify check clearance.* Periodically review the list of checks issued that have not cleared the bank, and contact suppliers to ask them to cash their checks. It may be necessary to place a stop payment on a check and issue a replacement check.

Analysis of Check Payment Processing

Check printing is not an especially difficult function, and usually does not require a large part of the total time of the accounts payable department. Nonetheless, many check batches are printed during the year, so the time involved can add up to a significant amount. For this reason, it is worthwhile to pay attention to the following points of inefficiency:

- *Bottlenecks*. A potentially major bottleneck is when a check signer is not available to sign checks. Another issue is the continual monitoring needed to ensure that all checks are cashed by their recipients; the accounting staff could potentially spend months badgering recipients to cash their checks.
- *Distance*. The check signer may be located some distance from the accounts payable staff. If the check signer is traveling, this may even require that checks be sent to the check signer by overnight mail.
- *Controls*. A case could be made that check printing is nothing but a large control, interspersed with a few actual processing steps. The large number of controls are needed to ensure that payments are not incorrectly or fraudulently issued.
- *Error rates*. The primary errors in this area are the inadvertent printing of checks that were not approved for payment, and printing checks with incorrect check numbers.

Supplier Payment Processing, Lean Approach

There is not a single recommendation in this section that will result in a massive improvement in the lean characteristics of the check payments process. However, we named this section "Supplier Payment Processing," rather than "Check Payment Processing" to point out that there are alternatives to paying by check, such as paying by ACH. We discuss ACH payments in this section, as well as several alterations to the check payment process that improve its efficiency to some extent.

Recurring Payment Automation

A small number of invoices are probably paid in exactly the same amount and on the same date each month, such as rent and equipment lease payments. If so, set up recurring payments for these items in the accounting software, with a designated termination date. It may not be necessary to attach any explanatory materials to these payments, as long as they are designated as recurring payments. Doing so slightly reduces the processing time required by the accounting staff.

Manual Check Reduction

There are a variety of rush-payment situations where employees demand that a payment be made at once. These payments fall outside of the normal batch-oriented check payment process, which increases the time required per payment, as well as the risk that the payment will not be entered into the accounting system (which causes bank reconciliation problems). There are a variety of ways to reduce the number of manual payments made, including:

- Charge the requesting department a large inter-company fee for each manual payment made.
- Follow up on each manual payment to see if similar payments can be addressed by the regular payment system in the future.
- Print manual checks through the computer system by creating batch sizes of one check (thereby ensuring that the information is at least properly recorded in the accounting system).
- Increase the frequency of scheduled check runs, so that more manual payments can be incorporated into a standard payment batch.

Signature Stamp or Plate

Check signing is intended to be a final review of payments, but most check signers are in too much of a rush to conduct an in-depth review of each check. Further, the company is likely already contractually committed to making each payment by the time the check signer reviews a check, which makes this control even weaker. A reasonable alternative is to use a signature stamp or plate to sign checks, as long as some sort of review was conducted earlier in the purchasing process (such as the issuance of a purchase order or the approval of an invoice by a supervisor). If management is uncomfortable with this leaner approach, a mid-way solution is to require a check signer only for larger checks.

ACH Payments

An ACH payment requires the use of the Automated Clearing House (ACH) system, which is a digital payment that is usually paid into the recipient's bank account in one or two business days. The ACH procedure is the same as the one used for check payments, through the point where payments are approved. After that point, the accounts payable staff either prepares a direct deposit file for transmission to the company's bank, or accesses the bank's secure direct deposit site and manually sets up each payment. The bank then sends a confirmation to the company, stating the amounts and payees associated with each direct deposit transaction. The accounts payable staff notes in the accounting system that the related invoices were paid by direct deposit. The singular advantage of direct deposit is that it eliminates all subsequent monitoring of check payments to verify that they have been cashed. Thus, an ACH payment eliminates the final step in the payment processing procedure.

Practices to Avoid

From the perspective of having a truly lean accounting system, we advise against the use of any practices that complicate the accounts payable process flow. For example:

- *Positive pay.* A company can mitigate the risk of check fraud by sending a file to its bank, detailing the checks it has issued and the amounts on those checks. The bank then matches the information in this file to the checks that are eventually presented for payment, and can reject those that do not match the file. This anti-fraud measure is called positive pay. While it may be useful from a control perspective, it does nothing from a lean perspective – the accounting staff must remember to send the information to the bank, not only for regular check batches, but also for manual checks; forgetting to do so will require more time to communicate with the bank regarding checks that are about to be incorrectly rejected. Consequently, a company controller should consider the negative impact of positive pay on the accounts payable process flow before deciding to install it.

Analysis of Lean Supplier Payments Processing

The following bullets point out that there are few good ways to bring about a significant enhancement in the efficiency of the supplier payments process flow.

- *Bottlenecks.* Targeting the reduction of manual checks can eliminate a potential annoyance in the payments process, though the improvement does not represent a large bottleneck reduction. Also, the use of ACH payments eliminates the subsequent monitoring of issued check payments. The use of signature plates eliminates the bottleneck that can be caused by dilatory check signers.
- *Distance.* The use of a signature plate to sign checks eliminates the problem with sending checks to a distant check signer.
- *Controls.* The level of control is relatively unchanged after installing the enhancements noted in this section.
- *Error rates.* The error rate is not noticeably altered by the changes noted in this section.

The following flowchart reveals the revised process flow when several improvements are incorporated into the supplier payments process. Any payments approved through the evaluated receipts or pay from receipt systems are assumed to be paid by electronic means. Check payments utilize a signature plate to avoid the time required to have someone sign checks. Process improvements are noted in bold.

Supplier Payments Lean Process Flow

Additional Improvement Concepts

There are a number of additional concepts that can be applied to the accounts payable process to enhance its performance or reduce costs. These concepts did not fit into any of the process flows noted previously or were considered minor elements, and so are noted here instead:

- *Approve based on supplier billing history.* If a supplier has a history of issuing flawless invoices to the company, assume that this trend will continue, and automatically approve their invoices for payment. If a pattern of billing flaws appears at a later date, remove this approval exemption from their invoices.

- *Create standard adjustment letter.* The easiest way to interact with suppliers over adjustments to their invoices is to create a standard adjustment letter that contains a list of the most common reasons why the company takes deductions on payments. The payables staff then checks off the appropriate box, provides additional commentary in a comments box as needed, and sends it to the supplier along with the payment. This is easier than constructing a custom letter every time there is a payment adjustment.

- *Examine invoices for discount offers.* Only a few suppliers offer early payment discounts, so there is typically no process in place for detecting them. Instead, include in the payables procedure a step to examine each incoming invoice for discount offers. If one is detected, route it through a more accelerated process, to ensure that the company pays in time to take advantage of the discount offer.

- *Set discount flag.* If suppliers routinely offer the same early payment discount, flag this discount in the vendor master file, so that the system automatically schedules an early payment for all invoices submitted by these suppliers, and automatically takes the specified discount.

- *Obtain procurement card discounts.* If the company spends a sufficient amount through its procurement cards, it may be possible to obtain a small purchasing rebate from the card supplier.

- *Restrict cash advances.* Cash advances require an inordinate amount of staff time, first to cut a manual check for the requesting person, and then to track whether the person has repaid the advance. This issue is best sidestepped by imposing a policy that strongly restricts the situations in which cash advances are allowed.

- *Restrict manual checks.* It takes far longer to process a manual check than one processed through the normal batch processing system. Further, a manually-created check may not be properly entered into the computer system (if at all). To avoid these issues, require that a senior manager in the accounting department approve all requests for manual checks.

- *Restrict wire transfers.* The fee for a wire transfer is many multiples higher than the cost of an ACH electronic payment. Accordingly, require the approval of senior management before a wire transfer will be initiated.

- *Review for open credits.* Ongoing transactions with suppliers may occasionally result in a few credits being granted by the supplier, perhaps as sales discounts or for returned goods. Request that suppliers send the company a quarterly statement of account, and review it for these open credits. The credits can then be used to offset other payments.

Accounts Payable Measurements

There are several excellent measurements for the accounts payable area that have a noticeable impact on the function's operations. The following measurements are intended to be reviewed daily and to trigger immediate corrective action by the accounting staff:

- *Remaining three-way matches.* If a business uses evaluated receipts, pay from receipt, and procurement cards, there should be relatively few remaining supplier invoices that are still being reviewed with the cumbersome three-way matching process. Consider creating a report that itemizes every invoice for which three-way matching was used, with the intent of finding alternative ways to review these invoices.

- *Invoices not mailed to accounts payable.* Whenever an invoice arrives that was mailed to someone other than the accounts payable department, include the supplier name on a contact list. The accounts payable staff should contact these suppliers to request that the contact name be shifted to the accounts payable department. Doing so eliminates a possible bottleneck where invoice recipients might not immediately forward invoices to the accounting staff.

- *Supplier late fees.* Any late payment fee charged by a supplier should be recorded in a separate general ledger account. The information in this account is reviewed regularly to determine what circumstances caused the late fee. The result may be procedural or other changes to keep the issue from occurring again in the future.

- *Manual payments.* Track every manual payment made (including payments by check, ACH, or wire transfer), determine the reasons why manual payments were mandated, and see if they can be converted to the regular payment system in the future.

The following measurement is of less importance, but could be tracked:

- *Number of suppliers.* When there are fewer suppliers, it is easier for the accounts payable staff to manage the correspondingly fewer records in the vendor master file. There will also be fewer payments to issue, since the remaining suppliers will tend to aggregate their deliveries and services provided into fewer invoices. However, the accounting department does not have direct control over the number of suppliers, making this a relatively less important measurement to track.

Note that none of these measurements involve ratio analysis. Instead, they mostly require that the accounting staff investigate individual transactions in detail, with the objective of locating transactions that either resulted in errors or which required an inordinate amount of effort to complete. The result of these investigations should be a continual improvement in the efficiency of the accounts payable function.

Summary

In this chapter, we described how a variety of changes could be used to arrive at a more lean accounts payable process, with the following three changes delivering most of the improvement:

- Evaluated receipts processing
- Pay from receipt
- Procurement cards

In addition, it is of use to dismantle the three-way matching process that exists in many accounts payable departments, for it is very labor-intensive.

Accounts payable represents an interesting two-level improvement from the lean perspective, for a massive improvement can be engineered for purchases relating to the cost of goods sold, with a considerably less lean outcome for all other types of purchases. The volume of payments can certainly be reduced through the aggressive use of procurement cards, but the underlying process can only be tweaked to create a somewhat more efficient outcome.

Chapter 5
Lean Payroll

Introduction

Payroll is one of the most data-intensive accounting processes, and one that lives and dies by payroll processing due dates. The concepts of lean accounting are particularly applicable here, since a variety of upgrades can convert the department into one where data entry requirements are reduced, shifted elsewhere, or automated. As a result, the payroll staff may find itself out of the data entry business, and instead spends its time trolling for payroll errors to correct, as well as maintaining a variety of computerized payroll systems.

In this chapter, we begin with a discussion of improvement concepts, describe the standard payroll system and its characteristics, and then show the impact of improvement concepts. We provide separate analyses for:

- Payroll data collection
- Commission processing
- Payroll processing
- Employee payment processing

The text includes flowcharts of processes after lean concepts have been applied, as well as those measurements that are most effective in achieving a lean payroll process.

> **Related Podcast Episodes:** Episodes 126 through 129 of the Accounting Best Practices Podcast discuss the streamlining of payroll. The episode is available at: **accountingtools.com/podcasts** or **iTunes**

Improvement Concepts

The application of lean concepts in this chapter involves the following improvements to existing systems:

- *Convert hourly to salaried pay.* Avoiding hourly time tracking by shifting hourly employees to salaried status.
- *Data collection minimization.* Collecting the absolute minimum amount of payroll and other data, thereby reducing the data collection task.
- *Computerized time clocks.* Using "smart" time clocks to automatically check time clock entries for accuracy and aggregate this information for payroll processing.

- *Web-based timekeeping.* Allowing employees to enter timekeeping information through an on-line form, thereby shifting data entry work away from the payroll staff.
- *Smart phone time tracking.* Allowing employees to enter timekeeping information through a smart phone timekeeping app, thereby shifting work away from the payroll staff.
- *Copy forward hours worked.* Giving employees the option to copy forward their last timesheet into the timesheet for the current period; this is useful when employees have few or no changes in their time reporting.
- *Automated time tracking reminders.* Issuing e-mails to employees, reminding them to enter their hours worked and other information in the timekeeping system. Doing so improves the odds of completing payroll data entry on time.
- *Commission plan simplification.* Reducing the complexity of the commission plan in order to reduce the number of iterations required to determine commission payments.
- *Standard commissions report.* Configuring a report writer to automatically generate commissions payable, thereby removing this task from the commissions clerk.
- *Incentive compensation management software.* Using software to calculate commissions, thereby removing this task from the commissions clerk.
- *Payroll cycle duration.* Reducing the number of payroll cycles per year in order to reduce the payroll processing workload for the payroll staff.
- *Off-cycle payroll elimination.* Stopping or at least reducing the number of off-cycle payrolls, which require a significant amount of payroll staff time to complete.
- *Outsource payroll processing.* Shifting the payroll processing and employee payment tasks to a supplier.
- *Payroll data entry by employees.* Making an on-line form available to all employees, who use it to update selected payroll information. This data entry reduces the work load of the payroll staff.
- *Payroll data entry by managers.* Making an on-line form available to managers, who use it to update employee pay rates and other information, thereby reducing the work load of the payroll staff.
- *Prohibition of employee advances.* Not allowing employees to be paid their wages in advance of the next payroll, thereby reducing manual processing by the payroll staff.
- *Prohibition of reimbursements through payroll.* Not allowing employees to make purchases through the business and then pay back the company through the payroll system, thereby eliminating some manual processing by the payroll staff.
- *Reduction of pay deductions.* Consolidating and eliminating the number of deductions from employee pay, in order to reduce the amount of data entry by the payroll staff.

- *Combine payroll systems.* Consolidating payroll systems into one system, thereby reducing overall payroll headcount and reducing other expenses.
- *Direct deposit.* Sending electronic payments to employees to eliminate the pay distribution task.
- *Pay cards.* Sending electronic payments to employees who do not have bank accounts, thereby eliminating the pay distribution task.
- *On-line access to W-2 forms.* Storing W-2 forms on a secure website, to eliminate the manual distribution of these forms to employees.

Payroll Data Collection

Payroll begins with the collection of data, which can include hours worked, bonuses, commissions, pay deductions, and many other items. In examining the payroll process flow, the principal hindrance is the collection of information about hours worked. Most other types of payroll data are not critical to the completion of a specific payroll – that is, they can usually be deferred and shifted into the following payroll cycle. In this section, we describe the basic timecard data collection process, followed by a discussion of various alternatives to and enhancements of it.

Timecard Data Collection

The following steps show the basic process flow for the collection of timecard information. The steps are:

1. *Issue reminder.* Issue a reminder to employees a few days in advance of the payroll to make sure their timecards are up-to-date. This is especially important for those employees who have a history of being late in making timecard submissions.
2. *Print employee list.* Print a list of all current employees who are supposed to submit timecards.
3. *Sort received timecards.* Sort all timecards received by employee last name. This makes it easier to match timecards received to the employee list for verification purposes.
4. *Determine missing submissions.* Compare the timecards to the employee list, and note which employees have not yet submitted their timecards.
5. *Determine missing employees.* Compare the employee list to the schedule of employees who are on vacation, and cross off the names of those employees who did not submit timecards and who are on vacation.
6. *Notify supervisors.* Notify management of the remaining employees who have not submitted timecards. Supervisors are responsible for obtaining these timecards.
7. *Review for errors.* Review all timecards for errors and return them to employees for correction.
8. *Approve overtime.* Forward all timecards containing overtime hours to management for approval.

9. *Verify timecard returns.* Verify that all timecards returned for correction or approval have been returned to the payroll department.
10. *Summarize hours worked.* Add up the time worked on each timecard and note the total hours worked on the card.
11. *Forward for processing.* Forward the approved and summarized timecards to the payroll clerk for entry into the payroll processing system.

Analysis of Payroll Data Collection

The number of steps involved in timecard data collection, and the numerous built-in bottlenecks, make it quite surprising that businesses are ever able to pay their employees on time. The following bullet points explain the problem:

- *Bottlenecks.* There are usually a few employees who give the payroll staff fits in every payroll, because they do not submit their timecards by the specified due date. It is also possible that supervisors are not tracking down these employees on a timely basis, so both supervisors and their employees can cause a bottleneck.
- *Distance.* There can be a major problem with the forwarding of timecards from outlying locations to the payroll department by the required due date. These cards may even be lost in transit.
- *Controls.* The need to approve hours worked requires that supervisors be involved in timecard processing, which adds to the duration of the process.
- *Error rates.* Much of the timecard process is involved with checking for errors, which happens after the timecards have been submitted.

In the next section, we will explore ways to improve payroll data entry.

Lean Payroll Data Collection

The problems with payroll data collection can not only be reduced, but even obliterated. In this section, we will address the reduction of information to collect, as well as the use of automated systems to collect and review payroll information. The result can be a situation where the payroll staff simply monitors the flow of timekeeping information into the payroll software, and only has to take action when information is missing or incorrect. The remainder of this section covers possible data collection upgrades and their impact on the entire payroll data collection process.

Convert Hourly to Salaried Pay

One of the reasons for recording hours worked is simply that employees are paid on an hourly basis, not that a business needs to track the types of work that they are doing. In these situations, it may be possible to convert some hourly employees to salaried pay, thereby completely eliminating the need to track their hours. However, if an employee is salaried but his time is billed to customers (as is the case for a consultant), then his time must still be tracked; in this situation, it makes no difference if the person is classified as hourly or salaried, since there must be a record of his hours worked.

Converting an employee to salaried status will likely only apply to a very small proportion of employees, since this status is governed by federal regulations. The key guidelines for designating a person as being eligible for a salary are as follows:

- *Administrative*. Those in charge of an administrative department, even if they supervise no one, and anyone assisting management with long-term strategy decisions.
- *Executive*. Those who manage more than 50% of the time and supervise at least two employees.
- *Professional*. Those who spend at least 50% of their time on tasks requiring knowledge obtained through a four-year college degree (including systems analysis, design, and programming work on computer systems, even if a four-year degree was not obtained). The position must also allow for continued independent decision making and minimal close supervision.

Data Collection Minimization

A time tracking system is a data collection system, and so can be used to collect information about *anything*. However, do not be tempted to overuse this capability, since collecting additional data requires more data entry time by employees. Instead, question the need for any additional data collection above the bare minimum amount. Ideally, this means the identification number of each employee and his time worked are being collected – and nothing else.

Above the baseline data collection level just noted, the next most common item to be collected is the pay code, which identifies hours worked as falling into a pay category, such as holidays, bereavement leave, jury duty, and vacation time. If the decision is made to use pay codes, do not overwhelm employees with a multitude of codes, since they will be more likely to record the wrong codes.

In the production area and materials management departments, it may be necessary to use activity codes for such tasks as receiving, putaways to stock, picking from stock, inventory counting, manufacturing, rework, and shipping. Resist the urge to use activity codes, because employees tend to spend their time in the same proportions on the same activities over time – collecting information to confirm that nothing has changed is a waste of time. Ideally, only require hourly production workers to clock in and clock out, and not waste their time recording any additional time tracking information – with the possible exception of the next item.

If the cost of production jobs is being accumulated, employees may be recording the time they spend on individual jobs. These systems can be quite elaborate, with every conceivable cost being assigned to jobs. Such detailed record keeping may be required by customers, but if it is not, is it really necessary to record the information? In a custom production environment, the answer may very well be yes, since it is useful to know how well the company is setting prices and controlling its production process. However, if the company is largely selling standardized products, consider strictly limiting the job tracking system to just those jobs that truly require custom work, and for which management regularly compares the budgeted to actual cost and takes action on this information.

> **Tip:** If possible, consider separating the job costing function from the timekeeping function. This means that employees only record their starting and ending times each day for payroll purposes, and then use a separate system to record their time spent on specific jobs. Doing so can eliminate a large amount of data entry work by the payroll department.

Computerized Time Clocks

The computerized time clock is a specialized computer terminal that is linked to the central payroll database, and which has an employee badge scanner attached to it. The scanner can accept a bar coded, magnetic stripe, or radio-frequency identification employee card. An employee swipes his badge through the scanner, and the terminal automatically records his time. The central payroll system periodically polls the terminal and downloads the recorded scans. Thus, the computerized time clock incorporates a very fast and error-free data entry system that requires no rekeying by the payroll staff, which represents a massive lean improvement.

The computerized time clock has been the time tracking device of choice for many years, but do not automatically assume that it is the *best* time tracking solution. It is one of the higher-cost solutions available, and so is most cost-effective only under certain circumstances, which are as follows:

- *Highly concentrated employees.* Given the high cost of an automated time clock, most companies only budget for a small number of them, which means that they are most cost-effective when there are a large number of employees using each one. Thus, the best environment for a clock is a facility with a large number of employees who pass through a choke point where the clock is located.
- *Computer interface.* There should be a payroll computer database which polls the various time clocks and downloads information from them. This may require the use of shielded network cables (for a heavy industrial environment), or a wireless connection, or even a cellular phone linkage.
- *Data rekeying reduction.* An automated time clock can eliminate a vast amount, if not all, of the rekeying of payroll data into the payroll system. This is a particular advantage where there are many employees, and when the time period between the end of a pay period and the pay date is very small.
- *Longer pay periods.* There is no theoretical limit to the duration of a pay period for which an automated time clock can accumulate information, so a company is not limited to the one-week pay period that is very nearly a requirement under a time sheet or time card system. A longer pay interval, such as once every two weeks, reduces the aggregate annual amount of payroll processing effort by the accounting staff.

The preceding list is based on a full-function automated time clock, which may cost in excess of $1,000 each. However, there are many lower-cost variations on this concept.

> **Tip:** Though the computerized time clock is certainly a high-speed data entry device, there is an upper limit to how many employees can use it at the start of a work shift. If the queue in front of the clock is too long, some employees will be late for work. Consequently, it may be necessary to install multiple clocks or stagger shift start times in order to reduce the queue in front of each clock.

Web-Based Timekeeping

A web-based timekeeping system is a website which employees can access to enter their hours worked. These systems are routinely offered by the larger payroll outsourcing companies, and can also be custom-designed by any company with a knowledgeable web design staff. A web-based time tracking system can be configured to accept any type of information, including task codes. These systems are also useful from an employee feedback perspective, because they can notify employees of any data entry errors, and may also allow them to view additional information, such as the time sheets from previous periods and their remaining unused vacation time. It is most useful under the following circumstances:

- *Dispersed staff.* Employees can access the system wherever there is Internet access, anywhere in the world.
- *Large staff.* Many of the available time tracking systems are massively scalable, so they can be used by very large numbers of employees.
- *Full integration.* If payroll is being outsourced to a supplier and the supplier's web-based time tracking system is also being used, there will be an interface between the two, so there is no need to rekey timekeeping information into the payroll system.

Web-based time tracking could work well in a professional environment, such as consulting or software development, where employees typically have Internet access and need to record some additional task information along with their hours worked.

Smart Phone Time Tracking

It is quite easy to track employee time using smart phones. Apps are available for the main smart phone operating systems, which allow employees to accumulate their hours worked, append a description of their activities, and then e-mail the results to the employer.

There are also time tracking systems available for non-smart phones that allow users to punch their time worked into the phone, which then sends a text message to a central server, itemizing the hours worked. If the phone is also GPS-enabled, the system can also track employee locations on a map. These systems are operated by a third party supplier, so there is a monthly charge for the service, as well as the usual monthly carrier fees for each phone.

Smart phone time tracking is enormously useful for very mobile employees, such as salespeople and field service personnel. These people may be in multiple locations per day, and so do not have time to access a more traditional fixed computer terminal to record their hours worked and tasks completed.

Time tracking with smart phones is constantly evolving, so one could reasonably treat a laptop or tablet computer with a wireless connection as a smart phone. These larger devices are more likely to be connected to a standard web-based time tracking system, and may also contain a great deal of information for mobile employees, such as product repair manuals, that make them a more versatile option than a smart phone, with its inherently limited screen size.

Cell phone time tracking has several restrictions that limit its use to more mobile employees, such as:

- *Computer interface.* There is no interface between the time recorded in a timekeeping app on a smart phone and a company's payroll computer system. This means that either someone must rekey the transmitted information into the payroll system, or a custom interface must be created to automatically port the information into the payroll system. The major payroll outsourcing suppliers have smart phone interfaces into their systems, so this is not an issue if payroll is outsourced to any of these suppliers.
- *Phone cost.* If employees are using their smart phones to submit time sheets, it is entirely possible that the company should be paying the monthly service charges for the phones. If so, this amounts to a hefty fee in exchange for giving each employee a portable data entry terminal.
- *Efficiency.* The small form factor of a cell phone represents an inherent limitation on the speed with which someone can enter information. This is a particular problem if employees are required to record descriptive information alongside their hours worked.

These constraints make smart phone time tracking an improbable choice for anyone working *within* a company location, where less expensive and more efficient alternatives are available.

Copy Forward Hours Worked

There are many situations where employees work essentially the same number of hours every week, and work on about the same tasks during that time. If the business has an on-line timekeeping system, consider taking advantage of the situation by providing employees with an option to copy forward their time from the previous time period. This automatic copying function makes it extremely easy for employees to record their time, which means that they will be more likely to update the timekeeping system by the specified due date.

Automated Time Tracking Reminders

Whenever a company adopts a time tracking system, it has an immediate and ongoing problem, which is getting its employees to remember to submit their hours worked in a timely manner. This can be a serious problem, especially when there are only a few days between the end of the pay period and the pay date in which to persuade employees to enter their time.

The traditional solution is to badger dilatory employees with phone calls, but a more advanced solution is to program the time collection system to automatically issue e-mails to employees at increasingly frequent intervals, and to copy their supervisors after the first one or two reminders. This approach keeps an annoying task away from the payroll staff, while ensuring that a proper amount of escalation will be followed at precisely defined intervals.

Analysis of Lean Payroll Data Collection

The ultimate solution for payroll data collection is to dispense with the need for payroll data. However, this is usually not possible, so the best alternative is computerized timekeeping solutions that review submitted information for errors and then forward the information directly into the payroll software. The following bullets expand upon these advantages:

- *Bottlenecks.* If employees use a computerized time clock to clock in and out each day, it will become immediately apparent which employees are missing time punches, which the payroll staff can follow up on immediately.
- *Distance.* The use of computerized timekeeping means that timecards are no longer sent to the payroll department, so there is no risk of losing timekeeping information in transit.
- *Controls.* Supervisors must still be involved in approving hours worked, but they can now do so from their computers, rather than manually reviewing timecards.
- *Error rates.* Timekeeping systems are designed to automatically spot time reporting errors, which can therefore be corrected at the point of data entry, rather than when payroll is about to be processed.

The following flowchart reveals an enhanced process flow for payroll data collection. Process improvements are noted in bold.

Lean Payroll Data Collection

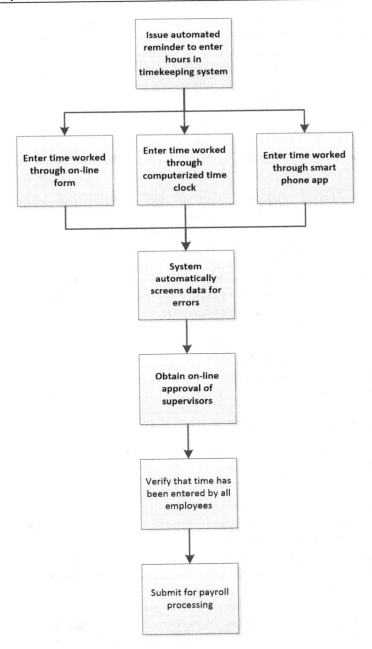

This section has shown that payroll data collection can be converted from a rushed scramble to collect information into a much more orderly process. In the next section, we turn to another type of payroll information – the calculation of salesperson commissions.

Commission Processing

Commissions are usually calculated immediately after the end of a month and paid in the following payroll. Since a commission expense number is needed to close the books and issue financial statements, the commissions clerk tends to be under a great deal of pressure to produce commission information. In this section, we present the outlines of a manual commission calculation process, followed by a discussion of the issues with this system.

Commission Processing

The following steps show the basic process flow for the calculation of commissions. The steps are:

1. *Obtain invoice list.* Obtain a summary of invoices issued during the calculation period, sorted by salesperson.
2. *Move information to spreadsheet.* Transfer report totals by salesperson to an electronic spreadsheet. In some cases, the detailed invoice information may also be included in the report.
3. *Adjust spreadsheet.* Update the spreadsheet for commission splits, additional bonuses issued, commission increases caused by target levels being met, and so forth. Also reduce commissions for invoices declared to be bad debts.
4. *Approve spreadsheet.* Send the completed spreadsheet to the sales manager for review. This may result in the adjustment of the spreadsheet to incorporate changes made by the sales manager.
5. *Forward for processing.* Forward the approved commission spreadsheet to the payroll clerk for entry into the payroll processing system.

Commission Processing Analysis

Commission calculations can produce some of the highest error rates found in any type of accounting transaction, and can also be a significant bottleneck in the production of financial statements. The following bullet points explain these issues:

- *Bottlenecks.* The process of transferring invoice information into a spreadsheet can be a major bottleneck, especially if the commissions clerk cannot automatically extract this information from the accounting system. Also, the sales manager is a bottleneck, since this person may make a number of changes to the spreadsheet and demand several iterations of the report until he or she is satisfied with the outcome.
- *Distance.* The sales manager is a key part of this process, and since sales managers travel more than other employees, it may be difficult for the commissions clerk and the sales manager to coordinate the commission review task.
- *Controls.* A review of commissions by the sales manager is essentially mandatory, since significant amounts of compensation are probably being disbursed through the commission system.

- *Error rates*. The commission error rate varies with the complexity of the commission plan. A highly complex commission plan will probably result in a multitude of commission errors that must be rooted out through several reviews of the commission calculations by the sales manager and commissions clerk.

In short, the sales manager causes commission errors by insisting on having an overly complex commission plan, creates a bottleneck by having to review commissions, and also cannot be removed from the commissions process for control reasons. In the next section, we will explore ways to change commission processing from one of the more annoying accounting areas to one that is largely automated.

Lean Commission Processing

There are several techniques available for converting commission processing into an extremely lean accounting function. The first two options noted below require some cooperation from the sales manager to simplify the commission plan. If the sales manager proves to be obstreperous, then a more expensive option is available.

Commission Plan Simplification

The single largest factor that leads to a convoluted commission process is a highly complex commission plan. The presence of a large number of splits, bonuses, rate changes, and so forth has the following effects:

- *Iterations*. The sales manager and commissions clerk may go back and forth several times with multiple iterations of the commission spreadsheet before there is mutual agreement that commissions have been properly calculated for the sales staff.
- *Opinions*. A complex commission plan may be subject to interpretation. If so, the sales staff may have a different opinion regarding what they should have been paid, which can lead to further iterations with the sales manager and commissions clerk, and possibly commission adjustments after commissions have already been paid. This may result in the issuance of manual checks to salespeople on a rush basis.

Both effects result in an inordinate amount of work within the payroll department. Clearly, the best path to leanness in this area is to simplify the commission plan. By doing so, the number of iterations is reduced, and commission payments will be subject to considerably less interpretation. However, the sales manager probably *created* the current convoluted commission plan, so expect a struggle that may only lead to a marginal reduction in the level of plan complexity.

Standard Commissions Report

If the rules for calculating commissions are reasonably coherent, it may be possible to enter the rules into the report writer used for the accounting system. The result should be an automated, detailed presentation of the commission calculation for each salesperson. This represents the ultimate lean approach to commission processing, for the following reasons:

- *Iterations*. The iteration loop between the commissions clerk and the sales manager is extremely short. Ideally, the sales manager can adjust commission information on-line, immediately run new versions of the report, and forward an approved copy to the commissions clerk.
- *Clerical labor*. There may no longer be a need for a commissions clerk, though there are usually a sufficient number of billing errors each month to still require one.
- *Formula simplification*. The use of a standard commissions report keeps the sales manager from wallowing in excessively detailed commission formulas, since the report writer may not accept some of the more convoluted rules.

> **Tip:** To ensure that all invoices have a salesperson assigned to them, set the invoicing form to require a valid salesperson identification number for each new invoice. If there is legitimately no salesperson to which an invoice should be assigned, use a default code.

Incentive Compensation Management Software

What if the sales manager does *not* agree to the simplified commission plan that we just advocated? Perhaps the sales manager likes to continually tweak the commission plan to drive the sales of specific products or regions, or to guarantee minimum commissions in difficult sales territories. These changes can make it nearly impossible to manually derive commission payments. In this case, an alternative is to acquire a software package that is specifically designed to track complex incentive compensation arrangements.

These software packages accept information from the accounting system through a custom interface, and incorporate the sales manager's complex commission rules to derive the exact amount of commission to be paid to each sales person. The commissions clerk essentially has nothing to do, other than verifying the accuracy of the reported results.

While an incentive compensation management package may seem like the ideal solution for both the sales manager and the commissions clerk, it is also extremely expensive. It is not a cost-effective option for smaller businesses, which must instead rely upon a simpler commission plan in order to achieve a lean commission processing solution.

Analysis of Lean Commission Processing

In essence, lean commission processing can only be achieved by simplifying the commission plan (a free option) or with incentive compensation management software (an expensive option). In either case, the result should be the near-total elimination of bottlenecks and reduced errors, while still including the sales manager in the commission review process. In particular:

- *Bottlenecks*. The elimination of a commission spreadsheet removes a major bottleneck from commissions processing. Also, there are likely to be fewer iterations of the commission review cycle, given the use of either a simplified commission plan or software that can handle complex commission rules.
- *Distance*. The location of the sales manager may still be a problem when commission reviews are needed.
- *Controls*. The sales manager is still the primary control over commission payments.
- *Error rates*. Error rates will decline with a simplified commission plan. Or, if an incentive compensation management system is installed and properly configured, errors should also be minimized.

The following flowchart reveals the altered process flow for commission processing. Process improvements are noted in bold.

Lean Commission Calculation Processing

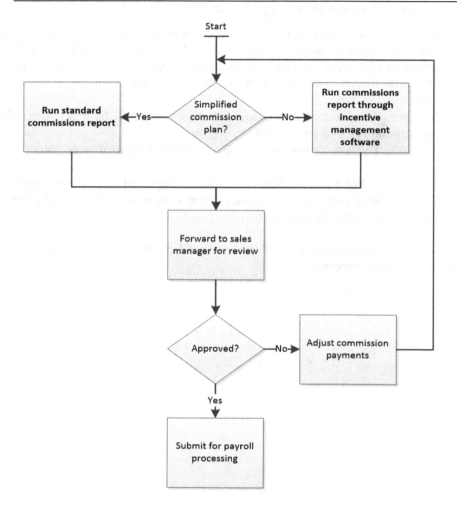

This section has shown that a combination of rules changes and reporting upgrades can yield an efficient, lean commission processing system.

Payroll Processing

Payroll processing involves entering a variety of information into a company's payroll software in order to generate payments for employees. This is a time-critical function, and is also subject to a high rate of error. In this section, we present the outlines of a payroll processing system, followed by a discussion of the issues with this system.

Payroll Processing

The following steps show the basic process flow for payroll processing. The steps are:

1. *Update employee master file.* Update the employee master file in the payroll software with all change notifications received, such as for changes of employee name, address, pay rate, marriage status, and so forth.
2. *Set pay period.* Verify that the payroll module is set for the correct pay period.
3. *Enter time worked.* Enter into the system the amount of regular and overtime hours worked by each employee.
4. *Enter manual payments.* Enter the amounts of any manual paychecks that have not yet been recorded in the payroll system.
5. *Calculate termination pay.* Manually calculate the amount payable to any employee who has left the company, including their unused vacation time and severance pay.
6. *Alter deductions.* Enter any changes to the standard deductions from employee pay, such as charitable contributions, insurance, garnishments, and pension plans.
7. *Calculate pay.* Have the software process all pay calculations for the period. If the company manually calculates pay, then use the tax tables provided by the federal and state governments to determine the proper amount of tax withholdings.
8. *Review payroll register.* Print a preliminary payroll register and review it for errors. Process payroll again until these errors have been resolved.
9. *Issue payments.* As described in the Employee Payment Processing section.
10. *Lock down the period.* Lock down the payroll period in the payroll module for the period just completed, to prevent unauthorized changes.
11. *Deposit taxes.* Deposit payroll taxes and verify their transmission to the government.

Payroll Processing Analysis

Payroll processing requires a significant amount of data entry into the payroll software within a short period of time. The real issue is not the volume of transactions, but rather the variety of data items to be entered and the brief time span within which they must be entered; the combination leads to an increased level of data entry errors. The following bullet points explain these issues:

- *Bottlenecks.* The real bottleneck in the payroll process is in the accumulation of timekeeping information (as described in the preceding sections); once this information has been aggregated, it is not especially difficult to enter it into the payroll software.
- *Distance.* Payroll updates sent to the company from outlying locations may not reach the payroll department in time to be processed in the next payroll.

- *Error rates*. The payroll data entry staff is effectively buried under a mound of disparate data items, and must somehow enter them all into the payroll software within a few hours. The result is a number of possible errors that must be rooted out by closely examining the preliminary payroll register. Also, there is a significant risk of not remitting payroll taxes to the government on a timely basis, which can lead to government-imposed fines.

In the next section, we will explore how to create a more lean payroll processing function.

Lean Payroll Processing

There are several ways to arrive at a lean payroll process – by having fewer payrolls, shifting some portions of the work to a supplier, shifting data entry to people outside of the payroll department, and/or by reducing the total amount of information to be entered. These alternatives are described below.

Payroll Cycle Duration

One of the more important payroll management decisions is how long to set the payroll cycle. Each payroll requires a great deal of effort by the payroll staff to collect information about time worked, locate and correct errors, process wage rate and deduction changes, calculate pay, and issue payments. Consequently, it makes a great deal of sense to extend the duration of payroll cycles.

If payrolls are spaced at short intervals, such as weekly, the payroll staff has to prepare 52 payrolls per year. Conversely, paying employees once a month reduces the payroll staff's payroll preparation activities by approximately three-quarters. Since paying just once a month can be a burden on employees, companies frequently adopt a half-way measure, paying employees either twice a month (the *semimonthly* payroll) or once every two weeks (the *biweekly* payroll). The semimonthly payroll cycle results in processing 24 payrolls per year, while the biweekly payroll cycle requires the processing of 26 payrolls per year. In addition, the semimonthly payroll coincides with the reporting period, and so makes it easier to calculate payroll expenses for the monthly financial statements.

An argument in favor of the biweekly payroll is that employees become accustomed to receiving two paychecks per month, plus two "free" paychecks during the year, which has a somewhat more positive impact on employee morale. Nonetheless, the semimonthly payroll represents a slight improvement over the biweekly payroll from the perspective of payroll department efficiency, and is therefore recommended.

Tip: If employees are accustomed to a weekly payroll cycle and they are switched to one of a longer duration, expect to have some employees complain about not having enough cash to see them through the initial increased payroll cycle. This problem can be mitigated by extending pay advances to employees during the initial conversion to the longer payroll cycle. Once employees receive their larger paychecks under the new payroll cycle, they should be able to support themselves and will no longer need an advance.

A further issue is when a company operates a different payroll cycle for different groups of employees. For example, hourly employees may be paid on a weekly cycle and salaried employees on a semimonthly cycle. To complicate matters further, a company may have acquired other businesses and retained the payroll cycles used for their employees. Retaining all of these payroll cycles places the payroll staff in the position of perpetually preparing payrolls, so that it never has time for other activities. To avoid this problem, convert all of the different payroll cycles to a single one that applies to *all* employees.

In short, paying employees at roughly half-month intervals and not allowing any additional payroll cycles can greatly reduce the work load of the payroll department.

Off-Cycle Payroll Elimination

Whenever the payroll staff must complete a payroll, it has to enter any necessary documentation, review preliminary payroll registers, print checks, finalize the payroll cycle, and so forth. Despite the extra workload, some managers insist on having additional off-cycle payrolls in order to make special bonus payments to their employees. Given the high labor cost involved, the payroll manager should insist on a large interdepartmental charge to run extra payrolls, or at least the approval of the chief financial officer. If an off-cycle payroll is needed to correct errors in a prior payroll, try to push the error corrections forward into the next regularly-scheduled payroll.

Outsource Payroll Processing

An in-house payroll department may have to issue paychecks for multiple locations, stay aware of changes in local payroll tax rates, remit taxes, and issue reports to the various government entities on payroll issues. All of these functions can be shifted to a third-party service provider. The company must still accumulate payroll information and enter it into the off-site payroll system maintained by the service provider, but nearly all subsequent activities are handled by the provider. Specifically, outsourcing payroll processing means that the payroll department no longer handles these items:

- Calculate gross wages
- Calculate tax deductions and withholdings
- Create paychecks, initiate direct deposit payments, and forward cash to payroll cards

- Remit taxes and withholdings to government entities
- Report new hire information to government entities
- Issue W-2 forms to employees following the end of the year

A payroll manager will undoubtedly find that outsourcing payroll represents a net increase in the costs of the department. However, outsourcing eliminates so many tasks that are subject to error that it can result in a significant improvement in the lean profile of the department.

Payroll Data Entry by Employees

Many payroll software packages and outsourced payroll providers have created on-line forms that employees can use to enter certain payroll information into the payroll system. Examples of information that an employee could enter directly are direct deposit information, tax withholdings, and address changes. Any business that has this option available should certainly take advantage of it, for the following reasons:

- Employees are more knowledgeable about the changes they want to make to their payroll records, and so are more likely to make accurate changes than the payroll staff (when assisted by error-checking routines in the on-line form).
- The data entry task for these items can be shifted away from the payroll staff, which reduces the bottleneck occurring during payroll processing and potentially shrinks the total amount of labor needed in the payroll department.

Tip: Run a cost-benefit analysis before constructing a custom data entry system for a legacy payroll system. Almost any change to legacy software is expensive, so it is possible that this change will not be worth the investment.

Payroll Data Entry by Managers

The on-line forms just noted for employees are also available for managers. These forms are of less importance from a lean perspective, for the amount of information entered into the payroll system by managers is less than what employees can potentially enter. If installed, a manager on-line form can be used to record employee pay rate changes, transfers of employees to different departments or locations, employee leave, and so forth. Given the impact on employee compensation levels, it may be necessary to append a workflow solution to the form, so that senior managers must give their approval before unusually large pay rate changes are accepted by the system.

General: Prohibition of Employee Advances

If employees are short on cash, they may request an advance on their next paycheck. When this happens, the payroll staff must cut a manual check, have it signed, manually record it in the accounting records, and then manually deduct it from the next paycheck. When the advance is quite large or the employee is in significant financial straits, the manual deduction may be spread over several subsequent paychecks. The extremely high level of inefficiency brought about by the request for an advance makes it necessary to have a corporate policy that prohibits *all* advances. This will not go over well with those employees who have been accustomed to treating the company as their personal bank in the past, and so will require reinforcement from senior management.

As a slightly less harsh alternative, an entity can prohibit all advances unless approved by the chief financial officer. For such a policy to be effective, the CFO should operate under strict guidelines regarding when advances can be granted.

General: Prohibition of Reimbursements through Payroll

Some companies purchase goods on behalf of their employees, or sell goods directly to employees, and allow them to pay the company back through a series of payroll deductions. It is time-consuming for the payroll staff to create these deductions and track them until the full amount has been paid off. Also, the more cash-poor employees may continually adjust the amount of the deduction, which creates even more work for the payroll staff. The clear solution is to have a company policy that prohibits all employee reimbursements through the payroll system. The only leeway that should be allowed is to have employees pay the company in full with a check payment as soon as the goods arrive that were ordered on their behalf.

General: Reduction of Pay Deductions

In a larger organization, it can take a considerable amount of time for the payroll staff to enter updates to employee deductions in the payroll system. This tends to be a larger problem where a business offers its employees a broad range of benefits, each one requiring a separate deduction for the employee share of the expense. The updating problem is especially severe whenever the cost of a benefit changes, since this means that the payroll staff must update the amount of the related benefit deduction for all employees. In addition, deductions may have been entered incorrectly, requiring periodic updates for any errors found.

There are several ways to reduce the number of pay deductions. One option is to offer a single benefits package to all employees, with a single deduction associated with it. Another possibility is to have the company pay the full amount of some benefits, so there is no deduction at all; this works well if the deduction is currently for a trivial amount. Or, consider completely eliminating some existing benefits in exchange for paying the full amount of other benefits (which is doubly effective from the perspective of eliminating deductions). Finally, consider instituting a policy that limits the number of benefits changes that employees are permitted to make per year. Any of these options will reduce the number of pay deductions.

General: Combine Payroll Systems

If a company has made a number of acquisitions, it may have retained the payroll system of each of the acquired businesses. If so, the company probably has the following problems:

- *Headcount.* The parent company is paying a full payroll staff at each subsidiary.
- *Software.* The parent company is paying for separate software maintenance at each subsidiary. Also, there may be multiple software packages in use throughout the company, which makes it difficult to create interfaces with the various systems, write standard procedures, and train employees on how to use the systems.
- *Payroll taxes.* If an employee moves from one subsidiary to another, the company may pay more than the normal amount of those payroll taxes that are capped at a certain compensation level per year.

The solution is to centralize payroll processing for the entire company. While this may require a robust and more expensive payroll system, it also eliminates overlapping payroll employees, the maintenance of a disparate set of payroll software packages, and the risk of paying an excessive amount of payroll taxes. It is also easier to impose the most efficient payroll improvements, since there is only one system to modify.

Analysis of Lean Payroll Processing

The revisions suggested in this section can put a substantial dent in the amount of data that must be entered, since the repayment of advances and purchases are eliminated, and the volume of deductions has been reduced or even eliminated. Further, the remaining data entry can be shifted to employees and managers outside of the payroll department. In addition, do not forget the use of computerized timekeeping systems that we advocated in an earlier section, since the information collected by those systems can be ported directly into the payroll software. The result may eventually be the complete elimination of data entry by the payroll department, other than error corrections.

In addition, the number of payroll cycles can be reduced to shrink the amount of payroll processing per year, while outsourcing may be a viable method for shifting compensation calculations, payments, and tax remittances to a supplier who is better equipped to handle these activities. The result can be a satisfyingly lean payroll processing function.

The following flowchart shows the revised payroll process flow. Process improvements are noted in bold.

Lean Payroll Processing

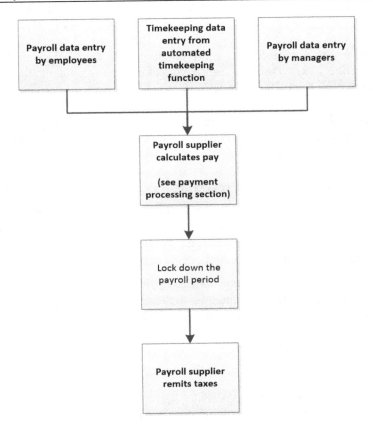

Employee Payment Processing

The employee payment process is not the most time-consuming task in the payroll department, but it contains a check signing bottleneck and an occasionally difficult payment distribution chore. In this section, we present the outlines of the employee payment system, followed by a discussion of issues with the system.

Employee Payment Processing

The following steps show the basic process flow for employee payment processing. The steps are:

1. *Obtain check stock.* Remove check stock from a locked storage cabinet.
2. *Print and review checks.* Print paychecks. Review and reprint them if necessary.
3. *Accept batch.* Accept the printed batch in the payroll software, which records the payments in the accounting records.
4. *Return unused check stock.* Return any remaining unused checks to the locked storage area, and log the range of check numbers that were used.

5. *Print and store final register.* The payroll software may require that a final payroll register be printed. If so, print and store it in the payroll archives area.
6. *Sign checks.* Have an authorized check signer sign all paychecks.
7. *Stuff checks.* Stuff the checks into envelopes for delivery to employees.
8. *Deliver checks.* Deliver the paychecks to supervisors for delivery to employees. For off-site locations, send paychecks by overnight delivery service.
9. *Issue W-2 Forms.* Shortly after the end of the calendar year, issue a W-2 form to each employee, on which is stated the amount paid to them by the company in the past year.

Analysis of Employee Payment Processing

The traditional process of paying employees by check is not especially difficult, but there has to be a check signer on hand when the checks are printed, and the payroll staff is responsible for distributing what may be quite a large number of payments to multiple locations. The following bullet points explain these issues:

- *Bottlenecks.* Paychecks are usually printed within a very narrow time window, after which they must be distributed at once. If an authorized check signer is not available during that time window, employees will not be paid on time.
- *Distance.* Paychecks may have to be sent to multiple locations, which calls for close coordination with overnight delivery services, with occasional payment failures.
- *Controls.* The controls applied to accounts payable check payments also apply to paychecks, which lengthens the time period required for this process.
- *Error rates.* The primary error in the payments area is the failure to deliver checks to employees on a timely basis.

In the next section, we will explore ways to eliminate the problems associated with check payments.

Lean Employee Payment Processing

The principle improvement to employee payment processing is to replace check payments with electronic payments. By doing so, the check signer bottleneck is eliminated and the problems associated with multi-location payment deliveries are removed. This concept, among others, is addressed below.

Direct Deposit

Direct deposit involves the electronic transfer of funds from the company to the bank accounts of its employees, using the Automated Clearing House (ACH) system. The payment process is to calculate pay in the same manner as for check payments, but to then send the payment information to a direct deposit processing service, which initiates electronic payments to the bank accounts of those employees being paid in this manner. Direct deposit is more efficient than payments by check, because it does not require a signature on each payment, there are no checks to be delivered, and employees do not have to waste time depositing them at a bank. Further, employees who are off-site can still rely upon having cash paid into their accounts in a timely manner.

Direct deposit can also be more efficient from the perspective of the remittance advice. A number of payroll suppliers offer an option to simply notify employees by e-mail when their pay has been sent to them, after which employees can access a secure website to view their remittance advice information. This approach is better than sending a paper version of a remittance advice, because employees can also access many years of historical pay information through the secure website.

Despite its efficiency advantages, direct deposit is not perfect, for it requires employees to have bank accounts. If this is an issue, consider using a blended solution with pay cards (see the next suggestion) for those employees who do not have a bank account.

The implementation of direct deposit can cause some initial difficulties, because each person's bank account information must be correctly set up in the direct deposit module of the payroll software (or software provided by the outsourced payroll supplier). This initial setup is prone to error, and also usually requires a test transaction (the *pre-notification*) that delays implementation by one pay period. Consequently, even if a new employee signs up for direct deposit immediately, a paycheck must still be printed for that person's first payroll, after which direct deposit can be used.

Tip: Consider paying all new employees by direct deposit as the default form of payment, so that they have to opt out if they do not want it. This ensures a high level of direct deposit participation.

Pay Cards

If there are employees who do not have a bank account and do not want one, they are either asking for payment in cash or are taking their paychecks to a check cashing service that charges a high fee. The situation can be improved for these workers by offering them a *pay card*, which is also known as a *payroll card* or *debit card*. The company transfers funds directly into the pay card, so there is no need for a check cashing service. Employees can make purchases directly with the card, or use it to obtain cash through an ATM. The company still issues a remittance advice to all pay card holders, so they can see the detail behind the amounts being paid to them. The advantages for the company are similar to those already stated for direct deposit.

Tip: To encourage the use of pay cards, consider installing an automated teller machine (ATM) on the company premises that will accept the pay cards. An ATM can be leased or purchased, and a monthly maintenance fee will likely be charged. An ATM also needs a dedicated phone line.

General: On-line Access to W-2 Forms

If a company has outsourced its payroll processing, the provider may offer the storage of W-2 forms on a secure website. This allows employees access to their annual pay information for multiple years, and takes the burden of issuing W-2 forms away from the payroll staff. In addition, the payroll staff no longer has to dredge up old copies of W-2 forms for those employees who need this information for mortgage applications and other purposes.

Analysis of Lean Employee Payments

Any form of electronic payment eliminates the bottleneck associated with check signing, though some form of review should be conducted to replace the control point represented by the check signer. The key improvement to the payment process is the complete elimination of distance considerations for the payroll department, since electronic payments can be delivered to any bank account where ACH transactions are accepted.

The following flowchart reveals the altered process flow for employee payments. Process improvements are noted in bold.

Lean Employee Payment Processing

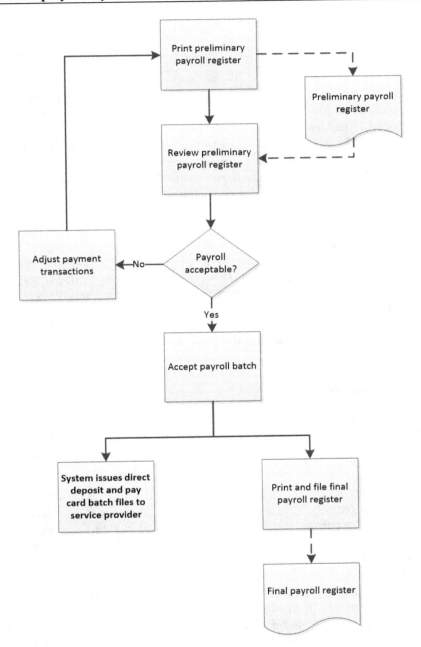

This section has shown that lean principles can be used to eliminate large portions of the labor involved in employee payment processing.

Additional Improvement Concepts

There are a number of additional concepts that can be applied to the payroll process to enhance its performance or reduce costs. These concepts did not fit into any of the process flows noted previously or were considered minor elements, and so are noted here instead:

- *Eliminate sick pay.* It can be quite time-consuming for the payroll or human resources employees to track the amount of sick time accrued and used. Instead, consider rolling sick pay into a paid time off account that aggregates all forms of time off into a single figure that needs to be monitored.
- *Eliminate vacation tracking.* An advanced concept is to allow employees to take paid time off whenever they need to, as long as their assigned tasks are completed on time. This concept eliminates the entire issue with tracking accrued and used vacation time, but can be subject to abuse by some employees.
- *Employ the common paymaster rule.* A multi-division company may have employees who work for several divisions during the calendar year, and are paid in turn by each division. If so, the company as a whole may be spending too much on matching payroll taxes for those employees whose total compensation exceeds the relevant wage cap for certain payroll taxes. In this case, consider using the common paymaster rule to pay all employees from a single location throughout the year, so that the amount of matching taxes paid is never too high.

Payroll Measurements

As the payroll function changes from a data entry organization to one that mostly reviews transactions and maintains payroll systems, its measurements must change to accommodate the new, leaner organization. The following two measurements are of most use to an enhanced payroll department:

- *Payroll errors.* Compile a list of all payroll errors uncovered (usually by paycheck recipients) and routinely work through the list to determine why the errors occurred, and to implement ways to ensure that they do not happen again. When there are many errors, it is useful to aggregate them by type, and then place the most emphasis on fixing the error types that contain the largest number of errors.
- *Staff entries per 1,000 employees.* Eventually, the payroll staff should have little transaction-level work to do, as more data entry is automated or shifted over to employees and managers. To view this decline, track on a trend line the total number of transaction entries made by the payroll staff per 1,000 employees. The intent of this measurement is not corrective, but rather to monitor the progress of the department toward a goal of having zero transactions entered by the payroll staff.

Note that these measurements focus on the twin goals of eliminating errors and getting the payroll department out of the data entry business.

Summary

In this chapter, we described how a variety of changes could be used to arrive at a more lean payroll process, with the following changes being the most important:

- Data collection minimization
- Computerized, web-based, and smart phone time clocks
- Standard commissions report
- Payroll cycle duration
- Payroll data entry by employees and managers
- Direct deposit and pay cards

The net result of these changes could be a situation where the payroll staff is shifted from the role of data entry clerks to monitoring the data entered by others. This scenario gives the payroll staff more time to investigate possible errors, which in turn drives down the number of errors experienced, thereby reducing the amount of payroll staff, and so on. In short, when the changes advocated in this chapter are implemented, the payroll function will have become more lean than most other parts of a business.

For more information about payroll, see the latest annual edition of the author's *Payroll Management* book.

Chapter 6
Lean Financial Statements

Introduction

The accounting department is responsible for many activities, but its best-known product is the financial statements. The financials contain time-critical information, so it is important to issue them as soon as possible after the end of an accounting period. A controller who is intent on achieving a lean accounting department might cut back on departmental funding to such an extent that it takes longer than normal to issue financial statements. This would be a mistake, for the information in the financial statements is of great value, and the utility of that information degrades the longer its issuance is delayed. Consequently, our definition of "lean" must change when dealing with financial statements. Instead of using minimal resources, a lean accounting department must focus on lean *timing* – that is, issuing financial statements as rapidly as possible.

In this chapter, we begin with an overview of improvement concepts, then describe how financial statements are usually produced, and finally show the impact of lean improvement concepts on financial statements.

Related Podcast Episodes: Episodes 16 through 25, 77, 160, and 199 of the Accounting Best Practices Podcast discuss closing the books. These episodes are available at: **accountingtools.com/podcasts** or **iTunes**

Improvement Concepts

The application of lean concepts in this chapter involves the following improvements to existing systems, with the intent of producing financial statements more quickly:

- *Financial statement avoidance.* Issuing financial statements on only a quarterly basis, possibly supplemented by "soft close" financials in other months.
- *Task interdependency analysis.* Being aware of the closing steps that prevent a faster issuance of financial statements.
- *Correct errors early.* Reviewing the financial statements for errors a few days before the end of the accounting period.
- *Reconcile accounts early.* Beginning the account reconciliation task a few days before month-end.
- *Adjust reserves early.* Updating period-end reserves as early as possible, to remove this task from the core closing period.

- *Alter overhead allocations early.* Adjusting overhead allocations as early as possible, to remove this task from the core closing period.
- *Review the shipping log early.* Examining the shipping log early, to see if there are any missing billings that can be corrected in advance of period-end.
- *Review billable hours early.* Reviewing billable hours in advance to adjust for any errors found.
- *Accrue early.* Making accrual entries early for all transactions where it is feasible to do so.
- *Accelerate depreciation calculations.* Running depreciation calculations prior to the end of the accounting period.
- *Examine commissions early.* Reviewing commissions in advance for possible issues.
- *Standardize the accounting system.* Using the same accounting software and procedures in all company locations.
- *Centralize the accounting system.* Shifting all accounting work to a single location.
- *Centralize travel bookings.* Having the company pay directly for travel bookings, thereby reducing the impact of missing or late expense reports.
- *Process centering.* Reducing the number of hand-offs of closing tasks between employees.
- *Mitigate information dependencies.* Altering systems to avoid the need for information coming from other departments.
- *Standardize the report layout.* Issuing a single, standard set of financial statements to all recipients.
- *Reduce the financial statements.* Issuing a reduced set of financial statement information to all recipients.
- *Collect report information early.* Obtaining information for accompanying reports as early as possible.
- *Electronic delivery.* Issuing financial statements by electronic means to all recipients.
- *Defer activities.* Deliberately delaying a number of routine activities until the financial statements have been issued.
- *Automation solutions.* Using several types of technology to enhance the closing process.
- *Ongoing process improvements.* Using an issue tracking system to continually improve the closing process.

How Financial Statements are Usually Produced

This section addresses the normal sequence of events that are used to create financial statements. Of particular importance is the timing of these activities. Note that the closing begins immediately *after* the end of an accounting period, and continues for a number of days. We will deal with the compression of this time interval in the following section.

The Production of Financial Statements

Most controllers have arrived at a reasonable set of processing steps that eventually yield an accurate set of financial statements. The exact steps required will vary by type of business, but the basic process flow is:

1. *Invoicing.* As soon as the accounting period has been completed, obtain all remaining shipping documentation from the shipping department and issue invoices to customers. If the company bills for services, then contact employees to enter their billable hours into the timekeeping system, and wait for them to do so before issuing invoices. In the latter case, this may require a delay of several days before invoices can be issued.

2. *Cost of goods sold.* Either conduct a physical count at month-end (under the periodic inventory system) or derive ending inventory from a month-end inventory report (under the perpetual inventory system). In either case, compare the resulting cost of goods sold to revenue for reasonableness, and investigate the ending inventory information if the gross margin varies significantly from historical results.

3. *Bank reconciliation.* Upon receipt of the period-end bank statement, conduct a bank reconciliation and book any differences to the company's accounts.

4. *Accrue payables.* If suppliers have not submitted invoices after a few days have passed, accrue expenses for the amounts estimated to be on those invoices, and set them to automatically reverse in the following period.

5. *Calculate depreciation.* Once the accounts payable portion of the closing process has been completed, update the fixed asset records with any fixed assets that were purchased (or disposed of) during the period, and calculate and record depreciation.

6. *Accrue payroll.* Wait for hours worked to be recorded by all employees through the end of the reporting period. If there were any unpaid hours as of the end of the period, accrue an expense for these hours, and set the entry to automatically reverse in the following period.

7. *Update reserves.* After sales, accounts receivable, and inventory have been finalized, review all related reserve accounts (such as for sales returns, doubtful accounts, and obsolete inventory) to see if they require adjustments.

8. *Reconcile accounts.* A prudent controller will at least examine the contents of the larger balance sheet accounts, to ensure that nothing should have been charged to revenue or expense in the period. This may call for the comparison of detailed reports to the accounts, such as the reports for accounts receivable, accounts payable, and fixed assets.

9. *Review financials.* Print the financial statements and review them for errors. At a minimum, there are likely to have been entries that were made into the

wrong accounts, which will require adjusting entries. Several iterations of this step may be necessary.

10. *Accrue taxes.* If the financial statements appear to be correct, accrue income taxes if there are taxable earnings.

11. *Create disclosures.* If the financial statements are to be distributed outside of the company, add any disclosures mandated by accounting standards. If the company is publicly held, also calculate earnings per share and add this information to the financials.

12. *Distribute financials.* Issue the financial statements to the distribution list. In many organizations, different reports may be issued to each person on the list. For example, the company president receives the entire financial statement package, while the sales manager receives just the income statement and a detailed report on the expenses incurred by the sales department – and so on.

13. *Close the period.* Most accounting software packages require that an accounting period be formally closed in the accounting records and the next period opened. Doing so ensures that the transactions related to the next period will not be inadvertently recorded in the wrong period.

In a larger organization, it may also be necessary to eliminate any intercompany transactions, where subsidiaries have sold goods or services to each other.

Analysis of Financial Statement Production

There is nothing inherently wrong with the preceding steps to create financial statements. However, the results may be quite delayed, with financials being issued possibly several weeks after the end of an accounting period. The reasons for the delay can be found in the following areas:

- *Bottlenecks.* There are many bottlenecks in the closing process. For example, invoices for services cannot be issued until employees record their billable hours. Also, expenses cannot be accrued until a suitable interval has passed, during which late supplier invoices may arrive. Also, if a physical inventory count is required, this must be completed before an ending inventory valuation can be derived. The sheer number of bottlenecks is bound to delay the release of financial statements.

- *Distance.* If subsidiaries maintain their own accounting records, then they must first close their books before submitting their results to the parent company – which delays the closing even more.

- *Controls.* Any responsible controller wants to issue financial statements that contain no material errors. Achieving this goal calls for a great deal of cross checking of information. In addition, the longer the closing takes, the more likely it is that the information being reported will be accurate, since the passage of time tends to clarify uncertainties (such as which customer invoices will not be collectible). Thus, the time involved can actually act as a control over financial statement accuracy.

- *Error rates.* The controller is always hunting for material errors that can impact the financial statements, which is why it is not at all uncommon for the financial statements to go through several iterations while the accounting staff picks through each line item, looking for mistakes. The same level of care should go into account reconciliations. The result is a delayed release of financial statements.

In short, the traditional method for issuing financial statements works, but there are so many bottlenecks and potential errors that controllers prefer to take their time and release financials after a number of days have passed, when they are sure of the results being reported. In the following section, we will discuss a more regimented approach to producing financial statements that can greatly accelerate their completion.

Lean Financial Statements

In this section, we focus on how to fine-tune the closing process with a variety of management techniques, with the goal of accelerating the production of financial statements. The core concepts are:

- *Financial statement avoidance.* There may be a few cases where management is willing to operate with fewer financial statements per year, or with statements that do not incorporate all of the adjustments required by accounting standards.
- *Task interdependency analysis.* This involves examining the work flow to determine which tasks are delaying the completion of the close.
- *Early activities.* This involves completing selected closing tasks prior to the core closing period at month-end. Such activities include early reconciliations, accruals, and commission calculations.
- *Standardize and centralize.* This is the imposition of identical accounting procedures in all locations, and possibly the complete centralization of the accounting function.
- *Reduce reporting.* This is the reduction of the information contained within the financial statements.
- *Defer activities.* This is the shifting of non-closing activities out of the core closing period.
- *Use automation.* This is the use of technology to enhance the efficiency of the closing process.

The net result of these changes should be a massive reduction in the number of days required to issue financial statements. We delve into these changes through the remainder of this section.

Much of the information in this section is adapted from the author's *Closing the Books* book, which provides complete coverage of how to create financial statements.

Financial Statement Avoidance

In nearly all cases, companies prefer to issue some sort of financial statements at the end of each month, since management needs continual feedback about the financial condition of the business. Nonetheless, there may be situations where a controller who is intent on achieving a very lean department can avoid issuing financial statements. Accordingly, we mention the following two possibilities in passing:

- *Quarterly financials.* It may be possible to only issue financial statements once every three months, thereby eliminating statement preparation for two-thirds of the year. However, the missing statements should be replaced with a set of reports that still give management a reasonable impression of how the business is operating in the meantime. Quarterly financials are probably not suitable in an emerging market where a business is gyrating through changes at a rapid pace, since there is an inadequate feedback loop. Conversely, this approach might work in a staid industry where there is little competitive pressure and financial results have been consistent for a long time.
- *Soft close.* A soft close does not bother with the use of period-end accruals or overhead allocations, and only estimates the amount of ending inventory. These are among the more time-consuming month-end tasks, so financial statements can be produced more quickly. Of course, the financials will not be as accurate, but may at least give management a general idea of the condition of the business. A soft close can work well if it is supplemented on a quarterly basis by financials that include all closing steps.

Task Interdependency Analysis

The simplest tool for closing the books more quickly is task interdependency analysis. In essence, this analysis seeks out the few processes within the entire system of closing activities that keep the accounting department from issuing financial statements more quickly. This concept is best illustrated with an example.

EXAMPLE

The accounting team of Lowry Locomotion finds that it can consistently issue financial statements in about six business days. The controller hires a process analyst, who constructs the following table to break down the start and stop times of some of the more important activities needed to produce the financial statements:

Lean Financial Statements

Closing Activity	Day 1	Day 2	Day 3	Day 4	Day 5	Day 6
Payroll	Collect timesheets	Accrue wages	Review billable hours			
Customer invoicing	Invoice shipments		Invoice billable hours	Accrue commissions		
Supplier payables		Accrue liabilities	Update fixed assets			
Fixed assets				Record depreciation		
Inventory valuation	Count inventory	Count inventory	Value inventory	Allocate overhead		
General ledger		Reconcile cash account	Reconcile other accounts			
Financial statements					Compile and review financials	Add commentary and issue

The chart of task interdependencies reveals that (obviously) the financial statements cannot be prepared until a variety of other closing tasks have first been completed. In particular, the accounting team needs to eliminate all of the activities appearing in Day 4 in order to accelerate the compilation and review of the financial statements by one day. To do so, it needs to address three issues:

- *Customer invoicing.* The accrual of commissions in Day 4 can be completed earlier if the invoicing of billable hours in Day 3 can be accelerated. That is achievable if the employees tasked with payroll activities can review billable hours in Day 2 instead of Day 3.
- *Fixed assets.* The recordation of depreciation in Day 4 can be shifted to Day 3 if the updating of fixed assets by the employees tasked with supplier payables can be moved from Day 3 to Day 2.
- *Inventory valuation.* The allocation of overhead in Day 4 can be moved to Day 3 by increasing the workload of the employees tasked with inventory valuation on Day 3.

The accounting staff enacts these changes, resulting in the following table that reflects the altered schedule, and which allows the company to issue financial statements one day sooner.

Closing Activity	Day 1	Day 2	Day 3	Day 4	Day 5
Payroll	Collect timesheets	Accrue wages, review billable hours			
Customer invoicing	Invoice shipments	Invoice billable hours	Accrue commissions		
Supplier payables	Accrue liabilities	Update fixed assets			
Fixed assets			Record depreciation		
Inventory valuation	Count inventory		Value inventory and allocate overhead		
General ledger		Reconcile cash account	Reconcile other accounts		
Financial statements				Compile and review financials	Add commentary and issue

As the example demonstrated, it may be necessary to shift the timing of a number of activities in order to issue financial statements more quickly. As the closing process is gradually refined, this will mean that a large number of activities will be compressed into a very small time period, which requires extremely tight scheduling of activities. As a result, the controller may find it necessary to adopt the role of master scheduler and shift a number of hands-on closing tasks to other people.

Correct Errors Early

Transactional errors can arise throughout the month, which means that the financial statements can be run a few days prior to month-end and examined for errors. This is a vast improvement over waiting until the middle of the closing process and *then* finding problems. By spotting errors a few days early, the accounting staff can research and correct items at their leisure, rather than doing so in a hurry at month-end. Also, a rushed error correction at month-end may not yield a proper fix, which means that someone has to research and correct the issue a second time – which may delay closing the books.

If early error correction is used, there will still be a few days near the end of the month where errors may arise, since the accounting staff will not have reviewed financial statements that include those days. Still, there should be far fewer errors to deal with.

Reconcile Accounts Early

One of the lengthier tasks at month-end is to reconcile all of the accounts in the balance sheet that have significant ending balances, to ensure that their contents are correct. The accounting staff could start these reconciliations a few days before month-end, and then update them for any transactions that occurred during the last couple of days of the month. This is not a cure-all by any means, since many accruals are generated at month-end, and so will not appear in early versions of account reconciliations. Nonetheless, it can remove a fair amount of reconciliation labor from the core closing period.

The concept of reconciling early is especially important for the bank reconciliation. The cash account may have many adjustments each month that are caused by unrecorded bank fees, transactional errors, not-sufficient-funds check rejections, and so forth. The bank accounts can be reconciled a few days early based on the on-line account information that most banks make available to their customers over the Internet. This leaves just a day or two of final reconciliation work during the core closing period.

> **Tip:** Many banks automatically generate PDF versions of monthly bank statements and post them to their web sites, where they can be downloaded. These statements should be available within 24 hours of the end of each month; the monthly bank reconciliation can be completed with this report.

Adjust Reserves Early

It may be possible to adjust reserves early, rather than waiting until month-end. For example, if the company maintains a reserve for obsolete inventory, a review of inventory can be scheduled at any time of the month, along with a reserve adjustment, rather than waiting to do so at month-end. This approach is less useful for the allowance for doubtful accounts, since proportionately more accounts receivable are generated at month-end than at any other time of the month; this makes it difficult to adjust that reserve early.

> **Tip:** Use the simplest possible estimation method to adjust the allowance for doubtful accounts, such as a simple percentage of the total amount of receivables outstanding. The simplest method may not be as accurate as a more complex method, such as conducting a review of individual receivables. However, the calculation of this allowance is difficult to move out of the core closing period, so it may make sense to trade time for accuracy.

Alter Overhead Allocations Early

If a company engages in production activities, it should allocate manufacturing overhead to its ending inventory and cost of goods sold. The usual method for doing so is to add up all manufacturing overhead costs during the period and allocate them based on an activity, such as direct labor hours or machine time used. The trouble with this approach is having to wait until the month has been completed to determine (for example) how many direct labor hours or machine hours were used during the period, which then forms the basis for the allocation. It can take time to compile this allocation information, so consider using the allocation information from the immediately preceding month, or perhaps an average for the preceding three months. By doing so, it is not necessary to wait for the compilation of any operational information for the month that was just completed, thereby shifting work out of the core closing period.

Review the Shipping Log Early

Some organizations have procedural difficulties in issuing invoices to all of the customers to whom they have shipped goods, resulting in some missed billings. This issue can be rectified by comparing all issued invoices to the shipping log that is maintained by the shipping department. In companies where missed invoices is a recurring problem, matching invoices to the shipping log is a key part of the closing process. It can be tedious to crosscheck invoices against the shipping log, and so can interfere with the closing process. To mitigate this issue, consider conducting the comparison shortly before the end of the month; doing so will spot any missed billing opportunities for the bulk of the month. It will still be necessary to conduct the review during the core closing period, but only for the last few days of the month.

Review Billable Hours Early

When a business earns revenue by billing its staff time to customers, an important part of the closing process is to ensure that those billable hours are correct. Thus, there should be closing activities to verify that:

- Hours have been billed to the correct customers
- Hours billed are for the correct activities
- The rates per hour are correct
- There is sufficient funding remaining on customer contracts to be billed

When billable time is the core revenue-generating part of a business, these verification steps are likely to be the most important of all closing activities. To keep this verification work from inundating the closing team, consider conducting a preliminary review of billable hours a day or two prior to month-end. Doing so will not spot all errors and adjustments, because many employees wait until month-end to enter their time in the timekeeping system. Nonetheless, catching even a few errors in advance will shift work out of the core closing period.

Accrue Early

There are likely to be a standard number of liabilities that should be accrued as part of every month-end close, so that liabilities are recorded even in the absence of a supplier invoice or other documentation. While these accruals are usually completed in the core closing period, it is possible to calculate and record some of them in advance. For example:

- *Interest expense.* If a company has outstanding debt, accrue interest expense for it, or else wait for the lender to send an invoice for the interest expense. It may be possible to estimate the amount of interest expense prior to month-end. Even if there are sudden changes in the debt level in the last day or two of the month, the amount of interest expense associated with this change is likely to be small, and will be immaterial to the reported results of the business.

- *Vacation expense.* If there is a large amount of accrued but unused vacation time, there should be an expense adjustment each month (or least every quarter) to update the expense. This can be a significant issue in companies that have a large number of employees, liberal vacation policies, and/or do *not* have "use it or lose it" vacation policies. Any one of these three circumstances can result in large amounts of accrued vacation expense. It is usually possible to make this accrual immediately after the last pay period of the month, when employees have recorded their vacation time taken through that date.

- *Wage expense.* If there are any employees paid on an hourly basis, there are likely to be a few days at month-end when those employees have earned wages but have not yet been paid for them. It is usually possible to estimate the amount of these hours worked but not paid prior to month-end and then accrue the expense. The estimate may be slightly different from actual results, but the difference should not be material. The accrual may be somewhat more difficult if the hourly staff is also incurring a significant amount of overtime that is not easily predicted in advance; if so, this accrual may have to wait until all time recording has been completed for the month.

> **Tip:** Have the company follow a policy of having employees record their time every day in the timekeeping system. This means that the wage information available for accrual purposes is very nearly current, which makes it easier to calculate a reasonably accurate wage accrual just prior to month-end.

- *Accruals in general.* Complete accruals early by estimation, rather than waiting for final information. Within a week of month-end, management has a good idea of what will happen in the next few days, so that the estimates used for accruals are likely to be fairly accurate.

Accelerate Depreciation Calculations

It is not necessary to wait until the core closing period to calculate the depreciation and amortization expense for the month. Instead, do so a day or two in advance for all fixed assets that have been recorded through that point. If any fixed assets are recorded subsequent to that date, consider the impact on the financial statements of *not* recording the associated monthly amount of depreciation:

- Missing $1/36^{th}$ of the expense for an asset depreciated over three years

- Missing $1/60^{th}$ of the expense for an asset depreciated over five years
- Missing $1/120^{th}$ of the expense for an asset depreciated over ten years

In short, the impact on a single accounting period is extremely small. Further, double the amount of depreciation can be recorded in the next month for any fixed assets that missed the prior month depreciation, so there is no impact on the financial statements at all over even a short period of time.

The only time of the year when it is not possible to accelerate the depreciation calculations is at the end of the fiscal year, since the auditors will certainly want to see depreciation calculations that link back to the ending fixed asset balance.

Examine Commissions Early

It can be quite difficult to prepare the commissions payable documentation prior to month-end, especially when a large part of the monthly invoices are not issued until month-end, and commissions are based on the invoices. Still, there are some tasks or system changes to consider that might ease the commission calculation work. They are:

- *Switch to commissions paid from cash receipts.* If commissions are paid based on cash received from customers, it is possible to reliably calculate commissions throughout the month, as cash comes in. This may work better from a closing perspective than paying based on invoices issued, since many businesses issue a disproportionate number of invoices at month-end, which delays commission calculations until month-end.
- *Ask about plan changes.* Commission plans are notorious for incorporating a vast array of arcane payment features, such as retroactive rate increases if quarterly or annual targets are met, altered commissions for certain products, bonuses, and splits between multiple salespeople. If the sales manager has made yet another change to these plans, it is useful to document the changes in advance.
- *Itemize trigger points.* If some salespeople are about to receive different commission percentages or bonuses because they have achieved certain performance targets, then ascertain these trigger points in advance and incorporate them into the commission calculations for the month.

Tip: The sales manager nearly always reviews and approves the commission calculations generated by the accounting department. This review process may be so lengthy that it interferes with closing the books. If so, it may be acceptable to close the books *without* the approval of the sales manager. This situation arises when the most likely alteration that the sales manager will make is to shift a commission payment from one salesperson to another. This does not affect the *total* commission expense, which is the only number to be concerned about from the perspective of closing the books.

Standardize the Accounting System

If a company has a number of subsidiaries that report their information to corporate headquarters for consolidation, it is quite possible that the headquarters accounting staff will spend an inordinate amount of time trying to consolidate the disparate results that it has received. Further, if the corporate staff detects a possible error in the results forwarded from a division, it must make inquiries with that division, which make take a long time to respond. Also, some subsidiaries may use different procedures that require more time to forward closing information to headquarters. The result of these issues is a slower close.

The solution is a high degree of standardization throughout the accounting operations of the business. The following areas could be standardized:

- *Software*. It is very useful to have a single company-wide enterprise resources planning (ERP) system, but that solution is so expensive that it may not be cost-effective. Instead, consider installing the same accounting software in all locations, so that common procedures can be designed around them.
- *Chart of accounts*. Use an identical chart of accounts in all locations. This makes it much easier to map the month-end results of the subsidiaries to the general ledger of the parent company.
- *Procedures*. Use an identical set of procedures for all accounting transactions. This can be difficult if some transactions are based on non-standard systems elsewhere in the company, so there will likely be some variability in procedures.
- *Policies*. Accounting policies should be the same in all locations, so that business transactions are treated in the same way. For example, different capitalization policies would mean that an expenditure would be recorded as a fixed asset in one location and as an expense in another location.
- *Journal entries*. There should be a standard set of journal entries that are used in all locations, and which use the same accounts. Thus, journal entry templates are standardized.
- *Calendars*. The same activity schedules are used everywhere, so that the managers of all accounting operations know when they are supposed to complete assigned deliverables.

Tip: Encourage the selective testing of new ways to streamline accounting processes further. This may involve the use of an in-house team of accountants, internal auditors, or perhaps a group of process consultants. If successful, the revised processes can be rolled out throughout the company.

When there is a high level of standardization within the business, it is much easier to compare the closing performance of each accounting area. This is useful for spotting promotion-worthy employees. In addition, closing metrics can be developed for all subsidiaries and used to improve the operations of those accounting units that persistently perform at sub-par levels.

> **Tip:** Allocate a large amount of time to the standardization task. This involves the construction of operational manuals, training classes, and follow-up system testing by the internal audit staff to ensure that standardized approaches are being followed. In a large company, this could be a multi-year task.

Centralize the Accounting System

When there are multiple accounting locations that forward their results to the corporate staff for consolidation, the closing process will be less efficient. The trouble is that some locations will be less efficient than others, due to different policies, procedures, training, staff availability, management skills, and so on. The result is that a few locations will always be late in forwarding their results to the headquarters staff, which delays the close.

These issues can be avoided by shutting down the local accounting operations and instead centralizing all accounting activities in one place. Doing so yields the following advantages:

- *Coordination.* The closing team is located in a single place, so there is tight coordination within the team. There is also no need for a workflow management system, since everyone involved in the close is likely sitting next to each other.
- *Intercompany eliminations.* When the entire accounting system is in one place, it is much easier to flag intercompany transactions and eliminate them as part of the consolidation process. This is a much more difficult issue when there are different accounting systems in every location, and no one tracks intercompany transactions at the local level.
- *Research.* If someone uncovers a problem during the closing process, it is much easier to research the issue in a centralized environment, since the closing team has on-site access to the detailed transaction, and so can investigate it at once.
- *Software.* The company only needs one accounting software package. This yields considerable benefits over a distributed solution, since everyone is trained on a single system and procedures can be tailored to that system. Though it does not relate to the closing process, a company will also likely realize cost reductions from having to pay maintenance on only one software package, as well as from only creating custom interfaces between other systems and that single accounting package.
- *Standardization.* It is much easier to standardize all accounting policies and procedures when there is only one accounting location. This means that the accounting systems can be more easily fine-tuned to close quickly.
- *Transaction factory.* It is much more efficient to deal with all of a company's credit, collection, customer billing, and accounts payable transactions

in one place – essentially creating a "transaction factory" to reduce transaction costs. This approach carries the added benefit of being so efficient that those aspects of the closing process related to transactions can be completed extremely quickly.

It is a major chore to centralize all accounting activities. The best approach is to do so gradually and by functional area. Thus, one could centralize all supplier invoice processing activities, and perhaps then move on to the centralization of customer invoices, payroll processing, and so forth.

> **Tip:** Local managers may be concerned about losing all local accounting employees, so it may be necessary to retain a few people at the subsidiary level to handle a few issues that are closely related to local business transactions. If it is necessary to maintain some local accounting staff, at least keep them away from any activities that could increase the time required for the closing process.

If the company routinely acquires other businesses, it is quite possible that any one of these acquisitions will delay the closing process for a long time to come. The reason is that the accounting staff of the acquired company may set a low priority on the closing process, and so routinely completes closing activities many days late. If this is the case, the easiest alternative is to standardize their closing processes by providing them with the company's standard closing procedures and as much training as is needed to comply with it. However, it is also possible that they never attain the standards at which the rest of the company operates, so it may be necessary to shift their accounting operations to the centralized company facility. The key point to remember is that any acquisition can severely delay the overall closing process if their accounting operations are substandard.

> **Tip:** If the plan is to shift the accounting operations of all acquired companies to the corporate accounting center, have a standardized plan in place that is enacted as part of the initial integration process for every acquired company. Though these transitions are painful, there is less impact on the closing process if everything can be shifted to the central location as soon as possible.

Centralize Travel Bookings

In some companies, the expense reports submitted by employees are substantial, and therefore can have a major impact on the financial results of the accounting period. Unfortunately, they also tend to be submitted late, so that expenses do not appear in the month in which they were incurred. While this issue can be mitigated through the use of employee reminders in advance of month-end, another option is to remove travel costs from employee expense reports. This can be done by requiring all employees to use an approved travel agency for all airfare bookings, if not for hotels, too. By doing so, these charges appear on a company credit card, which the accounting staff can easily access and record in the accounting system well before any employee expense reports arrive. The end result is that employee expense reports contain far fewer expenses, and so it is less important to have them submitted in a timely manner.

Process Centering

A significant problem with the closing process is the participation of too many people in the process, because there are too many hand-offs of closing tasks between employees. Every time there is a hand-off, there is a risk not only of a task being inadvertently dropped, but also of it waiting in the work queue of the person to whom it was given. Thus, if a task is passed through multiple hands, there is a strong likelihood that it will not be completed in time, and will delay the closing process.

The solution is to reduce the number of people who are involved in the closing process, and then have as many of the remaining employees as possible handle closing processes from end-to-end. This approach is called *process centering*. The intent is to reduce the number of participants in the closing process to the point where queue times have been largely eliminated, but without shrinking the headcount so much that they cannot complete the closing tasks within a reasonable period of time. Thus, there will be an optimum number of people on the closing team that minimizes the amount of time needed to close the books. If too many people are eliminated from the closing process, there may be no queue times left, but the burden of the close will be on so few people that the time required to close the books *increases*.

> **Tip:** When the entire accounting department assists in the closing process, this means that it does not have enough time for other ongoing activities during the close – such as issuing customer invoices. Process centering keeps a few accounting people away from closing activities, which means that they can return to their normal day-to-day tasks, thereby eliminating work stoppages elsewhere in the department.

The best way to determine the optimum team size for process centering is to review the entire closing process, ascertain where queue times are actively interfering with the production of financial statements, and take one of the following actions:

- If the queue time is caused by waiting for an approval, find a workaround to the approval
- Route the transaction to someone else who does not have a work queue
- Have the person currently working on the activity complete the additional task(s) for which it was to be transferred to another person

Once the point is reached where queue times are no longer interfering with the close, there is no need to continue with process centering; doing so would only impact other activities that are not crucial to the closing process.

Mitigate Information Dependencies

It is possible that the entire closing process is being delayed because another department is supposed to forward information to the accounting department and has not done so. Examples of this situation are the completion of a physical inventory count and the forwarding of shipping information for customer billing purposes. In these cases, the controller will have a difficult time improving the closing process, because the generation of the required information is simply out of his control. It may be possible to improve the situation with one or more of the following options:

- *Eliminate the information requirement.* It may be possible to exclude the information from the financial statements entirely. For example, if performance metrics from the production department are delayed, shift this information to a metrics report that is issued separately from the financial statements.
- *Upgrade information systems.* If the manual collection and forwarding of information is taking too long, install systems that automate these steps. For example, if the shipping log from the shipping department is delayed, have the shipping staff enter shipment information directly into a computer system that is accessible by the accounting staff. Similarly, switch to a perpetual inventory system in order to avoid a physical inventory count.
- *Assign data collection to accounting.* There may be a few cases where data collection activities can be assigned to the accounting staff. This gives the controller direct control over data collection.
- *Assign coordinators to source departments.* It can be helpful to assign an employee to the departments from which information is sourced, in order to gain insights into why the information flow is delayed. Having this interface can increase the cooperation between the departments in finding a better way to handle the situation.

Standardize the Report Layout

Some managers who receive the financial statements prefer them in a certain layout, with perhaps more detail in one area and less in another. If so, the controller must prepare a variety of different reporting packages for distribution to the management team, which can require a significant amount of additional time. This is a particularly pernicious problem if some managers want special calculations included in their financial statement packages (such as different forms of net profit, or operational metrics). The solution is to persuade senior management to adopt a single reporting package that is used throughout the company.

Having a standardized report layout can be difficult to achieve, because of pressure from report recipients. If so, a possible solution is to issue additional information to the most importunate managers *after* the basic financial statement package has been released.

Tip: It is very important to standardize the calculation of any measurements included within the financial statement package. Otherwise, some managers may apply pressure for the accounting department to use calculations that favor the reported performance of those managers. To avoid this, prepare a report stating how all measurements are to be calculated, and have the chief executive officer approve it.

Reduce the Financial Statements

The financial statements can be considered just the income statement and balance sheet, but tend to grow over time, eventually encompassing a cover letter, statement of cash flows, statement of retained earnings, departmental results, and a variety of operational and financial metrics. While a large and comprehensive financial statement package makes for plenty of in-depth reading by the management team, it also plays havoc with the closing schedule. The primary issue is that any report not automatically generated by the accounting software can require a great deal of time to prepare by hand. Further, it may be necessary to use separate information collection systems to obtain the data needed for these additional reports, and that additional information may not be ready at month-end.

The solution is quite simple. The contents of the primary financial statement package should only contain those reports that qualify under both of the following criteria:

- The reports are automatically generated by the accounting system; and
- The information from which the reports are compiled has been recorded in the accounting system no later than the scheduled issuance date of the financial statements.

These criteria exclude any manually-prepared reports. These additional reports do not have to be eliminated entirely, but their issuance should be delayed until after the financial statements have been issued. By doing so, the accounting team does not waste time on anything other than the primary product of the closing process – the financial statements. In particular, consider shifting to a separate reporting package any information about the cost or profit of specific products, services, or contracts, since these items are usually compiled manually.

Tip: The one exception to the report issuance rules just described is the cover letter to the financial statements. This letter can provide valuable insights into the financial results achieved by a business. As such, it is worthwhile to spend extra time preparing it, rather than issuing financial statements without any accompanying explanations.

Also, if there are a number of metrics related to the company's financial or operational results, consider shifting them to a separate report; they can take time to prepare, and so may delay the issuance of the financial statements.

> **Tip:** Many reporting packages allow for the inclusion of metrics within financial reports that are automatically compiled from the financial information in the reports. If so, these metrics are not interfering with the issuance of financial statements, and so can be included in the basic reporting package.

If there is some uncertainty about which parts of the financial statements and related metrics are being read by the recipients, interview them to find out. Based on this information, it may be possible to eliminate large blocks of information from the financial statement package.

Collect Report Information Early

It may not be possible to enact the preceding change involving a reduction of the financial statements, which means that there will be additional reports that accompany the financials. If so, there may be some line items in those reports that the accounting staff can complete or at least start work on prior to the closing period. For example:

- *Commentary.* If there is a cover letter or disclosures that accompany the financial statements, review them in advance and update any information, where possible. If there are areas that cannot be completed before printing the final version of the financial statements, highlight them in the word processing software to indicate that further updates are needed.
- *Variance analysis.* If there was a significant variance earlier in the month and its cause has been determined, document it in the financial statement package as soon as there is complete information available.
- *Metrics.* In a few instances, financial or operational metrics may be received or calculated prior to month-end. If so, include it in the reports as soon as it is available.

Electronic Delivery

The time required to produce financial statements can be considered to include the time it takes to deliver the financial statements into the hands of their intended recipients. If so, the least efficient method of delivery is to print out the financial statements and mail them to the distribution list. Instead, consider converting the entire financial statement package into PDF format and e-mailing the package. Many accounting systems create PDF-format financial statements, or the entire set of printed documents can be run through a scanner, which will convert them into PDF format automatically.

Defer Activities

The closing process can be seriously delayed if the accounting staff is forced to engage in all of its normal day-to-day activities at the same time. Instead, block out a certain amount of time in which the staff does nothing but close the books. For example:

- *Meetings*. If the staff is normally required to attend various meetings during the closing period, defer the meetings to a later date, or do not attend.
- *Accounts payable*. The payment terms with most suppliers are reasonably lengthy, so there is no need to enter them into the accounting system the moment they arrive in the mail. Instead, let them pile up until the financial statements have been issued.
- *Reports*. If there are standard daily or weekly reports that the accounting staff issues to other departments, make it clear that these reports will not be issued until the close has been completed.
- *Tax returns*. Government entities usually allow a reasonable number of days for the preparation of tax returns (20 days for sales tax returns is common), so defer the preparation of these returns until after the close.

There will inevitably be a few issues that need to be handled at once, irrespective of closing activities. Examples of these issues are depositing cash at the bank and handling rush requests for supplier payments. A good way to address these occasional issues is to keep a few of the accounting staff completely away from the closing process, and task them with all day-to-day activities. Doing so minimizes any interruptions of closing activities.

The deferral of some activities will likely mean that the intense pressure to close the books will be followed by the intense pressure to catch up on all items that had been deferred. Nonetheless, it should be possible to have closed the books and be caught up on all deferred activities within roughly one week of month-end.

Tip: Make it clear to the rest of the company that the accounting department is not available for *anything* during the closing period. While a few crises will still leak through to the department, it is likely that the request to be left alone for a few days each month will be honored by other employees.

Automation Solutions

There are many ways to create an efficient and cost-effective closing process, and few of them involve the use of automation. This is partially because the core improvements to the closing process involve scheduling and procedural changes (which are largely free), and partially because automated solutions involve the installation of comprehensive company-wide accounting systems (which are fabulously expensive and difficult to install). Consequently, do not place the solutions set forth in the following bullet points at the top of the closing agenda. Instead, implement the other solutions recommended in this chapter, and *then* scan through the following points to see if there are any topics of interest. Possible automation solutions are:

- *Intercompany transactions.* An area that can seriously impede the closing process is the reconciliation of intercompany transactions. If a company routinely buys and sells between its divisions, these transactions must be removed from the consolidated results of the parent company in order to avoid the recordation of sales that do not really exist. Given the difficulty of identifying and eliminating these transactions, it can make a great deal of sense to purchase software that tracks this information automatically. This is usually a separate module within an enterprise resources planning (ERP) system. All transactions between subsidiaries are flagged when they are initially generated, and this module backs them out of the consolidated financial results of the company. The main issue with this solution is cost – the underlying ERP system is quite expensive, and must be used by all subsidiaries that engage in intercompany transactions.

- *Consolidation software.* If the financial results of multiple entities must be aggregated into consolidated financial statements, then consolidation software could be useful. This is accounting software that takes the financial information from multiple sources, converts it into a single currency, maps the incoming information to the corporate chart of accounts, and produces consolidated financial statements. This is expensive software that can also be costly to install, depending upon the number and complexity of custom interfaces needed to link it to the company's various accounting software packages. Consolidation software is not of much use if there is a simple consolidation environment, with few subsidiaries that all use the same chart of accounts and the same currency.

- *Enterprise resources planning systems.* An enterprise resources planning system is a comprehensive company-wide system that ties together all of the operations of a business, possibly for all locations. Having such a system is a clear benefit for the closing process, since all intercompany transactions can be flagged when they are produced, and eliminated for the purposes of creating consolidated financial statements. An ERP system also makes it much easier to produce consolidated financial statements.

  ERP systems are enormously expensive and very time-consuming to install. When installed incorrectly, they can even put a company's operations at risk of failure. Given these issues, it is certainly not cost-effective to acquire an ERP system solely to improve the closing process. Instead, there should be many other reasons for acquiring an ERP system; its impact on the closing process should only be considered a useful side benefit of the installation.

- *Workflow management systems.* A workflow management system is a software application that routes work to specific people, and monitors their progress in completing assigned tasks. It can also re-route work items to a different person if the person who was initially assigned those tasks is not responsive. It can track the amount of time required for a person to complete a task, which is useful not only for calculating the duration of a process, but also for measuring the efficiency of the person assigned to the task. In essence, it is designed to improve the flow of complex processes through a business.

Will a workflow management system improve the department's ability to close the books? In most situations, it probably will not play a direct role in the process flow. The trouble is that workflow management systems were designed to aid in the completion of complex tasks that involve many people, whereas the closing process typically involves very few people. When there is a small closing team (see the earlier comments about process centering), there is little need for anything that monitors work flow, since everyone already knows their assigned tasks. Furthermore, they are likely located together within a small area, so that any issue can be addressed simply by walking over to someone and discussing it.

A workflow management system can be of considerably greater use when the closing process is distributed across multiple locations. Under this scenario, it is difficult to personally keep track of the work of people who may be on different continents, so the system could introduce a good oversight capability to the process.

In short, workflow management software is most useful for closing the books in a highly dispersed environment. If there is a small closing team that operates from one location, the system is probably not necessary.

- *Incremental automation.* The closing team may spot possible enhancements to the closing process that require extremely minor adjustments to the existing accounting systems. If so, prioritize them and then make programming requests to the information technology staff in an orderly manner; the intent is not to overwhelm the programmers with requests. Instead, try to implement the improvements at a measured pace over a period of time, ensuring that each one is properly tested and integrated into the closing process before proceeding to the next request.

Some of the automation choices noted in this section are quite expensive. However, they can also be a godsend for larger companies that have multiple subsidiaries and the cash to pay for fully-integrated accounting solutions. For these companies, it may be highly cost-effective to acquire computerized solutions to improve their closing processes. Nonetheless, that is not the case for smaller companies that are unable or unwilling to spend large sums on automation. This latter group should concern itself with the other solutions outlined in this chapter, and will still be able to achieve excellent results with their closing processes.

Tip: Before purchasing an automated solution, consider its cost in comparison to the benefit to be gained from the closing process. In most cases, few automation solutions are worth the corresponding improvement in the closing process. Instead, there must be benefits in other parts of the business to make them worthwhile.

A final consideration is to first improve a process to the greatest extent possible, and wring out all possible efficiencies. At that point, consider some additional level of automation. By taking this approach, it is possible to avoid the automation of a process that is fundamentally inefficient and quite possibly flawed. In short, do not automate a process too soon, thereby locking in a process that is still too inefficient.

Ongoing Process Improvements

A basic rule of any system is that it is either being improved or it is in a state of decline – there is no steady state. This is because even the most perfect system will be continually assailed by changes in other systems within the business, resulting in alterations that make the "perfect" system less perfect over time. Thus, if the ongoing review and improvement of the closing process is stopped, the amount of time and effort needed to close the books will soon begin to increase.

This degradation in the system can be avoided by adopting an issue tracking and review system. In essence, this means writing down every issue that arises during the closing process over multiple periods, and periodically examining these issues to determine how they can be resolved. In particular, consider aggregating these issues by type, so that it becomes apparent over time if there are recurring problems that require more immediate attention. Issues that do not recur can be considered outlier problems, and which can therefore be assigned a lower priority for resolution.

The error tracking system may be a simple spreadsheet on which the date of the issue is recorded, along with a description and a code that designates the type of issue. The spreadsheet can then be sorted by issue code to more easily determine which issues appear to be problems. It may also be useful to record on the spreadsheet how issues were resolved. A sample format for such a spreadsheet is shown below:

Sample Error Tracking Spreadsheet

Date	Code	Description
03/20x1	Accrue	Did not set wage accrual to automatically reverse
03/20x1	Accrue	Missing rent expense accrual
03/20x1	Cutoff	Incorrect month-end cutoff at receiving dock
04/20x1	Accrue	No termination set for royalty accrual
04/20x1	Cutoff	Incorrect month-end cutoff at receiving dock
04/20x1	Calculate	Over-depreciated fixed assets
05/20x1	Posting	Missed posting of final customer invoice batch
06/20x1	Cutoff	Incorrect month-end cutoff at receiving dock
06/20x1	Accrual	Double accrual of rent expense
06/20x1	Accrual	Did not set wage accrual to automatically reverse

In the sample error tracking spreadsheet, we can see that there has been a month-end inventory cutoff problem at the receiving dock that has occurred so many times that it is probably most worthy of attention. There is also an issue with wage accrual reversals that has arisen with less frequency, so it can probably be assigned second priority for examination.

It is particularly important to encourage the accounting staff to contribute to the issue tracking system as soon as possible, since these issues tend to be forgotten in the midst of the closing process. Accordingly, the controller may want to take charge of issue collection and walk through the closing team each day, asking for issues to include in the system.

Once a problem with the closing process is tracked down and corrected, be sure to document it. By doing so, a history is developed of which actions were taken in the past. This is a useful training tool for new accounting managers, and also may provide clues to how to resolve similar problems in the future. For example, if an inventory cutoff issue is resolved with a training class for the receiving department, it may be worthwhile to require another class at some point in the future if a cutoff problem were to appear again.

Another ongoing process improvement is to schedule an annual review of the closing process with the entire closing team. This review would examine all steps in the closing process, opportunities for automation, and the presence of any non-value added activities. Consider having an outside expert on the topic attend the meeting, if he or she can provide usable insights. These types of reviews should be scheduled at sufficiently long intervals to make them of some interest to the closing team.

Tip: Schedule an update of the closing procedures at least once a year, if not more frequently. This is less of a concern if the closing process is well-refined and has changed little, but may require more frequent revisions if there have been many changes, or if the closing team is inexperienced and therefore relies upon the procedures to complete the close.

Analysis of Lean Financial Statements

The changes advocated in this section call for the elimination of bottlenecks, shifting of workloads, and changes in the final product to achieve a massive reduction in the time needed to produce financial statements. What impact do these changes have on our lean criteria? The answers are:

- *Bottlenecks.* There are still bottlenecks in the process flow, but so much work has been shifted away from them that their impact on the process is negligible. However, the creation of financial statements may itself create a new bottleneck, in that the handling of normal daily transactions will probably be delayed by the more concentrated closing process.
- *Distance.* Centralizing the accounting function effectively eliminates the impact of distance on the financial statements.
- *Controls.* The same controls are used in an accelerated system, but they are usually of a two-stage variety, with error checking both in advance of period-end and after the preliminary version of the financial statements has been produced.

- *Error rates.* If financial statements are to be produced with great speed, doing so requires the increased use of estimates, some of which will eventually prove to be incorrect. This is not necessarily an *error* problem, but rather an *estimation* problem. Thus, it is reasonable to state that faster financial statement issuance is usually accompanied by some loss of precision in the reported results.

The following flowchart reveals the altered closing process. There is not a specific process flow that moves from one step to another; instead, the flowchart is designed to show how much work has been shifted into the period being reported on. More structural changes, such as centralizing accounting, are not included in the flowchart.

The Lean Production of Financial Statements – Process Flow

Two days prior

| Warn employees to complete timesheets | Reconcile accounts | Reconcile bank account(s) | Review financial statements |

One day prior

| Accrue wages | Update fixed assets | Record depreciation | Update reserves |

—End of Accounting Period—

One day after

| Verify that timesheets are complete | Complete invoicing | Accrue commissions | Accrue expenses | Value inventory |

Two days after

| Reconcile accounts | Review financial statements | Accrue taxes | Add disclosures to financial statements | Issue financial statements |

The flowchart shows a reasonable two-day closing process. In fact, the process can be reduced further, to a single day. The author has routinely issued financial statements for a multi-division company within one to two business days of the end of each month for a number of years.

Financial Statement Measurements

The following measurements can be used to monitor a lean financial statement process:

- *Time to issue.* Track not just the number of business *days* after period-end that it takes to release financial statements, but the number of *hours*. Once the accounting department works its way down to a two-day close, subsequent reductions will likely be in the hour range, and so will require this finer level of measurement detail.

> **Tip:** Once the closing process has been reduced to a few days, start tracking the time required to complete *each step* in the closing process, which will be needed to effect further reductions in the closing period.

- *Errors found during review.* When the first draft of the financial statements is reviewed, note all errors found. After the financials have been issued, use this information to devise ways to keep those errors from occurring again.

These measurements are of equal importance, since the time to issuance gives feedback on the performance of the department, while the errors found during review give essential information for how to reduce the time to issuance.

Summary

This chapter has described a variety of techniques that can help to accelerate the closing process. When deciding which ones to install, consider that there should not be too many changes to the closing process in any one month. If there is already a functional closing process, then there is already a closely-knit set of functional procedures in place that are about to be disrupted. Consequently, it is better to implement one or two changes per month, in order to measure their impact on the total closing process and figure out how to integrate them seamlessly into the process. If it takes several months complete the implementation of a specific modification, then so be it; do not try to rush these modifications. Over a period of time, an accelerated close will be achieved. The trick is doing so without disrupting the process along the way.

Since it may take years to implement all of the improvements suggested in this chapter, concentrate on those suggestions that will have the most immediate impact on the closing process. Accordingly, it is most useful to determine which suggestions will immediately improve the speed of the close, and implement them first. For example, if switching from a physical inventory count to a perpetual inventory system will immediately reduce the time needed to close the books and issue financial statements by several days, then that may be the best immediate improvement to pursue.

Chapter 7
Lean Credit Management

Introduction

The credit department is tasked with finding those customers that present a significant credit risk, and finding ways to still do business with them while mitigating the company's risk of loss. The background under which this task must be handled is an ongoing flood of customer orders and salespeople demanding immediate credit reviews. It is no wonder that the typical credit department is in a defensive mode, trying to stand its ground on those customer orders that really present a risk, while not impeding the overall flow of business. Creating a lean credit department in this environment can be quite a chore.

In this chapter, we begin with an overview of improvement concepts, then describe a typical credit management environment, and finally show the impact of lean improvement concepts on credit.

Related Podcast Episode: Episode 86 of the Accounting Best Practices Podcast discusses credit best practices. This episode is available at: **accounting-tools.com/podcasts** or **iTunes**

Improvement Concepts

The application of lean concepts in this chapter involves the following improvements to existing systems:

- *Credit granting consistency.* Using a decision table to grant a consistent amount of credit to customers.
- *Terms of sale consistency.* Using the same terms of sale for all customers, to prevent confusion.
- *Complete information gathering.* Collecting a consistent set of information for different levels of requested credit from customers.
- *Ongoing information gathering.* Using decision points to trigger the collection of additional credit information about customers at regular intervals.
- *Behavioral trigger analysis.* Using several types of actions by customers to trigger a credit review.
- *Skew credit terms.* Altering a variety of credit terms to give the company an advantage if there are subsequent collection problems.
- *Contact new customers.* Getting in touch with new customers to explain payment terms to them, which improves the likelihood of being paid in accordance with those terms.

- *Shift risk to credit insurance.* Offloading credit risk to a third party insurer.

The Credit Management Environment

The credit management function is typically added to a company after it suffers one or more large bad debt losses, with instructions to guard against these sorts of issues in the future. Thus, the credit manager is thrust into a risk mitigation role. Unfortunately, the department suffers from being placed squarely in the middle of the sales cycle, where the rest of the company tends to view it as a slow-down to the daily grind of creating revenue. We address the mechanics and results of this unusual role in the remainder of this section.

Traditional Credit Process

In a traditional credit process, the credit department is expected to pluck potential bad debt situations out of the flood of orders passing through its review process every day. This usually means that the credit staff evaluates each customer order on its own merits and refuses credit whenever the information "smells bad." To reiterate the point, the credit staff reviews *all* orders, and passes judgment upon each individual order.

Because every customer order is being examined, it is common for credit to be applied inconsistently. For example, a salesperson may have landed a massive order from a new customer, and the sales manager pressures the credit department into issuing far more credit than it should. This situation is especially common when the credit department has recently been added to a business, and management sees the department as an impediment to sales, rather than a valuable risk mitigation tool.

Inconsistency can also arise with terms of sale. Certain customers may demand longer payment terms, resulting in a mish mash of terms across the customer base. This makes it more difficult to create invoices, as well as to keep track of when to start contacting customers about late payments.

The long-term review process tends to be lacking in a traditional credit function, because the trigger for a credit review is the receipt of an initial order from a customer or a request for an increase in credit. Thus, common practice is to leave credit levels at their initial amounts without further review. This has the following implications:

- The credit level may have initially been set too high in order to accommodate a particular order, and was not subsequently reduced to a more appropriate level. The result is an ongoing credit level that exposes the company to an unusually high risk of loss.
- The credit level has not subsequently been adjusted upward to reflect any improved financial condition of a customer, or to reflect a solid history of timely payments. The result is the possible loss of some business to competitors.
- The initial credit level only reflects the financial condition of a customer as of the exact date when the credit was granted. Since that time, the condition

of a customer may decline – possibly precipitously – without any corresponding reduction in the credit level. The result is a significant risk of default. Really large bad debt losses can arise from this scenario.

Analysis of Credit Management

The traditional approach to credit management tends to be reactive; that is, the credit staff waits to see what terms customers want, and then passes judgment on an individual basis on these requests. The result is not consistent, with differing levels of credit and terms of sale granted to each customer. This work flow does not mitigate the risk of incurring bad debts as much as it should, and also means that the credit department is perpetually overworked, but without having sufficient time to review the credit levels of existing customers.

In the following section, we will discuss an alternative approach to credit that focuses on the imposition of better systems that keep the credit staff focused on the largest potential problem areas.

Lean Credit Management

To properly configure the credit department, we must first depart from the usual view of "lean" being the use of minimal resources. Instead, we must view the credit department as being close to a profit center, for it prevents losses from occurring. From this viewpoint, the funding for the credit department may need to be *increased*, as long as the heightened expenditure makes it more likely that the company will incur fewer bad debt losses. However, we cannot simply add funding to a department that operates under the model described in the last section. Instead, there should be a focus on the following changes:

- Enforce consistency in the treatment of credit
- Collect the correct amount of information for the level of credit requested
- Require a credit review when certain events occur that are indicators of potential default

The net result of these changes should be a department that can easily develop appropriate credit levels for most smaller orders, thereby concentrating the attention of the credit staff on the more problematic or large orders. The department collects progressively more information to support its decisions, depending on the amount of credit involved. We also include three other improvement suggestions that can enhance the results of the department. We delve into these changes through the remainder of this section.

Credit Granting Consistency

Adopt a consistent methodology for granting credit to customers. This means that a decision table can be used to grant credit. A decision table should be built to meet the specific needs and credit history of a business, so no generic table is supplied here. The table might incorporate the following factors:

- Is there a minimum order size below which it is acceptable to grant credit automatically, without any investigation?
- To what extent is there a willingness to grant credit, based on the financial stability indicated by the financial statements submitted by the customer?
- Should a certain amount of credit be granted that is based on the credit levels granted to the customer by other companies, as indicated on the third-party credit report?
- How should the amount of credit granted be adjusted, based on the payment delays reported in third party credit reports?
- At what proposed credit level should a credit request be escalated to someone higher in the organization?
- To what extent is management willing to override the credit levels indicated by the preliminary decision table by tightening or loosening credit policy? This point can be driven by management's expectations of upcoming changes in the economic environment, or simply a desire to gain market share by taking on riskier receivables.

The preceding factors address two main points: the boundaries within which the credit staff is allowed to grant credit, and what the amount of that credit should be.

> **Tip:** The questions noted here are intended to focus attention on one key item – creating a well-reasoned decision table that the entire organization is committed to supporting.

Everyone in the credit department should have been trained in the use of the decision table, so that any one of them can input customer information into the table and derive the same amount of credit.

> **Tip:** The level of credit consistency advocated here does not have to be that rigid. The credit staff should certainly be allowed to authorize modest alterations to calculated credit levels in order to attain the credit levels needed for specific customer orders.

Credit granting consistency also means knowing when to escalate a credit request to the credit manager for additional review. Trigger points for an escalation can include such factors as:

- The requested amount of credit exceeds a certain trigger point
- The customer lost money in the past year
- The customer has negative equity on its balance sheet
- The customer's credit score is lower than a certain trigger point

Thus, the goal of credit granting consistency is to bring some order to what can be a judgmental task.

> **Tip:** It may be useful to periodically compare the credit levels granted by the credit staff to the decision table to see if any employees are not following it consistently. This audit is good for remedial training, and also reinforces the fact that management is serious about following the decision table.

Terms of Sale Consistency

The credit department should insist on consistent terms of sale to the greatest extent possible, such as requiring 30-day payment terms for all customers. This makes it much easier for the billing clerk to generate invoices, without constantly having to adjust invoice terms. Similarly, it is easier for the collections staff to deal with the same terms of sale with all customers.

> **Tip:** A situation in which to ignore the preceding advice for credit and payment term consistency is when the company is trying to sell off obsolete stock. In this case, the alternative is scrapping the goods, so taking a risk on a customer with marginal credit may be acceptable.

Complete Information Gathering

The credit department cannot use a credit decision table or render more specific credit judgments unless it has access to the largest possible amount of credit information. The following suggestions can improve the situation:

- *Complete credit application.* Any customer that wants credit must complete every field on a credit application. If any parts of the form are not completed, send it back to the customer. It should be made clear to the customer that no credit will be granted unless the credit department has a sufficient amount of information from which to make a decision.
- *Complete financial statements.* If the amount of credit demanded warrants it, require that the customer supply a complete set of audited financial statements.

> **Tip:** Of particular importance is the statement of cash flows. It reveals the cash inflows and outflows of a customer, which can be a better representation of the true condition of a business than its income statement.

- *Subscribe to credit database.* The information provided by a prospective customer on a credit application is always skewed in favor of the customer. To obtain a more objective view, always subscribe to the credit reports of an independent third party. This subscription is expensive, but is justified if even a few bad debts can be avoided by using it.

> **Tip:** If the credit report provider issues automatic updates on the condition of customers, subscribe to the service. Doing so allows the credit staff to hear about a sudden credit downgrade in time to cut the company's losses.

- *Ties to sales department.* While the sales department can be vilified by the credit staff for bringing too much pressure to bear for a credit increase, it can also be an excellent source of information about customers. Consequently, the entire department should go out of its way to foster ties with the sales staff.

In general, information gathering should begin with a credit application for all but the smallest requests for credit, and then proceed to financial statements when reaching a decision regarding a larger amount of credit. A subscription to a credit database is useful for all levels of credit.

Ongoing Information Gathering

The initial level of information gathering just noted is not sufficient over the long term, for the financial condition of all customers change. Consequently, the credit manager should adopt a standard methodology for reviewing the finances of current customers. There are several variations on this concept, such as:

- *Active customer below threshold level.* Pull a credit report on the customer once a year.
- *Active customer above threshold level.* Pull a credit report and require updated financial statements once a year.
- *Non-active customer placing order below threshold level.* Pull a credit report when new order arrives, if last order was more than one year ago.
- *Non-active customer placing order above threshold level.* Require new credit application with financial statements.

These data collection options are designed to reduce the work load of the credit department, while still providing more current information about customers. The use of a threshold level is designed to not bother customers too much, so that most customers will not even realize that their credit is being reviewed – the basis for the review is a credit report provided by a third party. It behooves the credit manager to ensure that current information is on file for the few really large customers, who will be required to submit updated financial statements.

> **Tip:** If a large customer is publicly held, just download their financial statements from the Securities and Exchange Commission website; there is no need to bother the customer for this information.

Behavioral Trigger Analysis

Besides the ongoing review of customer credit that we just advocated, there are certain indicators of financial difficulty that a customer may display, and which the credit department should be looking for. Any of the following indicators may trigger a credit review:

- *Stops taking early payment discounts.* If the company offers an early payment and a customer stops taking it, this is a strong indicator that the customer no longer has the ready cash available to take the discount. An even better indicator is when this discount is skipped twice in a row, since a single skip may only indicate that a paperwork problem prevented the customer from having a payment ready in time to take the discount.
- *Increased deductions taken.* A customer in financial trouble will be motivated to make every possible deduction from an invoice, so if the percentage of deductions taken suddenly trends upward, treat it as a warning sign.
- *Not sufficient funds check.* A major warning indicator is when any customer check bounces. This should set off klaxons in the credit department, and trigger an immediate review, especially if a customer currently has a large line of credit.
- *Selective payments.* A canny customer may give the appearance of being current with payments by making routine payments for smaller invoices, while delaying payments for larger ones. This can be difficult to spot, but a discernible pattern should be considered a strong indicator of cash flow difficulties.

It may not be possible for a smaller business to create a program that automatically monitors these issues and issues warnings to the credit department. If so, assign each credit staff person to a set of customers, and task the assigned employees with an ongoing review for these issues.

Skew Credit Terms

The terms that the credit department offers to customers can be skewed heavily in favor of the company. These changes usually involve factors other than the amount of credit granted and payment terms, which are what customers focus on. Instead of these "hot" topics, consider making the following changes:

- *ACH debit.* Do the collections department a favor and attempt to impose ACH debit terms. This means that the customer authorizes the company to deduct payments from the customer's bank account with an ACH debit on the designated payment date.
- *Arbitration.* If the parties have a dispute over payment, require the use of an arbitrator. This approach compresses the timeline needed to arrive at payment by the customer.

- *Legal venue.* If the company is forced to file a lawsuit against a customer, it wants to reduce its costs by filing in a court near the company's location. Therefore, state the legal venue in the agreement.
- *Personal guarantee.* It may be possible to obtain a personal guarantee of payment, or a guarantee from the corporate parent of the customer. This can be difficult to obtain.
- *Reimbursements.* Have the customer agree to reimburse the company for collection fees and fees incurred for checks that bounced due to not sufficient funds in the customer's bank account.

Of the issues noted here, permission to use ACH debits is of the most use, since it eliminates the risk of nonpayment (unless the customer has no cash in its bank account). If that provision cannot be obtained, at least insist on the arbitration clause, which can help to accelerate payment in the more contentious cases.

Contact New Customers

If a company has just started doing business with a new customer, send the customer a document that outlines the number of days that the company allows for payment, as well as the details of where to send payments. If the customer is likely to be a large one (as evidenced by the size of the credit limit being requested), the credit manager may want to take a step further and call or visit the customer. Setting up personal contacts can go a long way towards gathering better credit information, and also gives on-site information about the condition of the customer. It also becomes more likely that the customer will verify that the correct terms are entered in its accounts payable system, rather than some default terms.

Shift Risk to Credit Insurance

Contact an insurance company that provides credit insurance for accounts receivable, to see if it will provide coverage for the company's accounts receivable. Under a credit insurance policy, the insurer protects the seller against customer nonpayment. The insurer should be willing to provide coverage against customer nonpayment if a proposed customer clears its internal review process. Credit insurance offers the following benefits:

- *Increased credit.* A company may be able to increase the credit levels offered to its customers, thereby potentially increasing revenue.
- *Faster international deals.* An international sale might normally be delayed while the parties arrange a letter of credit, but can be completed faster with credit insurance.
- *Custom product coverage.* The insurance can cover the shipment of custom-made products, in case customers cancel their orders prior to delivery.
- *Reduced credit staff.* Credit insurance essentially shifts risk away from a business, so it is especially beneficial in companies that have an under-

staffed credit department that cannot adequately keep track of customer credit levels.

As is the case with all insurance policies, be sure to examine the terms of a credit insurance agreement for exclusions, to see what the insurer will not cover.

> **Tip:** It may be possible to offload the cost of credit insurance to customers by adding it to customer invoices. This is most likely to be acceptable for international deals, where a customer would otherwise be forced to obtain a letter of credit to pay for a transaction.

Analysis of Lean Credit Management

A lean credit department is all about having a system for easily calculating appropriate credit levels for the vast majority of customer orders. This leaves more time for the credit staff to analyze requests for large amounts of credit, and to examine the requests of the more problematic customers. There must also be triggers in place that allow the credit staff to reach into the morass of customer credit ratings and pluck out those few that may require a change. Thus, the themes of a lean credit department are focusing on consistency, basing decisions on the correct amount of information, and having appropriate triggers for credit reviews.

Additional Improvement Concepts

There are several additional concepts that can be applied to the credit management process to enhance its performance or reduce costs. These concepts did not fit into any of the process flows noted previously or were considered minor elements, and so are noted here instead:

- *Aggregate credit risk.* When there are several subsidiaries in a company, each one may grant credit to the same customer. The risk of default may seem reasonable from the limited perspective of each individual subsidiary, but could be too large when aggregated for the company as a whole. Accordingly, consider having someone monitor aggregated credit levels for the largest customers, and notify the chief financial officer when aggregated risk is too high. This can result in an overall reduction in the amount of credit granted to certain customers.
- *Offload risk to a distributor or retailer.* When the credit department decides that the risk of granting credit to an applicant is too high, it can refer the entity to a distributor or retailer, who might be more willing to accept the risk of default. However, this can mean that the distributor or retailer will then suffer a bad debt, and will be unable to pay the company.
- *Subscribe to check verification service.* The company can subscribe to a check verification service, which matches the information on a check to a national bad debt database to see if the paying person has defaulted in the past. If so, the company can decline the check payment; this approach works

well in a retail environment. An expansion of this concept is a check guarantee service, which guarantees payment even if the customer defaults.

Credit Measurements

The following measurements can be used to monitor the performance of the credit management function:

- *Duration of longest credit reviews.* Despite the value of the credit function, it should not hold up the revenue-generation process to an excessive extent. Therefore, create a system that monitors the time that has passed since a credit request was received. Any credit review that has exceeded a certain threshold should be the subject of an immediate review by the credit manager.
- *Inappropriate credit levels.* It may be possible to have the computer system highlight all credit levels that appear to be inappropriate, given the fundamentals recorded for each customer in the system. This measurement requires not only automation, but also the recordation of the most important payment and financial information for each customer, and so may not be a viable option for smaller companies. If available, it can be a useful tool for determining which credit levels to review.

As has been the case in other chapters, we prefer to focus measurements on a detailed analysis of individual transactions, since a business can use this information to fine-tune its operations.

Summary

The general tone of this chapter has been to arrive at a lean credit department by imposing consistency on the credit granting process, with individual attention being given to unusual credit situations. Consistency can be enforced to a large extent with good credit systems, a credit decision table, and close adherence to a credit procedure.

Unfortunately, a lean credit department requires more than excellent systems – it also requires a considerable amount of backbone by the credit manager. This person is constantly being pressured to grant more credit than is necessarily wise, since other parts of the business are more focused on the probability of revenues than the possibility of bad debts. The presence of strong systems can be overshadowed by a weak credit manager, so be sure to evaluate the management aspects of the credit department.

Chapter 8
Lean Collections

Introduction

In many organizations, the collections function follows a regimented path that gradually escalates collection activities for all overdue invoices, with a long tail of collection efforts over many months to resolve a few remaining unpaid invoices. When we view the collections function from a lean perspective, a different approach presents itself.

In this chapter, we begin with an overview of improvement concepts, then describe a typical collections environment, and finally show the impact of lean improvement concepts on collections.

Related Podcast Episode: Episode 55 of the Accounting Best Practices Podcast discusses targeted collection activities. The episode is available at: **accounting-tools.com/podcasts** or **iTunes**

Improvement Concepts

The application of lean concepts in this chapter involves the following improvements to existing systems, where the first three concepts address ways to completely avoid collection activities:

- *Payment on receipt by customers.* Arranging with customers to pay the company based on units received, not an invoice.
- *Payment in advance.* Requesting payment in advance in order to eliminate the need for collection activities.
- *Payment by ACH debit.* Charging customer bank accounts by ACH, thereby eliminating the need for collection activities.
- *Focus on large dollar invoices.* Directing most collection activities toward the collection of the largest dollar amounts, so the focus is on total cash collected.
- *Accelerate small write-offs.* Writing off the smallest open balances quickly, so the collections staff can concentrate on the largest unpaid invoices.
- *Increase collection staff efficiency.* Using technology tools, support staff, and scheduling to increase the time spent on collections.
- *Notify sales staff.* Building relations with the sales staff, who can assist with collection activities.
- *Contact new customers.* Discussing payment issues with new customers to prevent payment problems in the future.

- *Problem working group*. Creating a cross-departmental team to investigate internal issues causing collection problems.
- *Prevent deductions*. Engaging in a variety of cross-checking actions prior to shipment to prevent subsequent payment deductions by customers.
- *Accelerated escalation*. Pursuing an aggressive escalation policy to push for more rapid payment by customers.

The Collections Environment

The collections environment is usually one in which a company assumes that customers will pay on time. This means that a grace period of a few days is granted beyond the scheduled payment date, after which a gentle reminder contact is made. After more time passes, the assumption of payment gradually changes, so that more aggressive collection measures are taken. This traditional approach to collections is addressed in more detail in the remainder of this section.

Traditional Collections Process

In the typical collections environment, the collection effort follows a specific, regimented path. Frequently, customers receive a dunning letter if an invoice goes a certain number of days past due, and probably a statement of account at the end of the month. After a few more days go by, the collections staff contacts all of the customers whose invoices remain unpaid, perhaps by e-mail. Then a few more days go by, and they escalate matters to a phone call. At this point, the company finds out if there are any actual problems that are preventing customers (or making them unwilling) to pay. A week or two of remedial activities then follow, after which the collections manager decides whether customers are being obstreperous and need to be reminded of their payment obligations by an attorney. If this stiff reminder does not work, then the company has the option of either litigating, sending the invoice to a collection agency, or writing off the invoice as a bad debt.

The process flow just described is a logical one, but can easily add a month to the time period required to collect cash. In fact, a canny customer who figures out the timing of this collection pattern can probably exploit the system to routinely pay invoices several weeks late.

Analysis of Collections

This process flow focuses on specific collection activities to engage in after certain periods of time have passed; it can be considered an industrial view of collections, where *all* customers and invoices are treated the same. It may at first appear to be an efficient way of dealing with what may be quite a large number of invoices. However, the process incorporates so many delays that the eventual receipt of cash may be quite protracted.

In the following section, we will discuss an alternative approach to collections that focuses on the volume of cash received.

Lean Collections

It would be a mistake to consider a successful lean collections department to be one that operates on the smallest possible budget, as would be the case with most cost centers. Instead, consider it to be one of the more productive aspects of the accounting department, where collections is expected to generate large amounts of cash receipts within the shortest possible period of time. To make collections more productive, our focus is on the following changes:

- Avoid the need for collections
- Focus collection activities on the largest invoices
- Improve the efficiency of the collections staff
- Improve communications with the sales staff
- Create a system for reducing the errors that lead to customer non-payment

We delve into these changes through the remainder of this section. The first three recommendations involve unique payment plans that essentially guarantee timely customer payment. These options are unusual ones in most industries, so we then assume that collections must still be made, and walk through a number of options for enhancing the focus, tools, and processes of the collections department.

Payment on Receipt by Customers

We have discussed in the Lean Accounts Payable chapter the concept of evaluated receipts, where a business pays its suppliers based on the quantities of goods received, rather than on supplier invoices. This concept is of particular interest from the perspective of collections, since payments are usually automated – if goods are received, then payment will almost certainly follow. Thus, there is no need for a collections function in this environment.

A company could meet with its customers to explain the evaluated receipts concept to them and request that they adopt it. If the company is using an evaluated receipts system itself, it can volunteer to arrange customer tours to view the system, and perhaps even provide guidance if they want to set up something similar. However, this is about as proactive as a business can be – the decision is still up to the customer. There are two other problems, as well:

- *Not a complete solution.* It is quite unlikely that *all* of a company's customers will adopt evaluated receipts, so the likely outcome is that only a small portion of a company's sales will be paid through these systems.
- *Only applies to cost of goods sold.* The evaluated receipts system is designed to only work with materials that are shipped from suppliers to be included in the production process of the customer (though there are variations on the concept). If a supplier is selling something other than raw materials or production components to its customers, it will not be included in their evaluated receipts system.

Payment in Advance

If customers can be encouraged to pay in advance for goods and services, all collection issues are immediately eliminated. Payment in advance can be accomplished by offering a small discount, and/or by offering a somewhat higher commission to the sales staff if they can obtain these kinds of sales. Alternatively, a business model can be configured so that this is the normal state of affairs, such as an on-line website where customers pay with credit cards in advance, before their orders are accepted into the system. However, payment in advance is a hard sell to customers in more traditional industries.

Payment by ACH Debit

In a small number of markets, it has become acceptable for customers to pay by ACH debit. This means that the seller triggers a debit transaction from customer bank accounts. Doing so virtually guarantees that funds will be collected on time, and eliminates the need for a collection function. However, it is usually only acceptable to customers when these debits are for small amounts and are on a recurring basis. A typical use of the ACH debit is a recurring monthly payment for a parking space.

Focus on Large Dollar Invoices

In many organizations, the vast majority of the cash tied up in accounts receivable is concentrated in a small number of large invoices. It is quite common for 80 percent of the cash to be tied up in approximately 20 percent of the invoices. In this situation, the collections staff should focus most of its efforts on collecting the large-dollar invoices, and doing so as quickly as possible. The following accelerated collection techniques could be used for a large invoice:

1. *Search for complaints.* Review the customer complaints database and the database for return merchandise authorizations every day, to see if the customers to whom the largest invoices have been issued are making complaints or want to return goods. This is the first indication that something may be wrong, and should trigger an immediate contact with the customer.
2. *Pre-contact.* Contact the customer before the invoice due date to ensure that the invoice is scheduled for payment. If the invoice is not scheduled, provide whatever assistance is needed. Contact the salespeople who made the sale for additional assistance, since they have other contacts within the customer's organization who may be able to help.

> **Tip:** If the collections manager usually allows a grace period of a few days before contacting customers about overdue invoices, waive the policy for large invoices. These invoices involve so much cash that it is not reasonable to allow customers extra time to pay them.

3. *Delivery assistance.* Contact the customer and volunteer to have a salesperson or courier pick up the check, or offer the use of the company's account with an overnight delivery service. At a minimum, make sure that the payment is being sent to the company's nearest bank lockbox. Other alternatives are to encourage the use of an ACH electronic payment, or allowing the company to debit their bank account with an ACH transaction. Any of these steps are designed to create an immediate transfer of cash into the company's bank account.

> **Tip:** Always assign the best collections people to the largest accounts, and keep them assigned to those accounts in order to build up close relations with their counterparts.

By taking all of these steps, the likelihood of on-time payment for the largest invoices is greatly enhanced. Even if there is no immediate cash payment resulting from these efforts, the collections staff will likely have an excellent idea of the issues that are holding up payment, and will have this information much sooner than would normally have been the case.

> **Tip:** The concentrated approach to collections that we are advocating mandates the clear assignment of responsibility for collections. Thus, there should be a lead person who is responsible for collecting from a customer. This person should be given a reasonable level of authority over collection steps to be taken and credits to be granted, with escalation for major issues.

Of course, these early payments come at a cost, which is the additional staff time required to research issues and contact customers, as well as the cost of any overnight delivery charges for the delivery of payments. Nonetheless, this concentrated approach to collections achieves the primary goal of a lean collections function, which is to collect the largest amount of cash within the shortest period of time.

The collections manager could still follow the more regimented and traditional collections path for smaller invoices, where more automated methods are used first. Doing so keeps valuable staff time centered on large invoices for as long as possible; if the use of automated collection techniques results in a slower payment interval, that is acceptable, since the amount of cash involved is not large.

Accelerate Small Write-offs

The reverse of assigning most collection department resources to large dollar invoices is being willing to write off quite small invoices and deductions. It is rarely cost-beneficial to attempt to collect small invoices or to investigate the validity of small deductions – so do not bother. Instead, they should receive only the most cursory of reviews before being written off. The result should be a tight focus on larger invoices.

Increase Collection Staff Efficiency

A skilled collections person is a valuable resource. This person can empathize with customers, ascertain the real reasons for nonpayment, and cajole them into paying – while still maintaining a friendly, long-term relationship. These particular skills are most in evidence during phone calls or in-person meetings. Unfortunately, these interpersonal communications form only a small part of the working day of a collections person. They spend much more time researching information, obtaining data from other parts of the company, issuing credits, and so forth. We can surmount this downtime for clerical work with one or all of the following methods:

- *Integrate with collections database.* There are several software packages available that are specifically designed to make the work of the collections person more effective. They use a custom-built interface to the accounting system to access information about unpaid customer invoices, as well as store information about customer contact information and prior promises to pay, and can even link to an auto-dialer. The collections staff can rapidly work through their call lists with the aid of this software, which presents all relevant information to them as they talk to customers. Ideally, this should result in a massive increase in the number of calls that a collections person can make. The downside is that the software and its installation is expensive, and so may only be cost-effective for a larger collections department.

> **Tip:** The auto-dialer in an integrated collections system can be structured to call customers at the optimum time of the day, depending upon the time zones in which customers are situated.

- *Specialists deal with deductions.* In some markets, it may be quite common for customers to take an array of deductions from their invoice payments, claiming such items as short shipments, damaged goods, incorrect prices, and returned goods. The collections staff can be overwhelmed by the multitude of these deductions. If so, consider assigning deduction management to a small number of specialists, who are most familiar with the types of claims, and who are authorized to resolve them. By doing so, the most talented collections staff can focus on collecting the bulk of the amounts on customer invoices, and can pass off the more detailed deductions work to others.
- *Payments applied immediately.* Ideally, the cashier should apply all cash received against outstanding accounts receivable as soon as the cash arrives. However, there are times when it is not clear how cash should be applied, so there is a temptation to set aside a payment and wait for more information. However, doing so means that the collections staff is wasting its time on collection calls for cash that has already been received. Consequently, the cashier should at least apply the cash to the account of the customer in general, even if there is doubt about exactly which invoice is being paid. By

doing so, the payment becomes visible on the accounts receivable aging report, where the collections staff can see it.

- *Clerical support staff.* Hire clerks and have them support the collections staff by dealing with all of the issues that prevent the collections people from being in constant contact with customers. This means that the clerks find customer files, research alleged payments, process credit memo paperwork, locate contact information, and so forth.

Tip: The clerical support staff should be responsible for researching customer payments for which the proper application is unclear. In addition, they should clean up all stray credits and debits on the accounts receivable aging report. These actions clarify for the collections staff which remaining invoices are worthy of collection activities.

Tip: Depending on the types of customers and the size of the collections department, it may be useful to hire a very specialized position – the skip tracer. This person tracks down customers who have changed addresses, and who in some cases do not want to be found. The skill set for a premier skip tracer includes significant research skills, which is different from the more extroverted skills required for a collections person.

- *Department activities.* The collections manager needs to realize that the efficiency of the collections staff is paramount, which means that all other activities within the department must be timed to not interfere with their work schedules. This should result in team meetings only being held during non-peak calling hours, and arranging work hours to suit the needs of the collections staff.

Notify Sales Staff

The sales department should not be pulled into every collection situation, because their primary task is to generate new sales. Nonetheless, they may be aware of issues with customers that are not readily apparent to the collections staff, since salespeople have different contacts within the customer organizations. The easiest way to stay in touch with the sales staff is to e-mail each of them a customized accounts receivable aging report each week that shows the unpaid invoices for just their customers. A salesperson may occasionally volunteer information about these invoices or even suggest that they might be of service in making a collection contact.

Tip: Consider setting up a shared database of customer contact names with the sales staff. This is extremely useful when the collections staff needs to go around their usual accounts payable contacts and reach deeper into a customer's organization for a decision maker who can authorize a payment.

It is also useful to build a relationship with the sales team in general. They can provide background information on the company's history with each customer and act as the on-site investigator for the collections staff.

> **Tip:** It is best to pair up one collections person with one salesperson for each customer. This will keep a number of collections people from badgering a single salesperson, and so will yield better cooperation from the sales staff.

Contact New Customers

If a company has just started doing business with a new customer, send the customer a document that outlines the number of days that the company allows for payment, as well as the details of where to send payments. If the customer is likely to be a large one (as evidenced by the size of the credit limit granted to it), the collections manager may want to take a step further and call or visit the customer. Setting up personal contacts can go a long way towards gaining a high level of cooperation with a customer, which in turn may yield faster payments.

Problem Resolution Working Group

Any experienced collections person will point out that many collection issues originate within a business, not its customers. These issues may involve incorrect invoices, shoddy products, damaged deliveries, incorrect order taking, and so forth. Because of these problems, customers refuse to pay for invoices without some prior problem resolution, which the collections staff can ameliorate only by granting a large number of credits. These internal errors can make the collections department look like a poor performer, since it cannot accelerate the collection of cash.

A fine solution to these internal errors is to form a working group within the company that meets regularly to discuss and resolve the issues found by the collections staff. The members of this group should include representatives from those departments that are causing the problems, as well as those being impacted by the problems. Thus, a typical working group might include members of the collections, production, purchasing, warehousing, and engineering departments. The participants should be mid-level, with enough authority to make minor decisions on behalf of their departments. More important issues are escalated to more senior people within their departments for resolution.

The purpose of this group is not just to resolve individual collection problems, which in many cases are resolved more quickly by issuing a credit to the customer, in the interests of being paid for the remaining balance of an invoice. At a more general level, the group is tasked with locating and correcting the underlying reason for a customer complaint, so that it will be permanently fixed.

> **Tip:** The working group should maintain a database of customer complaints, so that it can aggregate the complaints into categories and target those problems that are causing the largest number of complaints. As this tactic reduces the overall volume of complaints, the group can focus more of its attention on the few remaining issues.

> **Tip:** A variation on the working group is to have a formal review of the circumstances surrounding any large bad debt. The focus should be on whether a systemic change should be made that might have reduced the probability of having incurred the bad debt.

Prevent Deductions

A problem resolution working group is responsible for fixing problems *after* they have occurred. The flip side of this scenario is to prevent deductions during the ordering, shipping, and invoicing phases of a customer order. Typical prevention steps include:

- Verify that the customer contract terms are correctly represented in the invoice, such as available funding, a referenced purchase order number, and the correct period of time for payment.
- Verify that authorized discounts are included in the invoice.
- Verify that sales taxes are not charged to those customers who have provided valid sales tax exemption certificates.
- Verify that the shipment is sent to the address specified in the customer's order, and that the company follows all requested shipping instructions.

> **Tip:** If customers can send electronic orders straight into a supplier's order entry system, doing so eliminates the risk of issuing incorrect deliveries based on document transcription errors.

> **Tip:** If a company knows that a customer will take a deduction for a specific reason, and the amount can be ascertained in advance, then include the deduction in the original invoice. This eliminates the time that would otherwise be spent in processing a credit for the deduction after-the-fact, when the customer has made a deduction from its payment.

Accelerated Escalation

A common practice in a collections environment is to wait a fairly long time before taking the more drastic steps of either taking legal action against a customer or referring the matter to a collection agency. This delay is usually caused by a combination of hoping that the customer will unexpectedly pay, of wanting to defer the cost of the escalated action, and of not wanting to annoy the customer with more aggressive collection activities.

In reality, these escalations to more aggressive collection activities should be accelerated. Once the collections staff reaches the point where it has tried every reasonable technique to collect from a customer, it should immediately escalate the matter. Otherwise, the passage of time makes it more difficult to collect funds. Certainly, more aggressive collection activities may damage the relationship with a customer, but if a customer refuses to pay, then the real question is why the company is even doing business with the customer.

> **Tip:** When taken to its logical conclusion, the escalation concept also means that a company should immediately sell any claim it may have against a bankrupt customer, rather than waiting years for reimbursement.

Practices to Avoid

We find that a few collection practices introduce more inefficiency to the collections function, and so are not recommended. They are:

- *Problem escalation.* When the collections staff finds a payment issue that is caused by a problem within the company, they may be tempted to route the issue through the company controller, who should have sufficient authority to have the problem fixed. However, there will be so many of these issues that the controller will soon be overwhelmed by them all. Instead, use the problem resolution working group already described; this group is designed to fix internal problems on its own, and only escalates issues for the more intractable problems.
- *Outsource collections.* It is generally a bad idea to outsource the entire collections function or even a portion of it. The reason is that the supplier providing collection services is located at some distance from the company, so there may be problems with coordinating collection activities. Also, the third party is only concerned with collecting overdue accounts receivable, and not with the correction of any internal company problems that may have contributed to the overdue invoice. The transfer of individual invoices to a collections agency is still acceptable, if a company has been unable to collect the invoices through its internal efforts.

Analysis of Lean Collections

The main focus of the improvement suggestions in this section has been to increase the effectiveness of the collections department. Doing so requires a laser focus on collecting the largest amounts of cash first, and allocating any remaining collection resources to smaller invoices later. The result will likely be a cluster of seriously overdue smaller invoices, but as long as the department can rapidly collect most of the cash due to the company, the losses arising from these smaller invoices will be a minor issue.

Additional Improvement Concepts

There are several additional concepts that can be applied to the collections process to enhance its performance or reduce costs. These concepts did not fit into any of the process flows noted previously or were considered minor elements, and so are noted here instead:

- *Avoid marketing deductions.* The marketing department may sometimes allow customers to spend advertising funds on behalf of company products, and then take these expenditures as deductions when they pay company invoices. This approach wreaks havoc on the collections staff, which can have an exceedingly difficult time verifying that these types of deductions are valid. Instead, have customers bill these reimbursable items to the company, so that they are run through the accounts payable system instead.

- *Pay by fax.* An option for extracting a rapid payment from a customer is to have them fax or e-mail a scanned image of a completed and signed check to the company. Then, using check printing software, enter the information from the check into the software and print the check using check security paper, which can be obtained from a local office supply store. The software will include the following text in place of the signature line: "SIGNATURE NOT REQUIRED. Payee to hold you harmless for payment of this document. Absence of endorsement is guaranteed by payee's bank." Then deposit the check, which may require manual processing by a bank teller. Be sure to retain the faxed or e-mailed original check as proof of customer approval of the payment.
- *Use deduction tracking system.* If there are many deductions, consider installing a deduction tracking system that aggregates the amounts of deductions by customer, identifies each deduction by type, and notes the progress toward resolution of each one. Doing so provides a considerable amount of order to the messy deductions management area, and can be used to assign additional personnel to investigate the larger claims, as well as to forecast the likely amount of deductions that will have to be accepted.

Collection Measurements

The following collection measurements can be used to monitor the performance of the collections function:

- *Amount of deductions over __ days old.* This is a listing of all deductions that the collections staff is still processing, and which have exceeded a certain number of days in-house. The intent is to make a determination on these items as quickly as possible, so that deductions do not fester. Depending upon the number of deductions in process, it may be necessary to review this list every day.
- *Amount of receivables over __ days old.* This is a simple listing of the oldest accounts receivable. The collections manager should review it at least once a week, with the objective of reaching a final disposition on as many items as possible.
- *Cost of collections.* This is the entire cost of the collections department, divided by the amount of cash collected in the period. The intent is to track the percentage over time, to see if the collection efficiency of the department is changing. This metric places an emphasis on the volume of cash collected.
- *Days sales outstanding.* This is the average amount of accounts receivable outstanding during the period, divided by average sales per day. When

tracked on a trend line, it shows changes in the ability of the collections staff to bring in funds in a timely manner.

As has been the case in other chapters, we prefer to focus measurements on a detailed analysis of individual transactions. In addition, we have added measurements for tracking the efficiency and effectiveness of the collections department.

Summary

There are a massive number of possible collection techniques available, and we have *not* covered most of them in this chapter. Instead, we have stressed the type of *process* that leads to the faster collection of cash. Also, we have diverged from the normal assumption that a lean function is one that operates with fewer resources. Instead, we advocate the view that the collections function is more of a profit center, and so might require *more* resources in order to achieve its goal – which is to generate large amounts of cash receipts within the shortest possible period of time.

The process focus of this chapter is based on several themes, which form the core of an effective collections effort. Those themes are:

- *Follow the money*. The vast majority of all collection activities are used to collect the largest-dollar invoices.
- *Efficiency*. View the collections staff as highly skilled individuals, which means that they should be made as efficient as possible with a support staff and appropriate technology tools.
- *Communications*. Make sure that all people involved with customers readily communicate problems to the collections staff.
- *Error reduction*. Create a system for eliminating problems that are prolonging the payment of invoices by customers.

Supporting all of these themes is required to ensure that the largest amount of cash is collected as rapidly as possible. For more tips to assist in improving the organization's collection capabilities, see the author's *Credit & Collection Guidebook*.

Chapter 9
Lean Inventory Accounting

Introduction

Inventory accounting can be a non-event in some businesses where it is a minor asset category; it can also be the primary bottleneck in closing the books, when record accuracy is poor and it is the primary asset category. In the latter case, the need for a lean inventory accounting function may be of central importance.

In this chapter, we begin with an overview of improvement concepts, then describe a typical inventory accounting environment, and finally show the impact of lean improvement concepts on inventory.

> **Related Podcast Episodes:** Episodes 27, 56, 66, 119, and 192 of the Accounting Best Practices Podcast discuss inventory issues. These episodes are available at: **accountingtools.com/podcasts** or **iTunes**

Improvement Concepts

The application of lean concepts in this chapter involves the following improvements to existing systems:

- *Perpetual inventory system.* Recording inventory transactions in a database in order to maintain an accurate on-hand inventory count.
- *Cycle counting.* Counting small portions of the inventory each day and correcting any errors found.
- *Transaction backlog elimination.* Keeping inventory transactions current; this increases the relevance of cycle counting information.
- *Bar coded inventory transactions.* Using bar codes to record inventory transactions, thereby reducing the incidence of inventory errors.
- *Backflushing.* Multiplying bills of material by units manufactured to arrive at the raw materials consumed, and automatically deducting these amounts from the inventory records.
- *Ending inventory estimation.* Using an estimation methodology to derive the ending inventory valuation.
- *Minimal overhead allocation.* Simplifying the allocation of overhead to inventory and the cost of goods sold.
- *Lower of cost or market limitation.* Only applying the lower of cost or market rule to the more valuable inventory items, to reduce accounting work.

- *Obsolete inventory tracking.* Using a standard methodology to locate and track the disposal status of obsolete inventory, which avoids the risk of an unanticipated write-off.
- *Charge inventory to expense.* Shifting selected inventory items to the shop floor, removing them from the inventory database, and instead charging them to expense as purchased. This reduces the amount of inventory valuation work.
- *Just-in-time deliveries.* Having suppliers deliver frequently and in small quantities, thereby reducing inventory levels and mitigating the risk of a valuation error.
- *Drop shipping.* Having suppliers ship goods straight to a company's customers, thereby eliminating inventory ownership by the company.
- *On-site inventory ownership by suppliers.* Having suppliers own raw materials that is positioned on the company premises.
- *Reduce product options.* Shrinking the number of product options offered, thereby reducing the amount of inventory to track.

The Inventory Accounting Environment

If there is an accounting area that strikes fear into the heart of a controller, it is probably inventory. The information that the accounting staff uses for inventory is maintained by a different department (the warehouse), so there is no direct control over its accuracy. Depending on the industry, this can be the largest asset category of a business; if so, even a relatively small error can have a dramatic impact on the reported results of the business. Thus, the inventory area can be the source of substantial financial reporting problems.

In this section, we will describe the basic inventory accounting process, and point out issues with it.

Traditional Inventory Accounting

In a traditional inventory accounting system, there is no tight control over inventory transactions. Instead, all inventory purchases are compiled in a purchases account during the accounting period. Once the period is complete, the warehouse shuts down while the warehouse staff conducts a complete physical inventory count.

From the perspective of the accounting department, the main problem with a physical inventory count is that its results are inaccurate. There are many reasons for record inaccuracy, including:

- Parts may be mislabeled or miscounted
- Inventory tags can be lost
- Inventory tags can be incorrectly transcribed into the inventory database
- Inexperienced counters may be used who have little experience with inventory

The inventory counting process may also uncover inventory items that the company does not plan to use, or which cannot be sold at a price above their cost. If so, the accounting staff must set aside a reserve for the amount that the company expects to lose when it disposes of these obsolete items.

Once the inventory count has been completed, the accounting staff must value it. This involves using a cost layering technique (such as the first in, first out or last in, first out methods) or standard costs to arrive at a valuation. If cost layering is used, the valuation calculation can be quite complex and difficult to verify. This step can involve several iterations, as the accounting staff reviews valuation reports for errors and makes corrections.

The accounting staff also compiles factory overhead costs into one or more cost pools, which they allocate to the goods produced during the period. Some of these items will still be in inventory, while other produced items may have been sold. Consequently, some of the overhead will be charged to the cost of goods sold, and some will be added to the ending inventory balance.

The accounting staff then conducts a reasonableness test, where it compares the company's preliminary gross margin for the period to its historical gross margin. If the preliminary version is not similar to the historical margin, the accounting staff investigates further to see if there is an error in its inventory valuation or overhead application procedures that caused the problem.

In addition, the accounting staff sometimes runs a comparison of the cost of inventory to its market value, and writes down any inventory for which the market value is lower than its cost. This step is required by the accounting standards, but does not have to be examined as part of every month-end close.

Analysis of Inventory Accounting

In the preceding discussion, we alluded to several problems with inventory. First, the accounting staff is trying to establish a valuation based on quantity information that may very well be incorrect. Second, the use of a cost layering methodology can involve a massive amount of cost information, which makes it easy to assign an incorrect valuation to an inventory item. And finally, the sheer size of the investment in inventory in many organizations tends to amplify the impact of valuation errors. In short, a number of factors make it difficult to create an inventory valuation that a controller can support with confidence.

In the following section, we will discuss ways to overcome all three problems – inventory record accuracy, inventory valuation, and the amount invested in inventory.

Lean Inventory Accounting

To create a lean inventory accounting function, the controller must be concerned with three key areas:

- High inventory record accuracy
- Simplified inventory valuation
- Reduced inventory levels

If these areas can be improved upon, it should be possible to very nearly automate large portions of the inventory valuation function. In addition, a reduction in the amount of inventory reduces the impact of any remaining errors. We delve into these changes through the remainder of this section.

Perpetual Inventory System

It is vastly easier for the accounting department to close the books when the inventory records are *always* accurate. This result is possible when a business uses a perpetual inventory system. This method involves maintaining up-to-date records on the on-hand unit quantities and locations of all inventory items.

While the perpetual inventory system seems like an obvious solution, it does not yield sufficient inventory record accuracy in practice, unless a company is willing to engage in the rigorous enforcement of a number of items:

- Lock down the warehouse and keep all non-warehouse people out of the warehouse
- Properly label all inventory items
- Properly label all bin locations, and include location codes in all transactions
- Cycle count to continually review unit quantities (see the following cycle counting topic)
- Audit inventory to measure accuracy levels
- Follow up on the underlying reasons for inventory record errors

An organization that is committed to high inventory record accuracy will likely find that accuracy levels will rise gradually over a number of months – this is not a quick solution. During the period when record accuracy is still improving, the controller will probably have to continue mandating period-end physical inventory counts in order to obtain a reasonably accurate ending inventory valuation.

Tip: When buying inventory tracking software, only buy a package that allows for the recordation of multiple bin locations for each inventory item. Otherwise, the warehouse staff will only be able to store inventory in designated bins that may already be full.

Cycle Counting

As we noted in a preceding section, a physical inventory count can be laced with errors, which causes lots of trouble for any controller attempting to produce reasonably accurate financial statements. The best way to improve upon the situation is to replace physical counts with cycle counts.

Cycle counting is the process of counting small portions of the inventory every day. This task is always handled by experienced counters, not by people who have no familiarity with the inventory (as can happen for a period-end physical count). These counters are given a report stating the items to be counted, which can be based on any of a number of counting criteria, such as:

- *Count by physical location.* The most commonly used, this approach is designed to give equal counting coverage to each area of the warehouse on an ongoing basis.
- *Count by usage level.* This focuses counts on high-usage items, on the theory that the volume of transactions makes it more likely for these items to have inaccurate records.
- *Count by value.* This focuses on counting the most valuable items most frequently. It is favored by the controller, since it improves the accuracy of the total inventory valuation. However, it is less effective from the perspective of ensuring that the correct inventory items are on hand for production purposes.

The cycle counting report is derived from the information in the inventory records, which means that counters are verifying the information in the inventory database. In addition (and especially effective when counting by physical location), the counters match items in the warehouse bins back to the report, which provides information about items that may never have been recorded in the inventory records.

The work thus far is of great importance, since it provides a continual update to the accuracy of the inventory records. In addition, the counters should work with the warehouse manager to investigate why errors have appeared in the inventory records. This investigation can lead to procedural and other changes that gradually eliminate the underlying causes of errors, and thereby improve the overall accuracy of the inventory records.

Tip: All inventory transactions must be entered into the inventory records before cycle counting reports are printed; otherwise, the counters are working with potentially incorrect report information which they will then adjust, which *decreases* the accuracy of the inventory records.

Transaction Backlog Elimination

As just noted, there should be no backlog of inventory transactions when cycle counting reports are run, since this impairs the accuracy of the reports. The following are options for eliminating the transaction backlog:

- *Create clerk position.* In many warehouses, data entry is considered an incidental task that is handled by the staff only when they have spare time. Instead, consider creating a dedicated position within the warehouse that only handles inventory record keeping. The downside of this approach is that the regular warehouse staff must now write down all transactions and forward them to the clerk, which introduces a time delay, the potential loss of transaction documents, and possible transcription errors.
- *Real time data entry.* The reverse of the last suggestion is to install computer terminals throughout the warehouse, and train the entire staff to enter transactions immediately. This concept can (and should) be taken a step further by equipping employees with portable terminals, so that they can enter transactions as they engage in putaway and picking transactions anywhere on the premises.

Bar Coded Inventory Transactions

When anyone enters a transaction into the inventory database, there is a risk of entering information incorrectly. This risk can be reduced by converting as much inventory information as possible into bar codes. Once created, it is essentially impossible to derive incorrect information from a bar code.

Bar codes should certainly be used to record all warehouse bin locations. In addition, bar codes can be listed on a work sheet for easy scanning access, listing the various types of inventory transactions, such as a pick, putaway, or scrap transaction.

The only downside of using bar codes is the cost of adding bar code scanners to portable and fixed terminals, but the improvement in record accuracy should more than make up for this cost.

Backflushing

Some of the more advanced computer systems allow for the use of backflushing, which is the automatic reduction of inventory levels based on the amount of goods that have been produced. In essence, a business constructs bills of material that detail the contents of its products, and then multiplies the bills of material by the total of all finished goods produced to determine how many raw materials must have been used. This calculated total is then subtracted from the amount of raw materials on hand.

Backflushing is the simplest method available for recording inventory transactions, since only the amount of finished goods produced is entered into the system. In a well-organized production environment, this can massively reduce the data entry chore. However, be aware of the following issues with backflushing:

- Bills of material must be *very* accurate, or else the wrong amounts of raw materials will be subtracted from the inventory records.
- Unusual inventory usage, such as for scrap and rework, should be recorded separately and subtracted from the raw materials inventory.

- The method for counting finished goods completed must be *very* accurate, or else the derived amount of raw materials usage will be wrong.
- If a raw material is located in multiple bins, the system will not know which bin from which to deduct units, and so will likely do so from a default location that may not be where the raw materials originated.

There is a risk of implementing backflushing and finding that inventory record accuracy has declined precipitously, due to any of the preceding issues. To avoid this, first verify that bill of material records are extremely accurate. Also, conduct continual cycle counts of the inventory, so that any backflushing issues are spotted and corrected quickly.

Ending Inventory Estimation

There are many months during the year when the financial statements are only being distributed internally. During these months, it may be acceptable for the controller to report cost of goods sold that is based on an estimate of the ending inventory, rather than one that is based on a physical count or a perpetual inventory system. The calculation is to subtract scrap and the standard cost of items sold from the sum of beginning inventory and purchases made during the period.

Use this approach with extreme caution, and only when there is great confidence that all major inventory-related events have been properly recorded. Otherwise, there is a considerable risk that the ending inventory estimate will be wrong, which means that the cost of goods sold will be wrong, which in turn causes an incorrect profit or loss figure. In general, only estimate ending inventory under the following circumstances:

- When there is a reliable historical trend for the amount of scrap that will probably arise in each period
- When audits have confirmed that bills of material accurately reflect the number and types of parts used in products
- When the accounting system can reliably record all purchases received
- When the number and type of units sold can be accurately tracked

Also, it is inadvisable to estimate the ending inventory balance for too many months in a row without confirming it with cycle counts or a physical inventory count. Otherwise, the actual balance will diverge more and more from the estimate, resulting in a large adjustment at some point in the future.

Minimal Overhead Allocation

Accounting standards require that the recorded cost of inventory is the sum of the expenditures directly *or indirectly* incurred to bring a product to its existing condition and location. The "indirectly" part of the requirement means that we must allocate overhead to inventory. However, allocated overhead does not improve the decision making of management, so there is no reason to engage in a complex allocation. Instead, the focus should be on allocating overhead as quickly and efficiently as possible. Consider following these rules to create a simplified overhead allocation:

- *Use auditor-approved cost pool.* Include in the overhead cost pool whatever the outside auditors want. The point is to not waste time in the middle of an audit retroactively revising the contents of a cost pool.
- *Minimize cost pools.* There is no reason to maintain a large number of cost pools in order to arrive at a "precise" allocation. Instead, since we are only complying with an accounting standard, store all applicable costs in a single cost pool.
- *Use simplest allocation base.* There are a number of measurements that can be used as the basis for an allocation, such as direct labor hours used, machine hours used, and square footage used. Select the one that is simplest to compile, and which the auditors will not complain is an inadequate basis of allocation. The worst allocation base is the one that requires an entirely new measurement system to compile.

The end result of a minimized overhead allocation methodology may be an allocation that is not quite as precise as the allocation derived from a more elaborate system. This is acceptable, since the goal is to keep the allocation as simple as possible in order to save effort, while staying in compliance with the accounting standards.

Lower of Cost or Market Limitation

The accounting standards mandate that inventory be periodically evaluated to see if its recorded cost is higher than its market value. If so, the inventory valuation is supposed to be written down to the market value. This can be a time-consuming and cumbersome process, especially since the market value of some older or custom-designed items may not be readily discernible.

A simple way to reduce the work associated with the lower of cost or market rule is to limit it to the 20 percent of inventory items that generally comprise the top 80 percent of the inventory valuation. The other 80 percent of inventory items have such minuscule valuations that any write down in their valuations would not have a material impact on the financial statements, and so can be safely ignored.

Obsolete Inventory Tracking

One of the larger worries for a controller is to report reasonable financial results for most of a year, and then discover that there was a large write-off at year-end, due to the recognition of a large amount of obsolete inventory. This is not a lean accounting issue, but obsolete inventory can be discovered sooner in the year, thereby eliminating the year-end surprise. Follow these steps to create an obsolete inventory tracking system:

1. *Reports*. Create a report that states all inventory items that are in stock, but which are not listed on any bills of material. Also create a report that details historical usage levels for all raw materials in comparison to current inventory levels. Finally, create a report that shows planned usage levels for all raw materials in comparison to current inventory levels. Highlight all items on these reports for which there appears to be too much inventory in comparison to planned or historical usage levels.

2. *Review committee*. Form a review committee with members from the purchasing, materials planning, engineering, and accounting departments. Have this group review the inventory items revealed by the reports as being potentially obsolete. The committee should create a list of which items can be disposed of, and the amounts to be disposed of.

3. *Reserve*. The purchasing department estimates the amounts at which these inventory items can be disposed of and forwards the information to the accounting department. The accounting staff creates a reserve in the amount of the difference between recorded inventory values and estimated disposal receipts.

4. *Adjust*. The accounting staff adjusts the reserve for obsolete inventory as inventory items are disposed of.

5. *Repeat*. Conduct a new review for obsolete inventory at regular intervals throughout the year.

This process makes it much less likely that there will be any surprises at the end of the year, when a physical inventory count is conducted.

Charge Inventory to Expense

Among the most difficult inventory items to count are the nuts, bolts, washers, and so on that fall into a general category called fittings and fasteners. It can take an inordinate amount of time to count these items, even when simply estimating unit quantities by weighing them. In addition to this annoyance, the amount of money involved is quite small, perhaps just a few percent of the entire inventory valuation.

The easiest way to deal with this difficult inventory record keeping is not to do so at all. Instead, move all fittings and fasteners to a storage area next to or within the production area, where the parts are freely accessible. Since the items are no longer being formally tracked through the inventory system, the accounting staff will instead charge them to expense when they are purchased. This will create a small increase in the cost of goods sold when the first batch of fittings and fasteners is written off, but should not have a noticeable impact thereafter.

Fittings and fasteners are essential components, so it is not acceptable to let them inadvertently go out of stock and thereby be the cause of a production stoppage. Since their quantities are no longer being tracked by the warehouse, a visual reordering system must be installed. This involves keeping all items in standard-sized bins, marking a reorder line in each bin, and routinely examining the bins to see which items have fallen below the reorder line and must therefore be reordered.

The net impact of this recommendation on the total inventory valuation is quite small, since fittings and fasteners do not have a large aggregate value. However, their absence from inventory counts can substantially reduce the counting activities of the warehouse staff.

Just-in-Time Deliveries

One way to achieve a lean inventory accounting function is to have no inventory, or as little as possible. One possibility is to adopt a just-in-time system, where suppliers make a large number of small deliveries to a company's production facilities, rather than less frequent and much larger deliveries. Delivered goods are sent straight to the company's production area, where they are built into products at once.

While a just-in-time system may appear to be ideal, it requires considerable preparation to make operational. Consider the following issues:

- *Bill of materials accuracy.* It is impossible to achieve a high level of precision with supplier orders unless the company knows the exact composition of each product. This information appears in a bill of materials, which must be closely monitored to ensure that it remains accurate.
- *Production schedule accuracy.* The production schedule must be locked down for the time period required by suppliers to manufacture the components that go into the company's products. Any last-minute changes will cause problems with deliveries.
- *Information sharing.* The company must be willing to share real-time information with its suppliers. This usually means setting up a master purchase order with each one to set the pricing and general quantities for a long period of time, and then having the company's production system send electronic messages to each supplier, informing them of the composition and timing of deliveries for each day (or several times per day).
- *Supplier proximity.* It is nearly impossible to arrange for just-in-time deliveries with suppliers located thousands of miles away, unless expensive overnight delivery services are used. Consequently, most suppliers in a just-in-time system are located near the company. Also, the further away a supplier is located, the greater the need to maintain a buffer inventory in case deliveries are delayed.
- *Supplier quality.* It is usually necessary to certify each supplier in a just-in-time system for the quality and reliability of its deliveries. By doing so, the company's receiving function can be eliminated and goods can be delivered directly to the production area.

In addition, the use of just-in-time deliveries only means that there will be minimal amounts of raw materials on hand; there may still be substantial quantities of finished goods in storage, unless the company is truly only building products if there are firm customer orders in hand. Thus, just-in-time concepts are certainly laudable, and will absolutely reduce the amount of inventory, but there will still probably be some inventory on hand for which the accounting staff must compile a valuation.

> **Tip:** If just-in-time concepts can reduce inventory levels to a sufficient extent, it may be possible to eliminate a perpetual inventory system and cycle counting, in favor of a simplified visual review of on-hand inventory levels.

Drop Shipping

If a company only resells goods to its customers, it may be possible to have its suppliers ship directly to the customers. This is known as *drop shipping*. By doing so, the company never owns inventory, which eliminates all inventory valuation issues for the accounting department.

If a supplier agrees to engage in drop shipping, the company sends it a copy of the customer order, which the supplier uses as the basis for a shipment. Once the goods are shipped, the supplier bills the company. The receipt of a shipping notification triggers the issuance by the company of an invoice to the customer. Thus, the paperwork flow is different from what is used for a delivery from the company warehouse, but may be worth the effort in exchange for not having to invest in or record inventory.

On-Site Inventory Ownership by Suppliers

The purchasing department may be able to arrange with some suppliers to continue their ownership of raw materials and components while the items are stocked on the company's premises. Under this approach, suppliers visit the inventory storage area on a regular basis and add items whenever inventory levels are too low. They also track usage and invoice the company for the amounts used. To make this system work, it is usually necessary to sole-source materials with certain suppliers, so that there is no confusion about whose raw materials were used.

The advantage from the accounting perspective is obvious – there is no inventory to track, since it is still owned by suppliers. However, this approach usually only works for smaller parts that are consumed in high volumes, such as fittings and fasteners. The suppliers of more expensive items and goods that must be custom-built are less amenable to this approach. Also, it only works if suppliers are located quite close to the company's production facilities.

Reduce Product Options

The marketing department likes to offer a wide variety of product features to its customers. This can reach the extreme of offering a product in many sizes and colors, with different numbers of attachments. By doing so, it is presumed that customers will buy more products. However, the downside is a massive increase in inventory, since the company must maintain far more varieties of finished goods in stock, as well as the various raw materials and subassemblies needed to construct these items. This situation makes matters much worse for the accounting staff, for two reasons:

- The amount of inventory to be accounted for is greatly increased

- Some of the product configurations will sell only infrequently, so it may be necessary to maintain a reserve for obsolete inventory

The solution is a careful analysis of the various product configurations to eliminate those that are not selling, thereby reducing the overall amount of inventory.

Analysis of Lean Inventory Accounting

Of the changes advocated in this section, the use of a perpetual inventory system and cycle counting can bring inventory record accuracy to such a state of perfection that the accounting department does not need to engage in physical inventory counts again. Thus, inventory record accuracy is highly attainable.

Inventory valuation, however, remains a problem for the accounting department. It is possible to occasionally estimate the ending inventory valuation, but this approach is risky, especially when not supported by high-quality record keeping. Consequently, the accounting staff will probably resort to using simplified overhead allocation methods, restricted lower of cost or market examinations, and ongoing obsolete inventory tracking to put a small dent in its period-end valuation work.

Of more long-term value are a number of methods for either whittling down or completely eliminating inventory. Whenever inventory can be charged to expense or shifted to a supplier, the accounting staff has no valuation work to do. If the amount can only be reduced, such as with just-in-time deliveries or reducing the number of product options, the impact of a valuation mistake is reduced, but the accounting staff must still engage in valuation work.

Additional Improvement Concepts

There are several additional concepts that can be applied to the inventory accounting topic to enhance performance or reduce costs. These concepts did not fit into any of the process flows noted previously or were considered minor elements, and so are noted here instead:

- *Audit bills of material*. The basis upon which inventory is typically valued is the bill of materials, which is the detailed listing of the components required to build a product. If the bill of materials is inaccurate, then so too will be the inventory valuation. Accordingly, have the engineering staff regularly review bills of material to verify that they are accurate. In particular, have them verify any bills for which there has been a change to the underlying product, since it is quite likely that no one altered the corresponding bills to match the revised products.
- *Adjust for scrap*. Bills of material typically contain a small allowance for the amount of scrap expected to be generated by the production process. Changes in the production process can alter the amount of scrap generated, so it makes sense to periodically compare actual scrap rates to the amounts in the bills, and adjust the bills as needed. Otherwise, when the bills are multiplied by ending inventory balances, the resulting valuation could be incorrect.

- *Adjust for returns*. Materials are usually picked from stock based on bills of material and then forwarded to the production area for processing into finished goods. If the bill of materials used for picking purposes is incorrect, some materials may be picked in excess quantities, in which case the excess amounts will be returned to the warehouse. Have the warehouse staff make note of these returns, since they are evidence that the underlying bills of material are incorrect.
- *Transaction training*. There are a large number of inventory-related transactions, such as consignments, cycle counting adjustments, receiving, and so forth. It is not at all difficult for a poorly-training warehouse or accounting employee to incorrectly process a large number of these transactions because they have incorrect training in how to do so. To avoid these surges of errors, institute a training program for all new employees who will be involved in inventory recordation activities, and require additional training for anyone who has subsequently caused an error. It can be helpful to back up this training with a "cheat sheet" that summarizes how to process each type of inventory transaction in a summary-level format.
- *Standardize parts*. Many of the problems that bedevil inventory record keeping arise from the massive number of parts that are kept in stock. The underlying problem is that each product is built from a unique set of parts. If the engineering staff can be encouraged to design products from a common set of standard parts, it is possible to pare back the number of raw material items over a long period of time. The result is fewer units to track, which streamlines the record keeping process.

Inventory Measurements

The following measurements can be used to monitor the performance of inventory accounting:

- *Cycle counting errors*. Summarize all errors found by the cycle counters and aggregate them by error type. This information can be used to focus attention on eliminating the conditions causing the highest volume of errors.
- *Negative inventory report*. Run an inventory unit quantity report that only shows those inventory records that have negative unit counts. These balances are obviously incorrect, and should be investigated at once.
- *Unit cost trend line*. Create a rolling 12-month report that states the month-end recorded cost per unit of each inventory item. It is useful to scan through this report to see if there have been any unusual changes in unit costs. This is an excellent tool for locating valuation problems.
- *Inventory accuracy percentage*. If inventory accuracy is being audited at regular intervals, track the inventory accuracy percentage on a trend line. Better yet, calculate the percentage by warehouse area (such as by aisle) and post this information in the warehouse. Then assign record accuracy respon-

sibility to the warehouse staff for these count areas, so that measurements can be tied to specific employees.

As has been the case in other chapters, we prefer to focus measurements on a detailed analysis of individual transactions, since a business can use this information to fine-tune its operations.

Summary

There is a major problem in this chapter, which is that none of the improvement recommendations for inventory record accuracy or reduction are under the control of the accounting department. Instead, the controller must rely upon the warehouse manager to maintain accurate inventory records. While it is possible that the controller may be given supervisory control over the warehouse, most controllers will likely have to rely on good relations with the warehouse manager to achieve increased inventory record accuracy. The situation is even worse for the inventory reduction initiatives, for the marketing and purchasing departments must also be involved. Usually, the best way to achieve success is to obtain the support of a senior-level project sponsor who can force the various departments to cooperate. Otherwise, a controller who is working alone to achieve these recommendations will be lucky to succeed in just a few areas.

For a more extensive treatment of the inventory subject, see the author's *Accounting for Inventory* and *Inventory Management* books.

Chapter 10
Lean Cost Accounting

Introduction

Cost accounting is one of the most archaic accounting functions, with roots in the high volume manufacturing operations in the earlier half of the twentieth century. The emphasis at that time was on long production runs, adhering closely to predetermined standards, and spreading overhead costs over as many units of production as possible. The production environment has changed radically since that time, but the tasks that the cost accountant was accustomed to performing in those days have still lingered. We can do better.

In this chapter, we begin with an overview of improvement concepts, then describe a typical cost accounting environment, and finally show the impact of lean improvement concepts on cost accounting.

Related Podcast Episodes: Episodes 43-47 and 57 of the Accounting Best Practices Podcast discuss cost accounting issues. These episodes are available at: **accounting-tools.com/podcasts** or **iTunes**

Improvement Concepts

The application of lean concepts in this chapter involves the following improvements to existing systems:

- *Cost derivation with backflushing.* Using bills of material and labor routings to derive the cost of items produced, rather than collecting actual labor and material consumption information.
- *Terminate labor tracking.* Stopping the collection of labor information, given the amount of work involved and the lack of relevance of the resulting information.
- *Terminate materials usage tracking.* Halting the charging of materials to specific jobs, in favor of doing so automatically with backflushing.
- *Terminate variance reporting.* No longer reporting on variances, since doing so is labor intensive and the results are counterproductive.
- *Minimize overhead allocation.* Avoiding elaborate allocations of overhead, to minimize the labor associated with this task.
- *Pull system.* Initiating production based on customer orders or other triggers, rather than pushing job orders through a production system. Doing so can greatly reduce inventory levels and other types of waste in the production process.

- *Terminate work orders.* Eliminating the use of work orders, which are not needed in a pull system.
- *Cell-level measurement systems.* Shifting reporting from monthly reports to real-time information that is generated at production cells.
- *Constraint analysis.* Focusing on the analysis of a bottleneck operation, to maximize its use and thereby increase company profits.
- *Target costing.* Planning for specific profit levels when products are initially designed, using predetermined price points, targeted profits, and product feature sets.

The Cost Accounting Environment

In this section, we describe four of the more central tasks that the cost accountant has been expected to engage in for many years. We will then note how many of these tasks are no longer applicable in today's altered production environment.

Traditional Cost Accounting – Variance Analysis

One of the main tasks of the cost accountant has been to investigate a variety of variances of actual results from standard or budgeted costs, and report this information to management. These variances are:

- *Purchase price variance.* The actual price paid for materials used, minus the standard cost, multiplied by the number of units used.
- *Material yield variance.* The actual material usage, minus the standard usage, multiplied by the standard price per unit.
- *Labor rate variance.* The actual price paid for the direct labor used in the production process, minus its standard cost, multiplied by the number of units used.
- *Labor efficiency variance.* The actual labor hours used, minus the standard usage, multiplied by the standard labor rate per hour.
- *Variable overhead spending variance.* The actual variable overhead cost incurred per unit, minus the standard cost per unit, multiplied by the total unit quantity of output.
- *Variable overhead efficiency variance.* The actual units of activity, minus the standard units of activity on which variable overhead is charged, multiplied by the standard variable overhead cost per unit.
- *Fixed overhead spending variance.* The total amount by which fixed overhead costs exceed their total standard cost for the reporting period.

The full range of variances noted here should make it clear that a cost accountant could spend an inordinate amount of time on this single task. In a larger organization, a number of people may be involved in nothing *but* variance analysis.

Traditional Cost Accounting – Job Costing

A major cost accounting task is the compilation of cost information at the level of the individual production job. This means having a data recordation system in place that requires all materials and labor to be charged to specific jobs. This information may be recorded on paper, in which case a data entry staff must enter it into a database. The cost accountant reviews this information for anomalies, and reports to management regarding unexpected costs incurred on jobs.

The recording of job cost data introduces a large non value-added task for the production staff, whose primary task should be manufacturing – not filling out forms. Since it is not their primary task, job cost information tends to be completed less than thoroughly, which requires more investigative work by the cost accountant.

Traditional Cost Accounting – Inventory Valuation

When a business produces goods using long production runs, it will have very large quantities of inventory on hand, and in all stages of completion. It is the job of the cost accountant to tally the quantities of inventory at the end of each reporting period, which may require the coordination of a physical inventory count. In addition, the cost accountant must assign a value to all inventory items, which may require the use of a complicated cost layering system, such as the first in, first out (FIFO) method or the last in, first out (LIFO) method. In addition, accounting standards require that factory overhead be allocated to inventory for external reporting purposes. The cost accountant is responsible for this task.

Once a preliminary inventory valuation has been compiled, there will likely be errors that must be located, investigated, and corrected.

Inventory valuation is addressed at greater length in the Lean Inventory Accounting chapter.

Traditional Cost Accounting – Margin Reports

The cost accountant routinely compiles costs at the product or job level, matches this information to the related revenues, and issues margin reports to management. These reports state the actual results achieved in comparison to expected results, and reports on the reasons for any variances. The time required to investigate these variances can be substantial.

It may be necessary to issue these reports in multiple formats, depending upon the information that management wants to see. If management needs to determine margin information for long-term pricing, then a report is produced that includes fully-applied overhead costs. If the report is instead needed to reach a decision about the price point for a specific deal, the report usually excludes the overhead information.

A significant problem with these margin reports is that management may misconstrue the use of overhead within a report, and terminate a product because it does not appear to generate a profit. In reality, the overhead being allocated to a product will still be incurred by a business even if the product is terminated. Thus, margin reports can be misleading.

Analysis of Cost Accounting

The traditional cost accounting job was designed to support a mass production environment, where a business produces a small number of products in very large quantities for a long period of time. Common characteristics of this model include:

- A large amount of inventory in all phases of the production process
- Comprehensive data collection to determine the cost of the very large jobs running through the system
- Variance analysis to spot any changes from planned efficiencies and costs. Planning is based on specific (and large) production volumes.
- The assumption that all assets must be utilized to the maximum extent possible
- Each individual part of the production process must be optimized

In this environment, it may make sense to engage in *all* of the cost accounting activities just enumerated.

However, manufacturers do not necessarily follow the mass production model. Instead, they may operate in a much leaner environment, where they only produce in small batch sizes, and only when there is a customer order in hand. The cost accounting tasks just described are completely inappropriate in such an environment, because:

- Production runs are so short that there is no point in calculating variances
- Production jobs may be comprised of a single unit, which makes it far too expensive to compile costs at the job level
- There is so little inventory on hand that inventory valuation is a minor task
- Margin reports are based on job costs, and job costing information is no longer being compiled

Instead, a new, leaner approach to cost accounting must be found. In the following section, we discuss which traditional cost accounting tasks to eliminate and which ones to install in a production environment that does not involve the mass production model.

Lean Cost Accounting

All of the recommendations made in this section for lean cost accounting are driven by the radically altered dynamics of a lean production environment. The characteristics of a lean manufacturing company include:

- Units are produced when customers order them (a "pull" environment)
- Products are manufactured in production cells in very small batch sizes, so there is little work-in-process inventory
- Machine setup times are very short, so there is little setup cost associated with a production job

- Suppliers deliver goods on a just-in-time basis, so there is little raw materials inventory on hand
- There is a heavy emphasis on product quality, which minimizes scrap levels

Cost accounting tasks must change radically in response to this new production environment. We delve into these changes through the remainder of this section.

Cost Derivation with Backflushing

The traditional way to derive a cost for a production job is to manually assign a variety of costs to it, such as direct materials and direct labor. A great deal of cost collection work is needed under this traditional approach, which interferes with the efficient flow of work through the production and warehouse areas. Further, the cost accountant spends a great deal of time examining the compiled costs for variances from expected or standard costs, as well as adjusting the amounts if it appears that costs were mistakenly charged to a job or not charged at all.

The solution is to not bother with any type of manual cost application. Instead, consider using the backflushing concept, where the cost of a job is considered to be the bill of materials, multiplied by the number of units produced. Costs are assumed to match the standard costs that are documented in the bill of materials for a product. For example, if a business produces 100 units, and the bill of materials states that the materials cost of each unit is $50, then the total derived materials cost is $5,000. There is no detailed cost compilation.

> **Tip:** This solution requires that the cost accountant spend time verifying that the bills of material and production counts are accurate, since these two factors are used to derive costs.

This suggestion will not work if a company has a cost reimbursement contract with a customer, since the customer will want to see a detailed compilation of all actual costs that the company proposes to charge to the customer.

> **Tip:** If there is some uncertainty about the variability of scrap and rework costs, it may initially be necessary to maintain a cost tracking system for these items. Once these costs can be reasonably estimated, include them in the bills of material.

The backflushing concept can be taken one step further by also maintaining accurate labor routings for all products, and using them to derive the standard labor cost associated with production. Thus, if a business produces 100 units, and the labor routing states that the labor cost of each unit is $15, then the total derived labor cost is $1,500. Again, no detailed cost compilation is necessary.

> **Tip:** Both bills of material and labor routings can be verified on a project basis, where actual cost information is compiled for a specific job. Once the project has been completed, the cost compilation is terminated, and the company returns to deriving costs through backflushing.

Terminate Labor Tracking

The production staff can spend an inordinate amount of time recording the hours they spend on specific production jobs, as can the accounting staff that transcribes this information into a database. Once recorded, management usually finds that the information changes little from period to period, and so ignores it.

A reasonable solution is to terminate all labor tracking. This means that the production line workers, administrative staff, maintenance personnel, and so on can immediately stop tracing their hours worked to specific products or services. The only labor tracking they should be doing is clocking in and out of work each day, for compensation calculation purposes (and only if they are paid on an hourly basis).

The only exception to this recommendation is when hours worked are being billed to customers. If so, the billing function is a key aspect of revenue generation, and therefore must be maintained.

> **Tip:** If the cost accountant insists that labor costs must be assigned to products in order to fully absorb all manufacturing costs, then include the cost of labor in factory overhead, and allocate it to products along with all of the other types of overhead costs.

It is easier to implement this recommendation once the production management group realizes that the entire production process is an integrated system, and the best way to manage the system is to focus on the bottlenecks in the process, rather than the amount of labor applied to specific jobs.

> **Tip:** Terminating labor tracking means that a business can potentially remove a number of data terminals from the production area, thereby reducing clutter and saving on IT support costs.

Terminate Materials Usage Tracking

In a normal job costing environment, there is an expectation that materials will be individually charged to a job. This can involve a great deal of paperwork, as well as clerical verification to ensure that the amounts charged are correct.

An alternative is to stop charging materials to jobs. Instead, and as noted earlier, multiply the bill of materials by the number of units produced to derive the standard amount of materials that should have been used (known as backflushing). This approach is particularly useful in a production environment where materials are being delivered on a just-in-time basis directly to the manufacturing area, since the process flow will be so fast that there is no time to manually record material usage.

Further, a just-in-time environment already relies upon extremely accurate bills of material to order goods from suppliers, so using these bills to also derive the cost of materials should yield very precise results.

This recommendation is less plausible in an environment where bills of material are not regularly reviewed for accuracy, and may not even include all costs. In this latter case, the quality of the bills of material must be upgraded before the separate tracking of materials usage can be terminated.

> **Tip:** The termination of materials usage tracking can trigger the reduction or elimination of computer terminals for material picking operations.

Terminate Variance Reporting

A large part of the cost accountant's time is taken up with the reporting of variances from various budgets or standards, usually involving either prices paid or the efficiency of various resources. We advocate the complete elimination of *all* variance reporting, for the following reasons:

- *Late information.* The information is compiled after the end of each accounting period. By the time the cost accountant can report back to management regarding the reasons for the variance, so much time has passed that it is no longer possible to take remedial action. Besides, a properly functioning production system should have already spotted these issues as soon as they occurred, and made any necessary corrections at once.

- *Nature of a standard.* A standard is an expectation that is based on a number of assumptions, such as the expected amount of production, or purchasing goods in certain quantities. Standards can also be based on politics; for example, a manager's bonus may be based on buying merchandise at a cost lower than a certain standard, so setting a conservative standard is a key element of earning the bonus. Thus, the baseline upon which a variance is calculated can be *quite* questionable.

- *Likely reaction.* If there is an unfavorable variance and the performance evaluation of a manager is partially based on that variance, expect the manager to take steps to correct the variance. This is not always a good thing; for example, a labor efficiency variance may be based on a certain amount of production volume, and a manager can eliminate the variance simply by increasing the number of units produced – even if the company cannot sell the extra units.

- *Impact on a lean factory.* A lean factory is one that only produces the exact amount of goods needed, and does not manufacture *anything* if there is no immediate need for the goods. There is no place for variances in this environment, since they would undoubtedly reveal "inefficient" labor and equipment usage.

In short, it is not only unnecessary to calculate and report on variances, but it is counterproductive to do so. The manufacturing environment runs more smoothly when employees are not being diverted from their work to deal with reported variances.

Minimize Overhead Allocation

Accounting standards require that factory overhead costs be allocated to produced goods, but this does not mean that the cost accountant needs to go to elaborate lengths to complete an allocation. Instead, use the simplest possible methodology to allocate overhead, thereby remaining in compliance with the accounting standards. This recommendation is dealt with at greater length in the Lean Inventory Accounting chapter.

Pull System

The traditional method for managing the flow of materials through a production facility is the push method, where a sales forecast is used as the basis for releasing production orders into the manufacturing facility. Order sizes tend to be fairly large, since the production scheduler is trying to take advantage of economies of scale in the production process. These production orders wend their way through the facility, with sometimes-lengthy stops while work is still in process, so that higher-priority jobs can leapfrog them. In this environment, the cost accountant may have to engage in elaborate month-end counts and valuations of work-in-process inventory, because there is so much inventory stacked up on the shop floor.

From a cost accounting and many other perspectives, a pull system is much more efficient than a push system. The pull system mandates that units are only produced when they are needed. This means that production is triggered at the shipping end of a business, with either a customer order or some other type of visual or electronic request. The request then flows back through the production line, authorizing the creation of only the exact number of units required.

In a pull system, production tends to be in the quantities that are about to be sold – which are usually quite a bit smaller than the batch sizes used in a push system. The result is vastly less work-in-process inventory on the shop floor. The amount of inventory may be so limited that there is no point in counting or valuing it at all, or at least there is much less of it for the cost accountant to deal with.

> **Tip:** A pull system can reduce inventory levels to such an extent that there is no need to even engage in cycle counting, which is normally an excellent tool for maintaining a high level of inventory record accuracy.

Terminate Work Orders

We have thus far discussed why labor and materials tracking should be eliminated, along with variance analysis. We have also advocated the introduction of the pull system of materials management. If those concepts are acceptable, it also possible to eliminate the work order. A work order is used for the following tasks:

- *To initiate production.* This is not needed under a pull system.

- *To collect actual costs about jobs.* This can be replaced by backflushing costs.
- *To report on job performance.* This can be eliminated by focusing on production cell operations.
- *To derive the overhead assigned to a job.* This should be avoided except for external reporting purposes.

In short, the pull environment does not require work orders, so they can be eliminated. In fact, a case could be made that it is impossible to even use work orders in a pull system, since the vastly increased number of small batches would create many more jobs to track.

Eliminating work orders also makes the life of the cost accountant easier, since there is no longer any pressure to compile costs or report cost information for jobs.

Cell-Level Measurement Systems

We have thus far pointed out that the traditional role of the cost accountant in issuing variance reports is not only unnecessary, but counterproductive. While there are some reporting options available for the cost accountant (see the Cost Accounting Measurements section), most reporting should be done at the production cell. The reason is that reports issued by the cost accountant are generally issued after the end of each month, which is far too late for management to take remedial action. For example, if a variance occurs near the beginning of a month and is not compiled into a variance report until after month-end, an entire month may have passed before management receives the information.

A better approach is to shift status reports to the operators of production cells. These employees can list a small amount of key operating information on a white board next to their work areas, such as a comparison of actual to planned production units, equipment setup times, or units rejected. The information is updated continually. The production and industrial engineering departments can review and take action on this information at once.

Constraint Analysis

In the preceding section, we noted that two characteristics of a traditional mass-production environment were the assumption that asset usage is to be maximized, and that each individual part of the production process must be optimized. In a lean production environment, these assumptions are considered to be incorrect. Instead, the following two assumptions are used:

- A company is an integrated set of processes that function together to generate a profit; and
- There is a chokepoint somewhere in a company that absolutely controls its ability to earn a profit.

The chokepoint is also known as a bottleneck, or a constraint. It is usually possible to tell where a bottleneck is located, because it has a large amount of work piled up in front of it, while the work operation immediately downstream from it is starved for work.

The first concept, that of a company being an integrated set of processes, applies very strongly at the product line level, where a set of production equipment can be used to manufacture a variety of related products. The second concept is most typically characterized by a machine that can only process a certain number of units per day. To improve profits, a company must focus all of its attention on that machine by taking such steps as:

- Adding supplemental staff to cover any employee breaks or downtime during shift changes
- Reviewing the quality of work-in-process going into the operation, so that it does not waste any time processing items that are already defective
- Positioning extra maintenance personnel near it to ensure that service intervals are short
- Reducing the amount of processing time per unit, so that more units can be run through the machine
- Adding more capacity to the machine
- Outsourcing work to suppliers

A major part of the management of a bottleneck operation is the inventory buffer located immediately in front of it. Constraint analysis holds that there will always be flaws in the production process that result in variability in the flow of materials to the bottleneck, so a buffer must be built up to insulate the bottleneck from these issues. The buffer should be quite large if there are lots of upstream production problems, or much smaller if the production flow is relatively placid.

If production problems start to eat into the size of the inventory buffer, then the bottleneck is in danger of having a stock-out condition, which may cause it to run out of work. To avoid this, have a large *sprint capacity* in selected upstream production operations. Sprint capacity is essentially excess production capacity. There should be sufficient sprint capacity available to rapidly rebuild the inventory buffer. If an investment has been made in a significant level of sprint capacity, there is also less need for a large inventory buffer.

In summary, the bottleneck operation is the most important operation in a company. The management team needs to know where it is located, and spend a great deal of time figuring out how to maximize its operation so that it hardly ever stops. The cost accountant can assist in this effort by engaging in the following activities:

- Reviewing the throughput (revenue minus all totally variable expenses) of the products scheduled for processing in the constrained resource. Ideally, the best way to maximize the use of a constrained resource is to schedule its use for the processing of products that have a combination of high through-put and low processing times at the bottleneck.

- The intensive analysis of downtime at the bottleneck, to see what can be done to improve utilization. This has a direct impact on company profits.
- The analysis of scrap immediately downstream from the constrained resource. Any scrap identified at this point was probably defective before it entered the constraint, and so was a waste of crucial processing time.
- The review of alternatives to processing through the constraint, such as outsourcing work to suppliers instead.
- The analysis of the inventory buffer located in front of the constrained resource, to ensure that it is sufficiently large to keep the constraint from running out of work.
- The review of sprint capacity levels, to ensure that there is sufficient upstream capacity to overcome any production shortfalls that would prevent work from reaching the constraint.

Constraint analysis differs markedly from the more traditional variance analysis. It represents a complete redirection of much of the work of the cost accountant.

Target Costing

A fundamental flaw in the role of the traditional cost accountant is that he reports on the costs that *are* – the costs that are already in existence. Product costs tend to continue in the same proportions into the future, so the cost accountant cannot do a great deal to improve a company's profitability based on its existing cost structure.

The primary management concept that can change this situation is *target costing*, under which a company plans in advance for the product price points, product costs, and margins that it wants to achieve. If it cannot manufacture a product at these planned levels, then it cancels the product entirely. With target costing, a management team has a powerful tool for continually monitoring products from the moment they enter the design phase and onward throughout their product life cycles. The primary steps involved in target costing are:

1. *Conduct research.* Review the marketplace in which the company wants to sell products. The target costing team determines the set of product features that customers are most likely to buy, and the amount they will pay for those features. The team must learn about the perceived value of individual features, in case they later need to determine what impact there will be on the product price if they drop one or more of them. It may be necessary to later eliminate a product feature if the team decides that it cannot provide the feature while still meeting its target cost. At the end of this process, the team has a good idea of the target price at which it can sell the proposed product with a certain set of features, and how it must alter the price if it modifies or drops some features from the product.

2. *Calculate maximum cost.* The company provides the design team with a mandated gross margin that the proposed product must earn. By subtracting the mandated gross margin from the projected product price, the team can

easily determine the maximum target cost that the product must achieve before it is approved for production.

3. *Engineer the product.* The engineers and procurement personnel on the team now take the leading role in creating the product. The procurement staff is particularly important if the product has a high proportion of purchased parts; they must determine component pricing based on the necessary quality, delivery, and quantity levels expected for the product. They may also be involved in outsourcing parts, if this results in lower costs or higher quality. The engineers must design the product to meet the cost target, which will likely include a number of design iterations to see which combination of revised features and design considerations results in the lowest cost.

4. *Ongoing activities.* Once a product design is finalized and approved, the team is reconstituted to include fewer designers and more industrial engineers. The team now enters into a new phase of reducing production costs, which continues for the life of the product. For example, cost reductions may come from waste reductions in production, or from planned supplier cost reductions. These ongoing cost reductions yield enough additional gross margin for the company to further reduce the price of the product over time, in response to increases in the level of competition.

The cost accountant's role on a design team is to continually compile the projected cost of the product as it moves forward through the design process. The accountant compares this cost to the total target cost, and communicates the variance between the two figures to management, along with qualitative information about where projected costs are expected to decline further, what design changes are most likely to achieve further cost declines, and how these design changes will affect the value proposition of the final product. Management uses this information to periodically monitor the progress of the design project, and to cancel the project if it appears likely that the product cannot be designed within the cost and value parameters of the project.

A key part of the cost accountant's role is to obtain cost information from suppliers, which in turn is predicated on the assumption of a certain amount of purchasing volume, which may not ultimately prove to be correct. If there are significant cost differences at varying purchase volume levels, it may be necessary for the cost accountant to present several possible product costs, one for each volume level.

EXAMPLE

Active Exercise Machines is designing a new treadmill for the home exercise market, and is having trouble pricing the laminated rubber conveyor belt. Since Active is creating a treadmill in a non-standard length, the conveyor belt supplier will incur a setup cost, and must spread this cost over the projected number of treadmills to be produced. Since the setup cost is significant, the cost per unit will decline dramatically if Active orders more conveyor belts. The cost is $95 per unit if Active only orders 5,000 belts, and drops to $50 if Active orders 10,000 belts. Since the total cost of the treadmill is projected to be $500, this difference represents 9% of the total cost, which is significant enough to bring to the attention of management. Consequently, the cost accountant presents management with two projected costs for the treadmill – one at a unit volume of 5,000, and another at a unit volume of 10,000.

Cost information is likely to be vague when a project is initiated, since the team is working with general design concepts and rough estimates of production volumes. Consequently, initial cost reports are likely to be within a range of possible costs, which gradually tighten up as the team generates more precise designs and better sales estimates.

A final task is for the cost accountant to continue monitoring the cost of the product after its release and throughout its product life. This is a key role, because management needs to know immediately if the initial cost structure that the design team worked so hard to create is no longer valid, and why the cost has increased.

Analysis of Lean Cost Accounting

The impact of lean concepts on the cost accounting function is massive. In fact, the cost accountant job description is essentially replaced with entirely new tasks. The issuance of standard reports and variances is almost completely eliminated, in favor of targeted analyses that more directly impact company profitability. Also, most of the data collection and aggregation work related to direct labor, direct materials, and jobs is eliminated, in favor of a tight focus on highly accurate bills of material and labor routings that can be used to derive standard product costs. Finally, the cost accountant should be involved at a proactive level in designing new products, rather than reporting after the fact on the costs of existing ones. In short, we have replaced a function that emphasizes massive data entry and the repetitive release of boilerplate reports with one that requires a much higher level of value-added analysis.

Additional Improvement Concepts

There are several additional concepts that can be applied to the cost accounting topic to enhance performance or reduce costs. These concepts did not fit into any of the process flows noted previously or were considered minor elements, and so are noted here instead:

- *Terminate work-in-process tracking.* Materials being processed through the production area tend to move through it rapidly and be in a constant state of flux, as they are modified through various work stations. Given the transitory nature of this area, it is quite labor-intensive to determine the cost of work-in-process inventory. Rather than attempting to assign a special value to this type of inventory at the end of a reporting period, only record the cost of the materials sent into the production area. This means that the cost of work-in-process items will be somewhat undervalued, since production labor costs and overhead will be ignored. However, this costing exclusion will reduce the work of the accounting staff, and may even allow for a quicker closing process.

- *Report on landed cost.* Landed cost includes every cost incurred to bring materials to the company, which means that freight, customs duties, shipping insurance, shipping damage, and sales taxes are also added. These costs tend to be diffused among a number of accounts, and so are not readily apparent to management. The cost accounting staff can develop a comprehensive analysis of the total landed cost of materials, which may lead to decisions to reduce total costs by switching to alternative suppliers, materials, and/or freight haulers.

Cost Accounting Measurements

The following measurements can be used to monitor cost accounting issues:

- *Days of inventory.* This is a comparison of the amount of inventory on hand to a company's sales. It provides a high-level view of the impact of a variety of policies and processes on the amount of inventory kept in stock. To calculate days of inventory, divide the average inventory for the year by the cost of goods sold for the same period, and then multiply by 365.

EXAMPLE

Active Exercise Machines has average inventory on hand of $1,000,000 and an annual cost of goods sold of $6,000,000. Its days of inventory metric is calculated as:

$$(\$1,000,000 \text{ inventory} \div \$6,000,000 \text{ cost of goods sold}) \times 365 \text{ days}$$
$$= 60.8 \text{ days of sales in inventory}$$

- *Dock-to-dock time.* This is the amount of time that it takes for materials to flow through a business, beginning with their arrival at the receiving dock and ending with their departure from the shipping dock. The measure notes the time required to convert materials to a finished product and sell it. A faster dock-to-dock time implies that a company requires a smaller investment in inventory to support a given amount of sales. The calculation is to divide the total on-site inventory by the average rate of products shipped per hour.

EXAMPLE

In the past week, Active Exercise Machines shipped 1,000 units. The company maintains a 40-hour work week, so the rate of shipping was 25 units per hour. During the past month, Active had an average of 500 units in stock (measured in terms of equivalent finished units*), which was spread across the raw materials, work-in-process, and finished goods portions of its operations. The calculation of its dock-to-dock time is:

500 Units in production ÷ 25 Shipments per hour = 20 hours of dock-to-dock time

---

* Equivalent finished units is the number of partially completed units, multiplied by their percentage of completion

- *First time through.* This is the percentage of completed products that were not scrapped or require rework or recalibration. It reveals the ability of the production process to manufacture at a high quality level. Any products that do not make it through production on the first pass should be investigated in detail to determine the underlying cause of the problem.
- *On-time shipment.* This is the percentage of orders that completely ship by their unadjusted promise dates. It is an excellent indicator of a company's ability to control its processes. If the order entry staff sets a promise date that is derived from a company's normal planning systems, then it should always be able to ship by the promise date. If not, management needs to investigate what process failure caused the shipment delay.
- *Purchase cost trend line.* If a business depends on a certain number of key commodities, it may be useful to monitor them on a trend line. This should be only for those commodities that represent a significant proportion of total costs, and which have historically been subject to a certain amount of fluctuation. The trend information may be useful for target costing and price setting purposes.
- *Bill of materials and labor routing accuracy.* Audit the bill of material and labor routing records on a recurring basis, and publish their accuracy, along with the details of all errors found. A record should be considered in error if it contains an incorrect part, unit quantity, unit of measure, labor type, or labor amount. The industrial engineering staff should use this information to make corrections to the records. This measurement is useful for estimating the reliability of the records for backflushing purposes.

All of the measurements described in this section should be considered vital for a manufacturing organization, as well as the analyses noted earlier in the recommendation regarding the use of constraint analysis.

Summary

Many of the recommendations made in this chapter relate to changing how operations are conducted within the production department, rather than the accounting area. This means that the proposed changes cannot be enacted without the overwhelming support of the managers of the production, purchasing, and engineering departments. Only with their support will it be possible to achieve a truly lean cost accounting function. Otherwise, the best a controller can hope for is some limited changes, probably in the areas of overhead application and variance reporting, which are under the direct control of the cost accountant.

The cost accounting concepts described in this chapter are addressed at much greater length in the author's *Cost Accounting Fundamentals* book.

Chapter 11
Lean Fixed Asset Accounting

Introduction

Fixed asset accounting is governed by a number of accounting standards that mandate the use of depreciation, impairment testing, asset retirement obligations, and so forth for fixed assets. Because of these requirements, the amount of effort expended by the accounting staff to deal with each fixed asset is much higher than is the case for any expenditure that is immediately charged to expense. There are ways to sidestep or at least streamline the amount of this work.

In this chapter, we begin with an overview of improvement concepts, then describe a typical fixed asset accounting environment, and finally show the impact of lean improvement concepts on fixed asset accounting.

Related Podcast Episodes: Episodes 15, 109, 122, 139, and 196 of the Accounting Best Practices Podcast discuss fixed asset accounting issues. These episodes are available at: **accountingtools.com/podcasts** or **iTunes**

We do not include in this chapter any discussion of the decisions to acquire, finance, or dispose of fixed assets, nor of the analysis of capital budgeting proposals, since those are decisions that may be handled by the management team as a whole, not just the accounting department.

Improvement Concepts

The application of lean concepts in this chapter involves the following improvements to existing systems:

- *High capitalization limit.* Using a high threshold to keep from recording smaller purchases as fixed assets.
- *Minimal base unit aggregation.* Avoiding the aggregation of several expenditures into a single fixed asset record, thereby reducing the number of fixed assets recorded.
- *Minimum number of asset classes.* Operating with just a few asset classes, to reduce the number of ways to depreciate fixed assets and present asset information.
- *Minimum limit on salvage values.* Imposing a threshold on salvage value assumptions, so that smaller amounts are excluded from depreciation calculations.

- *Interest capitalization avoidance.* Not taking advantage of the interest capitalization rules in marginal situations, to avoid the associated paperwork.
- *Common depreciation method.* Using the straight-line depreciation method for all fixed assets, to simplify calculations.
- *Annual fixed asset audit.* Periodically confirming the existence of the more valuable fixed assets, to keep from recording unexpected losses at year-end.
- *Fixed assets manual.* Using a procedures manual that documents the more difficult aspects of fixed asset accounting, to make the accounting for these items more consistent.
- *Formal documentation.* Using a standard system of supporting documents, to clarify the amounts and classifications of fixed assets.

The Fixed Asset Accounting Environment

In this section, we will describe the possible range of accounting issues that may be addressed for a fixed asset, and point out why these tasks are so time-consuming for the accounting department.

Traditional Fixed Asset Accounting

The easiest way to reveal the accounting for a fixed asset is to describe the transactions that may be required over the life of a typical fixed asset. Those steps may include:

1. *Record initial entry.* Determine which expenditures are required to bring the fixed asset to its intended location and condition, and record them as a fixed asset. Factors to consider in this determination are whether the total expenditure exceeds the minimum capitalization threshold, and which expenditures to include in the base unit.
2. *Capitalize interest.* If the fixed asset was constructed, the company is allowed to include in the capitalized amount of the asset any interest expense that can be reasonably associated with the asset during the construction period. The accounting standards have specific rules and examples for how and when interest is to be capitalized.
3. *Set up and record depreciation.* Determine the useful life, salvage value, and depreciation method for the asset, and set up this information in a depreciation table. Record the depreciation in the accounting records. This may involve the assignment of the asset to an asset class, for which the company uses a standard set of depreciation assumptions.
4. *Determine any asset retirement obligations.* Some assets may require a large amount of site remediation following their retirement from service, such as nuclear power plants or mining sites. In these cases, the accounting staff must record an estimate of this asset retirement obligation, as well as charge off the liability to expense over the remaining life of the asset.

5. *Review of impairment.* Periodically review the fixed asset to see if it is impaired, which involves a number of criteria. If so, reduce the carrying amount of the asset in the accounting records. This will also likely result in a change to the calculation of any remaining depreciation.

6. *Review for revaluation.* If the company is using international financial reporting standards, it can revalue its fixed assets. This requires adherence to a review methodology, as well as changes to the accounting records, and likely alterations to the depreciation calculation.

7. *Asset disposal.* Upon the sale or other disposal of the asset, remove it and any related accumulated depreciation from the accounting records, and also recognize a gain or loss on the transaction, if needed.

Of all the asset types found on the balance sheet, fixed assets present by far the most accounting challenges for the controller. There are not only initial recordation issues, but also continuing reviews over the life of each asset, sometimes followed by a relatively complex derecognition entry.

Analysis of Fixed Asset Accounting

The main point in itemizing the preceding list of possible fixed asset accounting activities is to show the sheer volume of actions that must be taken over the life of a fixed asset. In addition, consider that the controller must carefully document all fixed asset information, if only to defend the related accounting transactions with the outside auditors.

Also, many fixed asset transactions can be quite complex, which means that there is a strong possibility of recordation errors. Given the size and frequency of these potential errors, any reasonably prudent controller will cross-check all fixed asset transactions, which means that this area consumes a fair amount of accounting management time.

In the following section, we will discuss ways to overcome the fundamental inefficiency of fixed asset accounting, primarily by avoiding it entirely.

Lean Fixed Asset Accounting

The basis of our discussion of a lean fixed asset accounting function is the recognition that it requires significant effort to properly record and account for a fixed asset over its life span. If we can keep expenditures from being recorded as fixed assets and instead charge them to expense as incurred, all of this labor can be eliminated. We also have other suggestions for reducing the accounting work associated with those expenditures that *are* classified as fixed assets, while also bringing some order to the procedures and documentation being used. We delve into these changes through the remainder of this section.

High Capitalization Limit

The simplest way to eliminate fixed asset accounting activities is to impose the highest possible capitalization limit on fixed assets. This means setting the capitalization threshold at a large number, so that all smaller expenditures will be written off as expenses in the period incurred.

To determine a reasonable point at which to set the capitalization limit, list all fixed assets in the company's accounting records on an electronic spreadsheet, along with their original costs, and sort the records by cost. It is quite likely that the company tends to acquire a large number of fixed assets in a cost range that is just above the current capitalization limit. Then experiment with what would happen if the capitalization limit were increased to a point that would exclude most of these low-cost fixed assets. It is entirely possible that anywhere from one-quarter to one-half of the recorded fixed assets could have been eliminated with a modest increase in the capitalization limit.

> **Tip:** Include a step in the year-end closing procedure to review the capitalization limit again, to make sure that the current capitalization limit is appropriate.

A high capitalization limit also reduces personal property taxes, since a business reports fewer fixed assets on its personal property tax reports to the local government.

> **Note:** The concept of a capitalization limit does not appear in Generally Accepted Accounting Principles (GAAP), so the auditors may object if they find that a very high capitalization limit is triggering skewed results in the financial statements. Consequently, it can be useful to discuss a proposed capitalization limit with the auditors before enacting it.

Minimal Base Unit Aggregation

A base unit is a company's concept of what constitutes a fixed asset. For example, it may consider a single item to be a fixed asset (such as a desk), or it may allow a group of assets to be clustered together and designated as a single fixed asset (such as a group of desks). When it is considered allowable for a base unit to include several assets, the following issues arise:

- *Effective capitalization limit.* When several assets are combined into a single fixed asset record, the effective capitalization limit has been reduced, which means that more assets are being transformed into fixed assets, rather than being charged to expense. This requires more accounting staff time to record and monitor. For example, a company may have a $5,000 capitalization limit, and decides to record the purchase of six $1,000 desks as a single base unit; it therefore capitalizes the assets, which would otherwise have been charged to expense as incurred.

- *Asset tracking.* It is much more difficult to locate a group of assets. These types of assets tend to be easily moveable (such as a group of desks), and may be split up and sent to different destinations, so the accounting staff may spend an inordinate amount of time tracking them.

Due to the issues just noted, it is best to minimize base unit aggregation. Instead, an asset should be evaluated for fixed asset status by itself, which means that more assets will be charged to expense at once. The result will be fewer fixed asset records for the accounting staff to monitor.

Minimum Number of Asset Classes

It is customary for the accounting staff to group fixed assets into asset classes. An asset class contains fixed assets that are of a similar nature and use. Asset classes are useful for reporting fixed assets on the balance sheet or within associated financial disclosures. For example, fixed assets may be reported as being within the office equipment asset class, or the furniture and fixtures asset class.

Asset classes are also an efficient way to use the same depreciation method and useful life for large numbers of fixed assets. However, the concept can be taken too far. A nitpicky controller could create several dozen asset classes, such as:

- Vehicles – Hybrid
- Vehicles – Pickup truck
- Vehicles – Sedan
- Vehicles – Sport utility vehicle

There may be slight differences between the assets contained within these precisely-defined classes; for example, perhaps a sport utility vehicle has a slightly longer useful life than a sedan. Nonetheless, the sheer volume of asset classes makes it more difficult to record fixed asset information, and may lead to a plethora of different depreciation methods and useful lives. In addition, some assets could be defined within several asset classes, which require a number of qualitative judgments regarding where they should be listed – and which may not be followed consistently.

Consequently, we recommend establishing the absolute minimum number of asset classes, and only grudgingly expanding the list over time. The definitions of these few asset classes should be broadly defined, so that a range of assets can be assigned to them. Generally, it is most efficient to assign a single useful life and depreciation method to all assets categorized within an asset class. However, given the wide range of asset types that may be included in one of these broader asset classes, the controller can certainly vary from the standard useful life and depreciation method for certain assets.

Consider using the following decision points to determine which asset classes to use:

1. *Monetary aggregation.* Make a preliminary aggregation of all fixed assets by asset class, and calculate the total dollar amount of the assets in each class. See if it is possible to eliminate those asset classes containing the smallest total dollar amounts by shifting them into related asset classes.
2. *Retain unique assets.* Review the list again and see if any assets are so completely unique in terms of their nature and use that it is impossible to classify them within one of the more general asset classifications. Create separate asset classes for these assets.
3. *Borderline assets.* Review all fixed assets that could potentially be recorded in more than one asset class, and alter the class descriptions to ensure that they fit more closely into one class than another.

Minimum Limit on Salvage Values

As already noted, we want to reduce the amount of accounting labor associated with fixed assets. One minor way to do so is not to include salvage values in the calculation of depreciation, unless the salvage value is for a substantial amount. This has two benefits, which are a reduction in the complexity of depreciation calculations and the elimination of any documentation supporting the use of a salvage value (which the outside auditors might otherwise want to review).

The controller should set a threshold level for salvage values, below which salvage values are not used in the calculation of depreciation. When setting this threshold, review the current set of salvage values already used in the company's depreciation calculations, and ascertain what threshold would have eliminated the bulk of the salvage values. Then take this proposed threshold to the outside auditors to see if it is acceptable to them.

Tip: Include a step in the year-end closing procedure to review the salvage value threshold again, to make sure that the current threshold is appropriate.

Note: Eliminating the use of salvage values is a paltry issue for those businesses that use fixed asset software to track their depreciation, since they merely input the salvage value information and the software handles everything from there. However, it is more of a concern where depreciation is calculated on a spreadsheet, since the calculation error rate can be quite high.

Interest Capitalization Avoidance

The accounting standards contain detailed rules for how a business is to capitalize the interest expense associated with constructed assets. When interest is capitalized, the accounting staff must document the time period over which interest is being capitalized, the calculation of the amount of expenditures to which interest capitalization is to be applied, and why it is using a certain interest rate for the calculation. Clearly, this is a great deal of work, and it is likely to be examined in detail by the outside auditors as part of the year-end audit.

If a business is engaged in the construction of an asset for a relatively short period of time, it may be possible to completely avoid interest capitalization. For example, if a concrete pad is being constructed for a large machine purchase, followed by several months of equipment testing, the controller could make a case that the amount of associated interest expense is so small as to not be worth the documentation involved. Conversely, the multi-year construction of a shopping mall might *demand* the use of interest capitalization, given the time period and expenditures involved.

Tip: Create a policy under which interest capitalization is only allowed if the construction period exceeds a certain amount of time. The policy may also restrict interest capitalization to certain asset classes, such as buildings.

Common Depreciation Method

There are a number of possible depreciation methods available, ranging from the simplistic straight-line method to ones that greatly accelerate depreciation. In some companies, different depreciation methods are used for different assets, or perhaps a single depreciation method is assigned to all of the assets within an asset class. There are several problems with mixing up depreciation methods, and with only using accelerated methods. These issues are:

- *Asset class changes.* An asset may be re-classified from one asset class to another. If the standard depreciation method is different for the two asset classes, the accounting staff must spend time adjusting the methodology assigned to the asset.
- *Simplicity.* If a controller is calculating depreciation on an electronic spreadsheet, there is an increased risk that the calculations for an accelerated method will be incorrect.
- *Financial results.* The use of accelerated depreciation methods artificially skews the financial results of a business, so that profits appear to be reduced over the near term and enhanced later on. The controller may have to make manual adjustments to these figures in order to back out the impact of the accelerated depreciation.

To sidestep these issues, use the simplest possible depreciation method – the straight-line method – for all fixed assets.

Annual Fixed Asset Audit

The controller does not want to be surprised at year-end if the outside auditors review fixed assets and find that some are missing. Besides the obvious control issue with missing assets, it also means that the company must record an unexpected loss and derecognize the asset. Depending on the size of the unrecorded asset loss, this can have an impact as large as the considerable hit that many companies take when they find unexpected amounts of obsolete inventory at year-end.

To avoid this issue, the controller should sponsor a fixed asset audit once a year, preferably timed to be shortly before the annual audit. This review does not have to be comprehensive – there is no need to examine immovable assets or ones that have minimal asset values. Instead, focus on verifying the existence of just those assets whose loss would have a noticeable impact on the financial statements.

Fixed Assets Manual

The accounting for fixed assets can be quite complex, especially when it involves any or all of the following items:

- *Asset retirement obligations.* Tracking the liabilities associated with the eventual retirement of an asset.
- *Disposal.* Removing a terminated asset from the accounting records and recording any associated gains or losses.
- *Impairment.* Determining whether the value of a fixed asset has been impaired, and writing down its carrying amount as a result.
- *Interest capitalization.* Including interest expense in the capitalized cost of a constructed asset.
- *Non-monetary exchanges.* Accounting for asset swaps, or where cash is only part of the purchase price.
- *Not-for-profit.* Special rules apply to the accounting for fixed assets in a not-for-profit environment.
- *Revaluation.* Altering the carrying amount of a fixed asset, which is allowed under international financial reporting standards.

It is helpful to record these transactions as consistently as possible, which reduces the need for adjustments to the fixed asset records at a later date. Accordingly, create a fixed asset procedures manual that states exactly how each transaction is to be handled, including any required forms, approvals, and examples.

Tip: When there are many fixed assets and/or specialized fixed asset transactions, hire a fixed asset accountant who will specialize in this type of accounting.

Formal Documentation

The fixed asset records of any business are most assuredly going to be reviewed in detail by the outside auditors. This can cause a fair amount of wasteful assemblage of fixed asset records by the accounting staff as part of the audit. The clerical work associated with this review can be mitigated by having a formal system of documentation already in place. The level of documentation will vary, depending on the complexity of the assets. For example:

- *Single asset purchases.* Make a photocopy of the supplier invoice that documents the amount paid for an asset, and store it in a fixed assets binder, sorted by purchase date.
- *Constructed assets.* Create a separate binder for each constructed asset. The binder includes photocopies of all supplier invoices recorded for the constructed asset. There is a summary sheet in the front of the binder that lists the invoice number and amount of each supplier invoice, with a grand total that matches the amount capitalized in the accounting records. If interest is capitalized into the asset cost, then the documentation supporting the amount capitalized is included in the binder.
- *Disposed assets.* Maintain a separate binder for all assets that were disposed of. It should include the authorization for disposal, a copy of the sales receipt (if any) from the entity that acquired the fixed asset, and the calculation of the derecognition entry that removed the fixed asset from the accounting records, as well as the recognition of any gain or loss on the transaction.

Analysis of Lean Fixed Asset Accounting

The accounting standards require that a number of ongoing actions be taken to monitor and account for fixed assets, all of which require detailed accounting work. To avoid this, we have made several recommendations that are designed to keep a number of expenditures from being recognized as fixed assets at all. Realistically, these changes will have no impact on a business that has a large investment in expensive equipment. However, they may have quite a noticeable impact in some industries, such as services, where it may be possible to eliminate nearly all expenditures from consideration as fixed assets. Thus, the impact of these changes will depend on the nature of the business implementing them.

Fixed Asset Measurements

The following measurements can be used to monitor the performance of fixed asset accounting:

- *Depreciation trend line.* If there are a significant number of fixed assets that were purchased at varying points in time, the amount of depreciation expense that a business incurs should not vary much over time. If there is a sudden change in depreciation, it may very well be due to an error. Accordingly, track the depreciation expense on a trend line and investigate any noticeable changes in the amount.
- *New fixed assets list.* There may be cases where expenditures are recorded incorrectly as fixed assets. The best time to spot these problems is up front, when they are first recorded. Consequently, always print a list of the newest additions to the fixed asset register, and verify that they exceed the capitalization limit, have been recorded within the correct asset class, have not been

inappropriately aggregated into a base unit, and are being depreciated correctly.

These measurements are designed to spot errors in the fixed asset records at once, so that the accounting staff does not have to make corrections at a later date that may have accumulated in size over time.

Summary

Several of the suggestions in this chapter will accelerate the recognition of expenses. The use of a high capitalization limit, minimal base unit aggregation, and a limitation on salvage values will either trigger the entire recognition of an expenditure in the period incurred, or at least increase the amount of depreciation recorded. However, these changes will only be noticeable when they are first implemented; over time, as expenditures are consistently treated under these new rules, there will be little discernible change in the reported results of the company. Over the long term, the primary difference will be that the accounting staff has less work to do in creating and maintaining records for fixed assets.

The fixed asset concepts described in this chapter are addressed at much greater length in the author's *Fixed Asset Accounting* book.

Chapter 12
The Lean General Ledger Environment

Introduction

When creating a lean environment, the general ledger may not at first be considered as a candidate for improvement. It is more commonly considered a basic record-keeping instrument whose structure and use varies little from company to company. However, as we will see in this chapter, there are ways to streamline the format and use of the general ledger to a considerable extent.

In this chapter, we begin with an overview of improvement concepts, then describe a typical general ledger environment, and finally show the impact of improvement concepts on the general ledger.

Related Podcast Episode: Episodes 163 and 168 of the Accounting Best Practices Podcast discuss the chart of accounts and account reconciliation, respectively. The episodes are available at: **accountingtools.com/podcasts** or **iTunes**

Improvement Concepts

The application of lean concepts in this chapter involves the following improvements to existing systems:

- *Account reduction.* Shrinking the number of accounts in use, thereby avoiding several account maintenance issues.
- *Meaningful account codes.* Using alphanumeric account codes to denote departments, thereby reducing the recordation error rate.
- *Standardized chart of accounts.* Using a single chart of accounts across an enterprise, to eliminate the task of correctly mapping the accounts of subsidiaries to those of the parent company for consolidation purposes.
- *Journal entry restriction.* Confining journal entry data entry to a small number of people, thereby avoiding a variety of errors.
- *Journal entry checklist.* Using a standard list of journal entries as part of the period-end close, to ensure that a specific group of transactions are always recorded.
- *Journal entry templates.* Using standard templates to enter journal entries, so that the same accounts are employed each time.
- *Recurring journal entries.* Creating recurring entries for those few transactions that are repeated through multiple accounting periods.
- *Account content review.* Investigating the contents of accounts on a regular basis to ensure that they contain the correct transactions.

The General Ledger Environment

The general ledger environment is one in which the accounting staff routinely enters adjustments to various business transactions, accrues revenue and expenses, reverses entries, and cleans up account balances – all in the general ledger. In short, there can be a virtual flood of entries assailing the general ledger. There are several inherent problems with this environment. First, there are so many accounts that it is easy to record a transaction in the wrong place. Second, the variety of accounts used in a company's subsidiaries makes it difficult to create consolidated financial statements. Third, some of the transactions contain errors that can impact the results reported by a business, and which must therefore be rooted out, usually at the cost of a large amount of staff time. And finally, the number of error-filled entries can yield a situation where some accounts are stuffed with errors. These issues are addressed at greater length in the remainder of this section.

Number of Accounts

The typical general ledger contains hundreds or even thousands of accounts, with most of the accounts concentrated in the area of expenses. Most departments have roughly the same accounts, which are copied forward into any new department that a company creates. This leads to the following issues:

- *Incorrect account usage*. It is quite common for an expense to be charged to the wrong account within a department, which is discovered when the first draft of the financial statements are printed and reviewed. The result is that someone must create a journal entry to move the incorrect charge to a different account.
- *Immaterial balances*. The majority of all accounts contain small balances that have little impact on the reader's understanding of a business. Instead, they tend to focus on just a small number of accounts that contain the bulk of all transactions.
- *Training*. New accountants may require extensive training before they are comfortable with recording transactions into the correct accounts.
- *Audit cost*. It takes longer for outside auditors to audit a lengthy chart of accounts, which can increase the cost of an audit.
- *Financial statement links*. If there are many account numbers, it can be difficult to map these accounts into a coherent set of financial statements. The result may be financial statements that incorrectly reflect the contents of the general ledger.

Mapping

When a business acquires another company, the new subsidiary always has a chart of accounts that differs from that of the acquirer. If the acquirer does not impose its own chart of accounts on the acquiree, it must go through a mapping process at the end of each reporting period to determine which acquiree accounts correspond to its own accounts. The same problem arises when a corporate parent allows any subsidiary to maintain its own chart of accounts. More complex accounting packages always have a built-in mapping function to handle this issue. However, smaller businesses that operate a variety of lower-end accounting packages at each location must engage in a manual mapping process, which can increase the time needed to produce consolidated financial statements. Also, if the mapping is not done consistently, the financial statements produced over time may not be entirely comparable from period to period.

The easy solution to the mapping problem is to load the final results of each subsidiary into a standard journal entry that converts the results into the account code structure of the parent. However, every account change by a subsidiary requires a corresponding change to this standard journal entry, which can be a continuing cause of concern.

Journal Entries

Many types of transactions are recorded in the general ledger through journal entries. There are several types of errors caused by journal entries, which require an inordinate amount of time to research and correct. In particular:

- *Multiple entrants.* There may be a number of people who are allowed to create journal entries. If so, there is a risk that several people will create the same journal entry. Alternatively, one person may assume that another person is creating an entry, with the result that no one makes an entry.
- *Incorrect entries.* Some employees are better than others at creating journal entries. Those who are not careful may use the wrong account numbers or the wrong subsidiaries, or swap debits and credits.
- *Reversing flag.* Many journal entries are supposed to be reversed in the following accounting period. Employees may forget to flag entries to automatically reverse themselves, so that journal entries linger in the general ledger until discovered months later.
- *Minutiae.* Some accountants persist in making journal entries to reflect very small issues that have no material impact on the financial statements, perhaps due to a misguided sense that the statements must be absolutely perfect. While these types of entries do not necessarily create errors that must be corrected, they *do* add time to the closing process, while also cluttering up accounts with needless entries.

All of these issues can make it a virtual necessity to investigate the contents of every general ledger account at the end of each reporting period, just to make sure that all incorrect entries have been located and flushed out of the system. Such an intensive level of investigation can greatly delay the production of financial statements.

Account Contents

The error rates just noted for journal entries make it quite likely that the contents of the various general ledger accounts are not entirely accurate. This built-in level of inaccuracy can cause problems in several areas. First, the financial statements may not accurately reflect the results of the business. Also, the outside auditors will investigate the contents of some accounts as part of their year-end audit program, and will undoubtedly uncover issues that may call for embarrassing adjustments to the financial statements. The problem is particularly pernicious for balance sheet accounts, since these accounts may contain errors from prior years. This is less of a problem for revenue and expense accounts, which are re-set to zero at the end of each fiscal year.

Analysis of the General Ledger Environment

In this section, we have established that the general ledger environment is complex, with a vast array of accounts that can become overwhelming if there are a large number of departments and/or subsidiaries. A number of error-filled journal entries may have been recorded somewhere in this labyrinth of accounts, which the accounting staff must locate and correct. Otherwise, the accuracy of the financial statements will be affected. In the next section, we address how to improve the situation to arrive at a lean general ledger environment.

The Lean General Ledger Environment

There are several underlying problems that contribute to the general ledger problems described in the last section. First, most companies record information in an excessively large number of accounts. In total, these accounts require a large amount of maintenance, and make it more difficult to locate errors. Second, the account numbers used are usually lengthy and numeric in nature; an accountant can easily enter the wrong account number in a journal entry, since these account numbers do not convey any meaning. Third, subsidiaries may have their own charts of accounts, which do not necessarily match the one used by the corporate parent. And finally, there is little structure to the journal entries that are created, so that a staff person may use different accounts to record the same transaction in successive periods. We delve into the solutions to these problems through the remainder of this section.

Account Reduction

It may be possible to drastically shrink the number of expense accounts in use. We are not talking about a reduction of a few percent, but rather a reduction in the vicinity of 95% or more of all the expense accounts currently in use. In particular, consider using just the following mega-accounts:

- *Direct costs*. This account will probably contain the cost of materials and supplies used in the production process, as well as freight costs, and not a great deal more.

- *Allocated costs.* The major accounting frameworks require that overhead costs be allocated. Therefore, have a single account that contains all factory overhead costs that are to be allocated. The account would include production labor, since this cost is not a direct cost of goods or services in most companies.
- *Employee compensation.* This account contains an aggregation of hourly wages, salaries, payroll taxes, and employee benefits. If anyone needs to drill down into this information, they normally go to the source documents (i.e., payroll register and benefits supplier invoices), which would have been the case even if the employee compensation expense had been broken down into a multitude of accounts.
- *Business operations.* This account contains all of the expenses required to operate the company on a day-to-day basis, such as non-factory rent, utilities, legal fees, and office supplies.

> **Tip:** If a highly compressed chart of accounts is used, first consider its impact on the form of the financial statements that are being issued. In particular, an income statement that is structured as a contribution margin report will no longer be possible, since fixed and variable costs will have been combined in the few remaining accounts.

In addition, there may be a need for a small number of accounts in which information is aggregated for tax reporting or other specialized purposes, such as entertainment expenses.

The result of these actions would be a highly compressed chart of accounts, of which a portion appears in the following sample.

Sample Compressed Chart of Accounts

300-10	Employee compensation – Administration department
400-10	Business operations – Administration department
100-20	Direct costs – Production department
200-20	Allocated costs – Production department
300-20	Employee compensation – Production department
400-20	Business operations – Production department
300-30	Employee compensation – Sales department
400-10	Business operations – Sales department

There are two key issues revealed by the sample compressed chart of accounts. First, the extreme reduction in the number of accounts reduces the required length of the account code. We use three digits in the sample, rather than the usual four or five digits, but the length could be reduced even more. Second, the full set of recommended accounts is only needed for the production department. In the sample, we only use two accounts for the administration and sales departments.

If this recommendation appears too aggressive, consider following these steps to at least achieve a reduced number of accounts:

- *Eliminate small balances.* If an account contains an extremely small balance, it is unlikely that anyone is using it to make decisions. If so, consider shifting the underlying transactions elsewhere and closing down the account. This also means altering the default account codes in the vendor master file, so that no new transactions are directed into the closed account.

> **Tip:** It is less work to close down accounts at the beginning of the fiscal year, when few transactions will have piled up in the small-balance accounts.

> **Tip:** Include a note in the year-end closing process to eliminate small-balance accounts. Doing so ensures that the closure issue will be reviewed on a regular basis.

- *Review non-standard accounts.* If a manager has insisted that certain types of information be recorded in a unique account, discuss the issue once a year to see if the manager still needs the account. Also, managers periodically move on to other jobs, so check with the new manager whenever this happens, to see if the account can be eliminated.

When reducing the number of accounts, be aware that this makes it more difficult to compare a company's financial statements to its historical financials. For example, an account may have been merged into another one that is now located in a different line item in the financial statements than was previously the case. This is a particular problem if accounts are being closed partway through a fiscal year, so that financial statement line items no longer show consistent results *within* the year. There is no easy workaround to this issue, other than only closing down accounts at the beginning of each fiscal year.

> **Tip:** If it appears that a wholesale consolidation of accounts will make it impossible to compare year-to-year financial statements, consider engaging in a multi-year account reduction project, where only a small number of accounts are eliminated each year. Doing so limits the comparability problem.

The concept of a massive reduction in the number of accounts might illicit cries of outrage from those accountants who are accustomed to breaking down expenses into a multitude of buckets, which makes expenses easier to analyze. However, consider these points:

- *Usage of account analysis.* Once the accounting staff has provided a detailed variance analysis to management of the contents of each account, does anyone act on the information? Usually, they do not.
- *Help or hindrance.* How much time is spent by the accounting staff in reviewing accounts and reporting variances to management, and how much time is spent by management in investigating these items without taking any significant remedial action? In other words, is account analysis really a continual cycle of uncovering "issues" and then explaining them away?
- *Requirements of accounting standards.* Accounting standards do not require a full panoply of accounts. On the contrary, the standard-setting organizations have largely kept away from the business of requiring the use of certain accounts.
- *Incorrect account entries.* When there are only a small number of accounts in use, it is highly unlikely that entries will be made to the wrong accounts, since the definition of each remaining account will be entirely different from the other accounts.

Even if these points are not sufficiently persuasive to result in a wholesale reduction in the number of accounts, at least use them as discussion points whenever anyone wants to *increase* the number of accounts – hopefully, these concepts will prevent the chart of accounts from becoming more bloated than its current state.

Note: We realize that the account reduction advocated here is not possible when a business is accumulating costs for a government-paid project. The accounting for these projects is governed by stringent government-imposed rules that make it extremely difficult to achieve any type of streamlining of the general ledger.

Meaningful Account Codes

Accountants are usually taught that the chart of accounts contains an entirely numerical structure. A common format is one that uses four or five digits to describe an account, such as a revenue or expense account. In a larger business, an additional few digits describe the department or location to which the account is assigned. For example:

Account Number	Accounting Meaning
7200-100	Office supplies expense – Administration department
7200-200	Office supplies expense – Engineering department
7200-300	Office supplies expense – Sales department

When an accountant is entering a transaction into the general ledger and enters the account number, any self-respecting accounting software package will show the full name of the account somewhere on the page, so there should be no question about which account is being used. Nonetheless, accountants occasionally do not review this information, and so are at greater risk of entering transactions into incorrect accounts.

A reasonable way to reduce the incorrect usage of account numbers is to assign meaningful account codes to some portion of the chart of accounts. The most likely candidate is the department code, where a short contraction of a department name can be used instead of a meaningless number. For example:

Account Number	Accounting Meaning
7200-ADM	Office supplies expense – Administration department
7200-ENG	Office supplies expense – Engineering department
7200-SAL	Office supplies expense – Sales department

This account naming practice makes it less likely that the accounting staff will incorrectly enter transactions into the wrong account, which in turn reduces the amount of time required to research and correct errors.

> **Tip:** Note that the extreme reduction in accounts that we have already advocated in this section can also yield a shorter account number for the remaining accounts, which tends to improve employee recognition of account numbers.

Standardized Chart of Accounts

The mapping problem alluded to in the preceding section is an insidious one, for it means that any number of corporate subsidiaries may be continually altering their charts of accounts, making it extremely difficult for the corporate accounting staff to consolidate financial statements. The best solution is to create a company-wide chart of accounts and force every subsidiary to use it, without any allowed variations. By doing so, the mapping problem is eliminated, making consolidations much easier to complete.

A perfectly standardized chart of accounts is certainly the ultimate goal for the corporate accounting staff, but it does not meet with such universal approval among the accounting staffs of the subsidiary businesses. These other organizations may have substantially different businesses than that of the corporate parent, and so need other accounts. In such situations, at least require each subsidiary to formally notify the corporate parent whenever it is creating a new account, so that the parent's accounting staff can develop a proper account mapping in advance of closing the books. A less intrusive approach is to supply each subsidiary with the parent's official chart of accounts, and require the subsidiaries to map their results to that chart of accounts before forwarding their information at month-end. However, this latter approach relies on the ability of each subsidiary to consistently map its accounts to the corporate chart of accounts over time, which may not be the case.

The most comprehensive way to ensure that a standardized chart of accounts is used is to operate a centralized accounting system, which all subsidiaries must use for their day-to-day transactions. This approach gives the corporate accounting staff complete control over the accounts being used, and how they map to the corporate-level accounts. Of course, centralization also requires a lengthy implementation, which can be difficult when a company is a serial acquirer. Doing so also mandates that subsidiaries give up their local accounting systems.

> **Note:** It is much easier to standardize the chart of accounts when only a few mega-accounts are used to record expenses, as advocated earlier in this section. With mega-accounts, even a subsidiary that operates an entirely different business from the parent company will probably be able to shoehorn its expenses into the existing account structure.

Journal Entry Restriction

Block all users from being able to create journal entries, except for a very small number of the most senior accounting staff – perhaps just a single general ledger accountant. This approach funnels all journal entries through so few people that it becomes much easier to monitor the entries being made, and spot any duplicate entries. Also, assigning journal entries to a senior person reduces the risk that an entry will be made improperly. Further, if an entry *is* made incorrectly, there is no question about who made the entry, so that remedial action can be taken.

Where there are subsidiaries, the same principle applies – funneling journal entries through just a few designated individuals at each location. The concept can be taken a step further, where the people allowed to create journal entries at the corporate level are *not* allowed to do so at the subsidiary level; this approach preserves the integrity of the information created at the subsidiary level.

Journal Entry Checklist

There should be a standard checklist of journal entries that the controller expects his or her department to generate in each accounting period. The person responsible for entering journal entries should check off each entry on this list as it is completed and entered into the accounting system. This approach introduces considerable consistency to the closing process.

> **Tip:** Include a space on the checklist where each journal entry number can be entered, and then retain the checklist in the monthly journal entry binder. This preserves a record of all entries made.

The checklist concept can be taken a step further by using it to exclude certain journal entries. For example, the controller may want to personally approve all journal entries made that are *not* on the checklist, with the general ledger accountant being automatically approved to enter all items *on* the list. Doing so introduces an additional level of review for all unusual proposed journal entries, and may lead to their elimination or revision.

Journal Entry Templates

All accounting software packages allow for the creation of a standard template for a journal entry, so that it can be used repetitively. A template locks in a journal entry, so that the same accounts are consistently used every time, thereby reducing the risk of errors. Ideally, all standard journal entries should be created with a template. It may make sense to create templates even for those journal entries that are only used at somewhat longer intervals, again to preserve their consistency from period to period.

> **Tip:** Note on the journal entry checklist the identification number of the template associated with each journal entry, so that the general ledger accountant can easily locate it.

> **Tip:** If the intent is to gradually reduce the number of general ledger accounts, keep in mind that this may require the alteration of any journal entry templates in which eliminated accounts are used.

Recurring Journal Entries

There may be a few instances where the same journal entry is made in every accounting period and in the same amount. In these cases, consider setting up recurring journal entries that the computer system automatically repeats until a pre-set termination date is reached. Recurring entries reduce the work of the general ledger accountant, but only by a small amount. In general, recurring entries represent a very small proportion of the total number of journal entries created.

Account Content Review

In general, there should be an ongoing review process where the contents of accounts are reviewed to ensure that all line items should be included. Given the large number of accounts that most companies maintain, it is impractical to live up to this general standard in every reporting period. Instead, consider using the following rules to review accounts:

- *Examine major balance sheet accounts every month.* These are the largest accounts *only*, where an error will have a material impact on the financial statements. Maintain a spreadsheet for each of these accounts, itemizing the exact contents of each one. These spreadsheets should be updated every month.
- *Examine minor balance sheet accounts quarterly.* These are the accounts whose balances are so small that even a massive error will not have a material impact on the financial statements. Maintain a spreadsheet for each of these accounts, itemizing the contents of each one. Updates should be at quarterly or longer intervals. At a minimum, be sure to examine these accounts prior to the annual audit.

- *Examine revenue and expense accounts on trend line.* It is usually sufficient to construct a trend line for the revenue and expense accounts (such as 12-month side-by-side income statements), and only investigate the contents of an account if a monthly result is unusually high or low.

> **Tip:** The major balance sheet accounts should be examined immediately prior to closing the books, since an error here could have a noticeable impact on the financial statements. However, minor account reviews can take place at any time, with adjustments taking place either before or after closing the books; any adjustments should be so small that the impact on the financials will be immaterial.

Practices to Avoid

The underlying theme of this chapter has been to keep the general ledger environment as simple and streamlined as possible. Consequently, the following practices are to be avoided, since they yield opposite results:

- *Keep activity-based costing on a project basis.* Activity-based costing (ABC) involves the allocation of costs in a manner that a company's system of accounting is not usually constructed to handle. There may be pressure from the advocates of ABC to create a number of accounts in the general ledger, in which ABC information is to be stored. This is not advisable, since it increases the size of the general ledger. Instead, it is usually sufficient to keep ABC on a project basis, where costs are compiled within and allocated from a temporary system that is only concerned with a small subset of a company's operations.
- *Avoid short-use accounts.* The accounting department occasionally receives requests to create accounts that will accumulate information for a certain amount of time, and then stop. These requests usually relate to the accounting for specific projects. Wherever possible, track the requested information outside of the general ledger. Otherwise, the chart of accounts tends to build up a debris field of unused accounts.

Analysis of the Lean General Ledger Environment

If a business can overcome any doubts about shutting down most of its expense accounts, it can greatly simplify the account structure to which it records transactions. When coupled with rigid adherence to a single chart of accounts and the preceding list of journal entry improvements, it is quite possible to nearly eliminate errors in the general ledger. The result is a more lean operating environment, since the accounting staff wastes far less time researching and correcting errors.

General Ledger Measurements

The following general ledger measurements are used to monitor the streamlining of the general ledger environment:

- *Number of accounts per entity.* Track the grand total number of accounts used by each entity owned by the business on an annual trend line. At a minimum, the number should not be increasing. Ideally, there should be a gradual decline in the number of accounts over time.
- *Journal entries not involving a template.* The use of journal entry templates is strongly encouraged, since they reduce the risk of error. Thus, all journal entries *not* involving templates should be reviewed to see if they arise with sufficient regularity to warrant the creation of a template.

The more useful of these measurements on a monthly basis is the tracking of journal entries not involving a template, since the general ledger accountant can use it to gradually build up an impressive array of standard journal entry templates.

Summary

We have advocated the pursuit of two goals within the general ledger environment:

- To reduce the number of general ledger accounts to the absolute minimum, both in the parent company and its subsidiaries.
- To ensure that transactions are recorded within the general ledger correctly on the first try.

The first goal is a hard one, for it requires that a controller overcome the common perception that a broad set of accounts is good. The goal is also difficult because of the labor involved, for it impacts the comparability of financial information between different periods, and may require that the financial statements themselves be reformatted. The latter goal requires the establishment of a chokepoint – the general ledger accountant – where all journal entries are examined before being allowed to pass through to the general ledger. This step, combined with several other improvements, can greatly increase the proportion of transactions entered correctly on the first attempt.

Chapter 13
Lean Budgeting

Introduction

From the perspective of the accountant, budgeting is an annual process of developing a model of projected company results, followed by a year of variance analysis to show how actual results varied from expectations. From the perspective of the rest of the company, budgeting is quite a bit different – it imposes a strict financial and planning regimen on management that allows for little variation from the plan. There are also a number of adverse ethical effects that are driven by linking bonus plans to the budget, where managers game the system and sometimes bend the rules to achieve their planned goals. Consequently, this chapter focuses on how to create a lean budgeting environment *throughout* a business, as well as within the accounting department.

In this chapter, we begin with an overview of improvement concepts, then describe the problems with a typical budgeting environment, and then show two variations on budgeting improvements.

Related Podcast Episodes: Episodes 45, 71, 76, and 130-131 of the Accounting Best Practices Podcast discuss many aspects of budgeting. These episodes are available at: **accountingtools.com/podcasts** or **iTunes**

Improvement Concepts

The application of lean concepts in this chapter involves the following improvements to existing systems:

- *Error checking.* Using several methods to locate and correct errors in the budget model.
- *Summarization comparison.* Summarizing the budget in different ways to locate totaling errors.
- *Verification rules.* Reviewing the budget model for specific issues that might make it untenable.
- *Capacity verification.* Seeing if the budget contains sufficient planned expenditures to allow the business to achieve budgeted revenue levels.
- *Step cost verification.* Ensuring that the budget includes the amounts and times at which step cost changes can be expected.
- *Cash flow verification.* Calculating the amount of cash flow generated by the budget model, and verifying that the company has the financial resources to offset any planned cash shortfalls.

- *Budget simplification.* Reducing the number of line items and compensation details in the budget in order to simplify the overall model.
- *Budget procedure.* Using a budget procedure to increase the efficiency of model development and ensure that it is completed by the expected date.
- *Budget pre-loading.* Completing many or all of the budget line items before issuing the preliminary budget to department managers; this tends to increase the speed of model development.
- *Operating without a budget.* Using a rolling forecast, independent goal setting, and group compensation plans instead of a budget, thereby eliminating the flaws inherent in the budgeting system.

The Budgeting Environment

The budget is a standard part of the operational structure of a vast number of companies. Their chief executive officers will point out at great length that the budget is an essential tool needed to maintain control over their businesses. Nonetheless, we will spend this entire section pointing out a number of major problems with budgets. After reading these points, the reader may conclude that the budget is the *least* lean part of a business.

Control Basis

The single most fundamental problem underlying the entire concept of a budget is that it is designed to control a company from the center. The basic underpinning of the system is that senior management forces managers throughout the company to agree to a specific outcome (that portion of the budget for which they are responsible), which senior management then monitors to control the activities of the managers. This agreement is usually a formal agreement under which each manager commits to achieve a fixed target in exchange for receiving a bonus. Typical targets are for certain revenue, profit, or cash flow goals.

These targets may be combined to further control the actions of managers. For example, there may be a combination geographic revenue target and profit target, so that a manager is forced to commit resources to sales in a new sales region while still maintaining overall profitability. When there are many targets to achieve, managers find that their actions are entirely constrained by the budget – there is no time or spare funding for any other activities. Thus, the combination of the budget and a bonus system create an extremely tight command and control system.

Formal performance agreements are the source of an enormous amount of inefficiency within a company, and can also reduce employee loyalty. They require a great deal of time to initially negotiate, and may be altered over time as changing conditions give managers various excuses to complain about their agreements. Further, if the recipient of a bonus agreement misses out on a substantial bonus, how does he feel about the company? He may complain bitterly that the bonus system was rigged against him, and leave to work for a competitor.

In short, when budgeting is used within a command and control management system it imposes a rigid straightjacket on the actions of any managers who want to earn their designated bonuses. This level of rigidity makes it particularly difficult for a company to react quickly to changes in its competitive environment, since managers are constrained by their performance plans from proceeding in new directions.

Behavioral Impacts

The command and control nature of the budget results in an immediate behavioral change in the management team before the budget has even been completed, because managers understand that they can influence their bonus plans in advance by negotiating the amount of improvement that they will be required to achieve. This calls for fierce protection of their existing funding, as well as committing to the lowest possible improvement levels in their areas of responsibility. They will have an excellent chance to earn maximum bonuses, because their performance commitments under the budget are so small. In short, the concept of the budget forces managers to fight for *minimal* improvements.

The marketplace changes over time, so that a manager struggling to meet his budgeted targets must also somehow meet competitive pressures by altering products and services, changing price points, opening and closing locations, cutting costs, and so forth. This means that a manager is faced with the choice of either earning a bonus by meeting his budget, or of improving the company's competitive position. A manager's willingness to work in the best interests of a company's competitive position is further hampered by the sheer bureaucratic oppressiveness of the budgeting system, where a manager has to obtain multiple approvals to achieve a reorientation of funding. It is simply easier to not deviate from the budget. Therefore, the budget priority wins out and a company finds that its competitive position has declined specifically because of a tight focus on achieving its budget.

The pressure to meet a budgeted target can cause managers to engage in unethical accounting and business practices in order to control their reported results. Examples of such practices are:

- Recording revenue that was shipped after the month-end deadline
- Using a discount offer to stuff sales into a sales channel during a bonus period
- Overbilling customers
- Not entering supplier invoices in the accounting system during a bonus period
- Taking unwarranted discounts from supplier invoices
- Firing employees and using contractors to meet headcount targets

Unethical behavior is a poison that can spread through an organization rapidly; unsullied managers may leave, while the remainder engage in increasingly egregious behavior to meet their performance commitments.

Bureaucratic Support

Once the budget and bonus plan system takes root within a company, a bureaucracy develops around it that has a natural tendency to support the status quo. Here are several such areas:

- *Human resources.* Bonus agreements may include specific budget-based goals, due dates, and resources to be allocated; this can be one of the largest tasks of the human resources department.
- *Accounting.* The accounting staff routinely loads the budget into its accounting software, so that all income statements it issues contain a comparison of budgeted to actual results. Thus, the accounting staff incorporates the budget into its system of reports.
- *Analysts.* The budget may be used as a baseline for cost controls, where financial analysts investigate why costs are higher or lower than the budgeted amounts. These analysts report to the controller or CFO, who will therefore want to retain the budget in order to keep tight control over costs.
- *Investment community.* If a company is publicly held, the investor relations officer may routinely issue press releases, stating how the company performed in comparison to its budget. The investment community may rely on this information to estimate a share price for the company's stock, and will want the same information to be reported to it in the future.

Consequently, there are many constituencies, both inside and outside of a company, that have a vested interest in retaining the budget and bonus plan system.

Information Sharing

A related issue in a command and control environment is that senior management has a propensity to only release financial information pertinent to the operations of each manager. This means that there is a great deal of information available at the top of the organization, but very little at the bottom. In addition, managers have a tendency to massage information as they pass it down to their subordinates. The result is a paltry amount of actionable information in the hands of front line employees.

We can only presume that managers engage in this information filtering because they assume that employees below them in the corporate hierarchy are not capable of making their own decisions. Instead, the system is designed to hoard information with those people authorized to make decisions. Therefore, by default, those people receiving a *minimum* amount of information are *not* authorized to make decisions.

This type of restricted information sharing has a profound impact on the budget, because most employees never know what their budgets are, or how they are performing in relation to the budget. Since there is no knowledge of the budget, there can be no acceptance of it by employees, and therefore little chance that it will be achieved.

Inaccuracy

A budget is based on a set of assumptions that are generally not too far distant from the operating conditions under which it was formulated. If the business environment changes to any significant degree, the company's revenues or cost structure may change so radically that actual results will rapidly depart from the expectations delineated in the budget. This condition is a particular problem when there is a sudden economic downturn, since the budget authorizes a certain level of spending that is no longer supportable under a suddenly reduced revenue level. Unless management acts quickly to override the budget, managers will continue to spend under their original budgetary authorizations, thereby rupturing any possibility of earning a profit. Other conditions that can also cause results to vary suddenly from budgeted expectations include changes in interest rates, currency exchange rates, and commodity prices.

Analysis of the Budgeting Environment

Our usual approach to analyzing a system or process is to focus on its inherent bottlenecks, controls, error rates, and the like. However, a proper analysis of budgeting calls for a broader view of the situation. Budgeting imposes a rigid outlook on how a management team operates a business, and allows little operational leeway. It also engenders infighting to see who can corral the largest amount of budgeted funds, irrespective of who *needs* the funds. Finally, it nearly mandates a short-term mindset, where everyone is completely focused on making their numbers. In short, to consider a traditional budget model to be any part of a lean organization is ludicrous.

At the level of just the accounting department, the budget requires a great deal of staff time to construct. After its completion, the accounting staff spends the rest of the year comparing it to actual results, delving into the reasons for variances, and issuing reports to management concerning these findings. Thus, the controller must allocate a significant part of the department's resources to creating and maintaining something that is counterproductive to the company as a whole.

The discussion of budgeting in this chapter has cast serious doubts on the need for a detailed and rigorously-enforced budgeting system, especially one that integrates the budget model with bonus plans. Nonetheless, the decision to install a budget is up to the reader. In the following two sections, we present two ways to deal with the budget – either use a number of techniques to make an existing budget easier to construct and use, or eliminate it entirely and use alternative systems that have a less pernicious impact on a business.

A More Lean Approach to Budgeting

Depending upon the level of detail, a budget is one of the most complex documents that a business will create, while the budgeting process needed to create it is equally difficult to manage. Consider using some or all of the error reduction, data verification, and both model and process simplification suggestions in this section to increase the level of efficiency in the budgeting process.

Error Checking

One of the fundamental sources of flaws in a budget is that nearly everyone creates it using an electronic spreadsheet. The electronic spreadsheet is a magnificent tool, but it is all too easy to inadvertently introduce an error with an incorrect formula or cell reference. If a spreadsheet has been created, have someone else review it in detail. This person should verify that the ranges for each subtotal and total are correct, that the totals across the bottom of each spreadsheet (for individual months or quarters) correctly sum to the total down the right side (the line item totals), that any information being automatically pulled from a different spreadsheet page is linked to the correct cell, and that formulas are correct.

This error review work should absolutely *not* be done by the person who created or currently maintains the spreadsheet, since they are so familiar with it that they are unlikely to spot what might be considered a glaring error. Instead, use someone who is familiar with spreadsheets, but who does not interact with the budget on a regular basis. This task could even be handed off to an auditor, who likely has the necessary skills and no vested interest in covering up an error.

Summarization Comparison

It is useful to summarize the budget model in two ways, to see if the totals of the two methods are the same. If there is a difference in the two summarizations, there is probably a summarization error within the model. One summarization should be by department, and the other by expense line item, as follows:

- *Department totals*. This takes the grand total expense for each budget period from the individual department budgets and aggregates them on a single page. Thus, the summarization could include totals for such departments as administration, engineering, and production.
- *Expense totals*. This takes the line item expense for each period from the individual department budgets and aggregates them on a single page. Thus, the summarization could include totals for such expenses as office supplies, payroll taxes, and salaries.

The problem being located is a summarization error at the department level. Since the summarization by expense line item does not use these department-level summarizations, any disparity between the two methods should be caused by a departmental summarization error. The following example illustrates the problem.

EXAMPLE

The controller of Quest Adventure Gear wants to know if there is a summarization error somewhere in the company's budget. To find it, he summarizes the budget results of all five company departments in a separate section of the budget, along with a separate

201

summarization of all expenses by individual expense line item. The result appears in the following two tables:

Summarization by Department

	Quarter 1	Quarter 2	Quarter 3	Quarter 4
Accounting department	$83,000	$86,500	$79,250	$84,500
Engineering department	320,000	324,000	317,500	321,750
Production department	840,000	901,000	894,000	903,000
Purchasing department	95,000	103,000	98,000	105,750
Sales department	210,000	215,000	203,000	217,000
Total expenses	$1,548,000	$1,629,500	$1,581,750	$1,632,000

Summarization by Expense

	Quarter 1	Quarter 2	Quarter 3	Quarter 4
Depreciation	95,000	98,000	102,000	105,000
Office expenses	42,000	40,500	43,000	46,000
Payroll taxes	97,500	104,000	99,750	103,500
Salaries	1,133,500	1,192,000	1,147,000	1,190,500
Travel and entertainment	180,000	195,000	200,000	187,000
Total expenses	$1,548,000	$1,629,500	$1,591,750	$1,632,000

There is a disparity of $10,000 between the totals of the two tables. The problem appears to originate in the third quarter, where the summarization by department is lower by $10,000. Upon further investigation, the controller finds that the expense budget for the engineering department contains an error in the summarization total in the third quarter, as shown in the following table.

Engineering Department Budget Containing Error

	Quarter 1	Quarter 2	Quarter 3	Quarter 4
Depreciation	15,000	15,000	16,000	16,000
Office expenses	7,000	7,500	8,000	8,500
Payroll taxes	24,000	24,500	21,000	20,250
Salaries	274,000	277,000	272,500	277,000
Travel and entertainment	0	0	10,000	0
Total expenses	$320,000	$324,000	$317,500	$321,750

The total expenses line for the engineering department contains a summarization formula that does not include the final row of expenses, which is the travel and entertainment line. Since only the third quarter contained a budgeted expenditure for this line, the error was not apparent in the other quarters.

Upon correction of the summarization total, the controller finds that the summarizations by department and expense match. It is unlikely that any other summarization errors exist in the budget model.

Verification Rules

How can an entire budget be reviewed? For a larger corporation, there may be masses of line items on dozens or even hundreds of pages, so how is it possible to ascertain which items are either not correct or at least in need of serious additional review? Here are several ways to address the issue:

- *80/20 rule.* Only do an in-depth review of the 20 percent of all line items that comprise 80 percent of the revenues and expenditures in a budget. Any other items are so insignificant that even an egregious error is unlikely to cause much of an impact on the total amount of a budget.
- *Fixed cost continuance.* A fixed cost may not continue at the same historical expenditure level through the entire budget period. Such costs are sometimes subject to cost escalation clauses (especially multi-year rent agreements), so consider creating a separate list of all contractually-mandated cost changes, and compare it to the budget.
- *Contract expirations.* Does a long-term agreement expire during the budget period? If so, it is entirely possible that the cost will change significantly, so obtain the best possible estimate of the new cost from the purchasing manager or legal counsel.
- *Compare spending to events.* There may be a number of events during the budget period for which major expenditures are required, such as a trade show or a company Christmas party. If so, verify that expenditures in the budget are aligned with these events, and that sufficient funds have been allocated for them.

Capacity Verification

Perhaps the most common conceptual problem in a budget model is that management alters planned revenue levels and does not also alter the capacity of the business to generate the revenue. This usually means that not enough money has been set aside for the necessary capital improvements, or for the hiring and training of additional personnel. The classic situation is when the budget includes a sharp increase in revenue, but assumes that these sales will somehow be generated by the existing sales staff, which is supposed to become more productive during the new budget year.

A very important improvement to the budget model is to define key capacity points in the business, and automatically report on them within the budget model. For example, it may have been historically established that the average salesperson can generate $500,000 of sales per year. If so, note this fact in a separate capacity table within the budget, and use the information to sprinkle capacity line items throughout the budget model. The following sample illustrates the concept.

Sample use of Capacity Verification

	Quarter 1	Quarter 2	Quarter 3	Quarter 4
Budget revenue	$10,000,000	$12,000,000	$14,000,000	$16,000,000
Standard sales staff needed	20	24	28	32
Budgeted sales staff	20	21	22	23
Variance	0	3	5	9

The sample budget shows that management is scheduling a large ramp-up in sales, but has not budgeted for a similar increase in the sales staff in order to effect the change. The variance information in the sample would then be used to budget for an increase in the sales department's headcount.

The concept of capacity verification can be used in a number of areas besides the sales staff. Here are other areas in which capacity should be considered:

- Capacity of the production bottleneck operation
- Number of computers that can be maintained by each computer support person
- Number of engineers needed per new product to be developed
- Number of picks per warehouse person
- Number of production employees per assembly line
- Number of shipments per shipping person

Tip: A similar issue to review is the ramp-up time needed to bring new capacity on line. For example, a salesperson may not be fully productive on the job for at least a year. Similarly, it may take three months to set up and test new production equipment. Ramp-up time usually requires manual review of the budget – it is difficult to build this analysis into the model.

A particular concern for anyone building the budget model is to look for the central bottleneck that is limiting the ability of a business to generate more revenue. This is traditionally located in the production area, but can be elsewhere. Other possibilities are a limitation on raw materials, or a cap on quantities sold under a royalty agreement, or the number of specialized sales staff on hand. Knowing the severity of this bottleneck and how to work around it is central to the development of a budget whose results can actually be achieved.

Step Cost Verification

As a follow on to the last subject, there will be points at which changes in activity levels will require that an entirely new level of costs be incurred. For example, headcount or inventory storage requirements may reach a point where rent on new facilities must be paid.

There is usually a certain amount of "wiggle room" around the concept of step costs, so that a company can continue at its current expenditure level even when the incurrence of a step cost is clearly warranted. Nonetheless, the accounting staff should investigate whether the activity levels in a proposed budget will impact step costs, and provide feedback regarding the probable changes in those step costs that will be required, as well as the approximate timing of when the new expenses must be incurred.

Cash Flow Verification

A company may create a budget that appears to deal correctly with capacity levels and step costs, and be free of errors, and yet have one key failing that renders it inoperable – cash flow. It is necessary to estimate the timing of cash inflows and outflows associated with all budgeted activities, as well as the amount and timing of any changes in debt levels or the issuance or repurchase of stock. If the budget reveals a cash shortfall that the business simply cannot overcome through its funding sources, then the budget must be revised downward to the point where cash is not a limiting factor.

> **Tip:** When estimating the timing of cash flows associated with the collection of accounts receivable, it is unwise to assume a faster collection rate than the historical collection rate. If anything, add an extra day or two to the historical number of days outstanding to arrive at the most likely level and timing of cash inflows.

Budget Simplification

The budget model is a complex document that requires a substantial amount of effort to maintain. The maintenance issue can be mitigated by periodically simplifying the model, using block budgeting, eliminating accounts, and aggregating compensation information. We will discuss these issues below.

A key problem with a spreadsheet-based budget model is that it tends to become more complex over time as more departments, assumptions, revenue and expense types, and so forth are added to it. This increased level of complexity makes it easier for errors to find their way into the model. To avoid this problem, include a step at the beginning of the annual budgeting procedure to examine the structure of the budget model from the preceding year and simplify it where possible.

In some companies, there is a budgeted amount for every line item in the chart of accounts (or at least those accounts appearing in the income statement). The accounting staff likes this level of budgeting, since it can insert a budgeted amount in the financial statements next to each line item and show variances between actual and budgeted expenditure levels. If senior management insists that department managers only spend the funds specifically authorized for each line item, this is called *line item budgeting*.

Line item budgeting is a very restrictive format and is not recommended, for it forces managers to monitor expenditures at an oppressively detailed level, as well as document any requests to shift budgeted funds between accounts.

A much better approach is the *block budget*, where funds are allocated to an entire department or other functional area, and managers are given authority to expend the funds as they see fit. This approach is much less restrictive and easier to manage. Also, it accommodates the natural variability in expenses that will arise from year to year, where some line item expenses will inevitably vary from expectations due to factors outside of the control of management.

The main reason why there are so many expense line items in a budget is because the budget is designed to mimic the structure of the chart of accounts. Therefore, if there is a desire to simplify the budget, a good way to do so is to reduce the number of accounts in the chart of accounts (see the Lean General Ledger Environment chapter). It will be necessary to verify which accounts are no longer needed, move the balances (and perhaps the underlying detail) out of those accounts and into other accounts, and then modify company reports to reflect the change. This is a slow and tedious process, so consider eliminating just a few accounts per year, thereby gradually simplifying both the chart of accounts and the budget model over time.

An alternative to eliminating accounts is to simply remove them from the budget model. This means that there will be no budget associated with some financial statement line items. This may be acceptable for minor or rarely used types of expenses.

Another area in which budgets tend to be overly complex is in the calculation of compensation for every employee on the payroll. If the company has a large number of employees, this can result in a massive amount of data entry to ensure that the correct pay rates and annual pay review dates are included in the budget. In such cases, consider aggregating compensation by title, job function, work group, or department. By doing so, the amount of information in the budget can be reduced by several orders of magnitude. However, this requires the use of averages for the amount of budgeted compensation, as well as estimates for the timing of changes in compensation (though a policy can be instituted for altering pay levels so that it always occurs on the same date of every year). The use of estimates always results in less accuracy, but this may be a worthwhile tradeoff if a large part of the budget model can be eliminated.

In short, a certain amount of budget model simplification can be achieved by requiring a periodic simplification review of the budget model, switching to block budgeting, reducing the number of accounts, and aggregating the calculation of employee compensation.

Budget Procedure

One of the problems with the annual budget is that the accounting staff only uses it during a specific time period, once a year. Because of the long intervals between usage, employees may forget how to use the system, and so will have to re-learn it the following year. To reduce this level of inefficiency, consider having the accounting staff create a short procedure that touches upon the key points of operating the model, which they can use to refresh their memories when they begin using the model again at the start of the next budgeting cycle.

Consider creating an extensive budgeting procedure and calendar for the entire annual budgeting process, to be distributed to all participants in the process. This procedure specifies the due dates for all budget-related deliverables, who is responsible for each deliverable, and what the deliverable should look like. There should also be a qualified manager who can drive the budgeting process through to its completion as of a targeted date. Further, continually review and update the procedure every year to adjust it to match changes in the business and the requirements of the budget model. Only after multiple iterations and refinements of the procedure over several years can a business attain a process that generates a high-quality budget with the least amount of company-wide effort.

Budget Pre-loading

It takes time for a department manager to fill out a blank budget form that outlines his estimates of expected costs during an upcoming budget period. Completing the form takes managers away from their usual operational responsibilities, so it may be quite some time before they can attend to it. This delay can be reduced by issuing a pre-loaded budget form to the department managers. This form contains the accounting staff's best estimate of what a department will expend, based on its historical results and as adjusted for expected changes in activity levels and the inflation rate. This approach works well in most situations, since the bulk of expense line items are essentially fixed or at least do not vary much over time.

When a department manager receives a pre-loaded budget, all that he has to do is make a few adjustments and return the completed document. The adjustment will likely involve step costs, such as the hiring of new staff or the acquisition of new equipment, which the accounting staff might not have been aware of. The only problem with the pre-loaded budget concept is that department managers might try to avoid responsibility for their budgets on the grounds that they were following the dictates of the accounting department.

Analysis of the More Lean Approach to Budgeting

If it is necessary to have a budget, the suggestions noted in this section will improve the accuracy of the budget model, as well as introduce some modest levels of efficiency to the budgeting process. In particular, we recommend extensive error checking and verification work while a budget is being constructed, thereby keeping the model from generating misleading results that will interfere with corporate planning. The extra time required for error checking is far less expensive than having to reformulate and reissue a budget in which flaws have been found.

The Ultimate Lean Budget

If the reporting system, decision making, and organizational structure of a business can be modified, it is entirely possible to not only operate without a budget, but to thrive while doing so. Thus, the ultimate lean budget is to have no budget at all. This section discusses the changes needed to operate without a budget.

Operating without a Budget

In order to have a properly functioning organization that operates without a budget, it is necessary to make alterations in four areas. They are:

- *Forecast.* The forecast is a rolling forecast that is updated at frequent intervals, and especially when there is a significant event that changes the competitive environment of the business. The forecast is simply the expected outcome of the business in the near term, and is intended to be an early warning indicator of both threats and opportunities. It is completely detached from any compensation plans.
- *Capital budgeting.* Requests for funds to buy fixed assets are accepted at all times of the year. Funding allocations are based on expected results and the needs of the requesting business unit. There is no formal once-a-year capital budgeting review.
- *Goal setting.* Employees jointly set targets that are relative to the performance of other business units within the company, and against other benchmark organizations. If there is a bonus plan, it is based on these relative results.
- *Compensation.* Bonuses and other compensation are based on the ability of the company as a whole to improve its performance relative to its competition or some other relevant performance baseline.

A key point is that the forecast and capital budget are not related to targets. By separating these processes from any corporate targets, there is no incentive for employees to fudge their forecasts or fixed asset funding applications in order to earn bonuses.

From the management perspective, it is critical that senior managers step away from the traditional budget based command-and-control system and replace it with a great deal of local autonomy. This means that local managers can make their own decisions as long as they stay within general guidelines imposed by senior management. The focus of the organization changes from short-term budgets to medium-term to long-term financial results. There is no emphasis on budget variances, since there is no budget.

Also, senior management must trust its employees to spend money wisely. The expectation is that an employee is more likely to question the need for any expenditure, instead of automatically spending all funds granted under a budget allocation.

From a more general perspective, if a company abandons budgeting, how does it maintain any sort of direction? The answer depends upon the structure of the business and the environment within which it operates. Here are several examples of how to maintain a sense of direction:

- *Margin focus.* If a business has a relatively consistent market share, but its product mix fluctuates over time, it may be easier to focus the attention of managers on the margins generated by the business, rather than on how they achieve those margins. This eliminates the structural rigidity of a budget, instead allowing managers to obtain revenues and incur expenses as they see fit, as long as they earn the net profit margin mandated by senior management.

- *Key value drivers.* If senior management believes that the company will succeed if it closely adheres to specific value drivers, it should have the company focus its attention on those specific items, and not hold managers to overly-precise revenue or profit goals. For example, the key to success in an industry may be an overwhelming amount of customer support; if so, focus the entire company on maximizing that one competitive advantage.
- *Few products and very competitive environment.* If a business relies upon only a small number of products and is under constant competitive pressure, then decisions to change direction must be made quickly, and the organization must be capable of reorienting its direction in short order. This calls for a centralized management environment where a small team uses the latest information to reach decisions and rapidly drive change through the organization. In this case, a budget is not only unnecessary, but would interfere with making rapid changes. Thus, keeping employees focused on the operational direction given by senior management is vastly more important than meeting revenue or expense targets; taken to an extreme, employees may never even see the financial results of their areas of responsibility, because the focus is on operations, not financial results.

Forecasting without a Budget

A good replacement for a budget is the rolling forecast. This is a simple forecast that contains information only at an aggregate level, such as:

- Revenues by product line
- Expenses aggregated into a few line items
- Customer order backlog
- Cash flow

The intent is to create a system that is easily updated, and which gives the organization a reasonable view of what the future looks like for at least the next few months. A key reason for having a rolling forecast is to bring up issues as soon as possible, so that a company can initiate corrective actions to deal with them. Thus, the goal of a rolling forecast is not to attain a specific target, but rather to provide early notice of problems and opportunities.

Employees should update their parts of the rolling forecast about once a month, and should only spend a short time doing so – a fine level of detail is not expected. Since the forecast is updated regularly, it does not have a great deal of impact on the organization if the forecast proves to be incorrect – after all, a new version will replace it shortly, so there is very little time during which a bad forecast can impact the business.

While it is customary to update a forecast at fixed periodic intervals, an alternative approach is to update it whenever there is a significant event that impacts the business. There may be events that trigger a forecast update only for a local business unit, and not for the entire company, while other events may be so significant that they warrant a complete review of the forecast. Such events should be rare, but should trigger an immediate response from the company, so that employees know what to expect.

Given the extremely short time line and minimal time allocated to updating a forecast, it rarely makes sense to derive multiple forecasts that also address best case and worst case scenarios. Instead, since the time period covered is so short, there should be minimal divergence from the best case scenario, to avoid creating extra forecasts.

The time period covered by the rolling forecast depends upon the ability of a company to project its activities into the future. If there are many long-term contracts, it may be entirely reasonable to compile a rolling forecast that extends more than a year into the future. However, if the company has a bad history of projecting results, do not waste time doing so excessively far into the future. Instead, only forecast for the period when there is a reasonable expectation of achieving a prediction. If this means that the forecast period is only a few months, then that is sufficient – generating a longer-term forecast is a waste of time.

Another way of formulating the correct period for a rolling forecast is to estimate the amount of warning that employees need to trigger ongoing business activities, such as altering product prices, and launching new products and related promotions.

The rolling forecast is accompanied by a rough work plan that is adjusted as frequently as the forecast. No one has to submit the work plan to a higher authority for approval. Instead, employees formulate their direction, document it in the work plan, and adjust it to compensate for both current and expected future events.

Capital Budgeting without a Budget

The process of reviewing and approving capital expenditures can be lengthy and complex. How does this mesh with an environment in which there is no formal budget? Even if there is no budget, there should still be a rolling forecast. Given the presence of a rolling forecast, three prospects for dealing with capital expenditures suggest themselves:

- *Fast track approvals*. Many capital budgeting proposals are positioned at the lower end of the range of possible dollar amounts, and so require both fewer funds and less analysis. For these items, senior management should maintain a pool of funds at all times, and fast track the review process for any capital budget proposals submitted. This process is designed to support the bulk of all capital expenditures needed by front-line teams.
- *Near-term projections*. The treasury staff should maintain a short-term forecast of available cash flow, so that managers can see if cash will be

available for capital budget requests. If the forecast indicates a cash flow problem, then projects can be delayed until more funds are available.

- *Long-term projections*. Senior management should maintain a rolling five-year forecast. This can be quite a brief document, showing general estimates of where the market will be, and the company's position within it. Based on this forecast, the company can determine its long-term capital expenditure plans for high-cost items.

Those capital expenditures designated as fast track approvals require no attention from senior management, since the funds involved are not large. However, the largest expenditures should be labeled as strategic commitments, and therefore fall within the responsibility of senior management.

A good way to limit profit centers from demanding an excessive amount of funds for capital projects is to designate them as investment centers and charge them the corporate cost of capital for all invested funds. This arrangement should keep them from requesting funds for projects whose returns are below the cost of capital. If the availability of funds to the company as a whole becomes restricted, consider increasing the cost of capital, which should reduce the flow of capital budgeting requests.

Goal Setting without a Budget

The senior management team typically integrates its corporate goals into the budget – so what happens to the goals when the budget is terminated? If there are no goals, how do employees know what to do?

The answer is to use continual improvement goals that will place the company in the top quartile of those companies or internal profit centers against which it measures itself. For example, a retail chain can measure the profitability of its stores, and have the lowest-performing stores attempt to match the performance already reported by the top 25 percent of stores. Further, the same company can benchmark the performance of other "best in class" companies and have its top-ranking stores attempt to attain benchmarked performance levels.

For large companies having many similar profit centers, tracking performance against peers within the company can be the best basis for such goal setting, for several reasons:

- *Internal support*. Everyone works for the same company, so employees of the top-performing profit centers should be willing to assist other profit centers to improve their performance.
- *Similar environment*. The various profit centers presumably work within the same industry, and deal with similar customers and suppliers, so their results should not only be quite comparable with each other, but their business practices should be readily transferable to other profit centers.
- *Been done*. Employees may baulk at the idea of being measured against the performance of another company that may not even operate in the same industry; but this objection does not apply if the benchmark originates with-

in the company – the benchmark has already "been done," and within the same industry.

The tracking of internal peer performance can result in an extensive reporting system where employees can readily access the results of profit centers by geographical region, or store size, or product line, or customer. The result can be an exceptional internal database that reveals who conducts business the best, and how to contact them for advice.

The trick to goal setting in this environment is to not make such goals appear to be fixed targets that are agreed upon in advance, but rather goals to aspire to achieve, with compensation being paid on the extent to which they *are* achieved.

Compensation without a Budget

If a company's budget is eliminated and along with it the traditional bonus contract, then how are employees to be compensated? Here are the key issues to consider when designing a new method of compensation:

- *Unit of measure.* The unit of measure for a traditional bonus plan is probably profitability, but that does not have to apply to a situation where management wants to focus the attention of employees on other key success factors. For example, in a rapidly-expanding market, the most important issue may be revenue growth, even if there are no profits. Or, if a company has gone through a leveraged buyout, debt reduction (and therefore cash flow) may be the most important concern. Or, a niche strategy may mandate a high level of customer support. The central point in the selection of the unit of measure is that it provides a measure of progress toward the company's strategic objectives.
- *Team basis.* The traditional model favors bonuses for individuals. However, when longer-term goals are paramount, it requires the ongoing efforts of a large team to achieve above-average performance. Thus, it makes more sense to eliminate individual bonus plans in favor of group-based bonuses. Ideally, there should be one bonus plan, and it should include *every* person in the company. With one bonus plan, every employee has an incentive to help everyone else to optimize their performance. Conversely, if there were to be localized bonus plans, it is more likely that employees in different bonus plans would not assist each other, since they would have no economic reason for doing so. The worst situation is to only have individual bonuses for a small number of managers, since the rest of the company has no reason to work hard so that someone else can earn a large bonus.
- *Bonus calculation.* The calculation of a bonus can be a nefariously difficult and arcane formula under a traditional budget plan which sometimes results in no bonus at all, despite the best efforts of an employee, or an inordinately large bonus because the circumstances were just right. In a no-budget situation, it makes more sense to not establish a detailed compensation plan in advance. Instead, create a baseline for measurement (such as the perfor-

mance of competitors), and pay out an appropriate amount based on changes from that baseline. In general, this approach means limiting bonus payments to a certain percentage of profits or cash flow, so that the company is not crippled by inordinately large payments. Also, paying all bonuses from existing profits or cash flow means that compensation will always be supportable, since the company has already earned the money.

- *Nature of the bonus.* A company that wants to *really* focus the attention of its employees on long-term performance should consider *not* immediately paying out the bonuses that it grants to employees. A better alternative is to pay all or a portion of the bonus into a fund, which in turn invests at least some of the money in the company's shares. The fund then pays out both the accumulated bonuses and any earnings to employees when they retire. By taking this approach, a company is ensuring that employees have a significant interest in the performance of the company's stock, which in turn is driven by their ability to improve its earnings and cash flow over time.

- *Comprehensive evaluation.* A traditional bonus contract focuses on the achievement of very few targets – perhaps just profits – in order to trigger a bonus. This can lead to "gaming" to twist the system to achieve only the specified targets, perhaps to the long-term detriment of the business. A better approach is to establish a large group of performance factors that an evaluation committee can use to ascertain the improvement (or decline) of the business during the measurement period. Such a comprehensive system may start with profitability, but then go on to measure (for example) backlog, customer turnover, employee turnover, absentee levels, average accounts receivable outstanding, the debt level, and new product launches to obtain a more well-rounded view of how the organization has changed.

Compensation under this system should be based on *relative* improvement, rather than performance against a fixed target. This is a key concept, for it does not tie employees to a number or other metric that may be increasingly irrelevant over time. Thus, if there is a steep economic decline, it may still be quite reasonable to issue a bonus to the members of a profit center even if their profits dropped, because the profit decline was less than the median rate of decline for other parts of the company. Conversely, if the market is expanding rapidly, it may not make sense to issue bonuses to the members of a profit center that earned fewer profits than the median rate of profit increase for the company.

Analysis of the Ultimate Lean Budget

The ultimate lean budget is an environment where the budgeting concept has been replaced. Instead, we use a rolling forecast, requests for expenditures as needed, and continual improvement goals. This replacement system no longer requires managers to rigidly adhere to a predetermined target. Instead, they do the best they can, with a general improvement goal in mind. This considerably looser view of "budgeting" requires that local personnel take on much more responsibility for running the business, which can be a rude shock if a business has heretofore been run in an authoritarian, top-down manner.

From the perspective of the accounting department, the new approach is considerably more lean than the old budget model. No time is spent constructing or maintaining a budget, nor is there any variance analysis. However, the accounting team will likely be deeply involved in preparing and issuing a multitude of highly targeted reports. This type of reporting, known as *responsibility accounting*, mandates that employees be given complete information about the areas for which they are responsible. Thus, the janitorial services manager will receive detailed information about actual historical expenditures for every aspect of janitorial services. As a result, the accounting staff may find that its time has been redirected from budgeting to reporting.

Summary

In this chapter, we have presented a number of problems with the traditional budgeting system. If management still wants to cling to a budget, we have provided a number of improvement suggestions that are primarily designed to make the budget model simpler to work with and relatively free of errors. However, the truly lean approach to budgeting is to completely eliminate the concept. Instead, we suggest using a rolling forecast and performance metrics that are based on relative levels of improvement. This replacement system eliminates all of the pernicious effects that accompany a budget.

Even if the accounting management group is not convinced of the qualitative improvements that we have stated in this chapter, consider the situation from a quantitative perspective. There are fewer employees when there is no budget, since many of the corporate staff and mid-level managers who used to maintain the command and control environment are gone. Thus, the reduction in corporate overhead associated with budget elimination is a valid reason for trying this alternative approach.

For more information about budgeting models and the alternatives to budgeting, see the author's *Budgeting* book.

Chapter 14
Lean Filing

Introduction

Our final functional area may be unique to the accounting department – paperwork. Accountants can be overwhelmed with a massive amount of documentation, which brings up the issues of how to organize, reduce, and store it while still keeping key information close at hand.

In this chapter, we begin with an overview of improvement concepts, describe a typical filing environment, and then show the impact of improvement concepts on the filing of accounting paperwork.

Improvement Concepts

The application of lean concepts in this chapter involves the following improvements to existing systems:

- *Report purge.* Eliminating most month-end reports once the current fiscal year has been completed, to conserve storage space.
- *Copy elimination.* No longer printing an extra copy of accounting documents, to avoid the related storage requirements.
- *Folder creation policy.* Standardizing the point at which an additional folder is to be created.
- *Record presorting.* Presorting records before they are filed in order to reduce filing time.
- *Document destruction policy.* Using a standardized method for eliminating documents.
- *Off-site storage.* Shifting as many documents as possible to a lower cost off-site location.
- *Filing cabinet locations.* Moving filing cabinets so that they are adjacent to the work areas of those people most likely to use them.
- *Filing carts.* Issuing carts to those employees most likely to need continuing access to files, so they can keep the files near their work areas.
- *Longer archiving intervals.* Extending the on-site storage interval to keep people from having to travel to long-term storage.
- *Storage improvements.* Using a variety of storage techniques to arrive at a more organized long-term storage area in which research can be conducted more easily.
- *Document imaging.* Creating digital images of documents for easier data storage and retrieval.

- *Document consolidation and clarification.* Organizing records to match customer name changes, as well as adding folders to compensate for high volume.
- *Tickler file.* Using a tickler file to remind users when to take certain actions.
- *Mis-filing solutions.* Using coding and tracking systems to reduce the number of mis-filed documents.

The Traditional Filing Environment

Documentation does not usually receive a great deal of attention from the accounting staff. The level of filing organization is typically set at a level where it is not an active annoyance, but where the situation is hardly world class. We will expand upon the basic filing issues in this section.

The Filing Environment

The accounting profession appears to harbor a number of pack rats. These individuals do not like to throw out *any* documents, which means that the filing system is bursting at the seams. For example, a customer folder that should only contain invoice copies may also be burdened by copies of sales orders, bills of lading, comments received from customers, and collection notes. Similarly, every report printed is retained in a binder, rather than being thrown out. Examples of such reports are payroll registers, check registers, invoice registers, and fixed asset registers.

The accounting area is usually designed to have a cubicle farm in the center, with a few offices on the periphery. Document storage is usually a secondary consideration, so it is set up off to one side of the main accounting area, typically as a row of filing cabinets. If someone wants to access a file, they have to walk to the cabinets to retrieve the file, return to their desk to review it, and then bring the file back to the cabinet. Anyone doing extensive document research may build up an impressive number of miles of travel over the course of a year.

There is usually a step in the year-end closing procedure that requires the accounting staff to load many accounting documents (such as payroll registers, supplier invoices, and customer billings) into storage boxes. Though the accounting staff is usually concerned with the organization of incoming documents, it tends to be less so with the proper storage of outgoing documents. For example, several types of documents may be stored in a single box, with an inadequate summarization of its contents on the box label. Further, these items are frequently stored on a pallet, where the box labels are not necessarily pointing outward, and then stored on a distant shelf in the warehouse where they can only be accessed with a forklift.

Analysis of the Filing Environment

From the discussion of the typical filing environment, we can see that there are several areas of inefficiency, which are:

- *Volume of documents filed.* There are too many copies of the same document being filed, as well as a large number of documents that will probably never be accessed again.
- *Location of documents filed.* Those documents that are likely to be needed again for reference purposes are located too far away from the accounting staff to result in minimal travel times.
- *Recordation of documents filed.* Documents are not being properly recorded for easy retrieval, especially in regard to those items kept in long-term storage.

The Lean Filing Environment

There are a number of ways to improve on the bloated and disorganized filing system just described. In this section, we make suggestions that follow these themes:

- *Document reduction.* Many documents will never be referenced for research purposes, and there is no legal need to retain them. If so, they should either not be allowed into the storage area or pruned from it.
- *Document organization.* Organize documents prior to filing them, and also use a considered approach to creating additional folders in which to store documents.
- *Document locations.* Do not force the accounting staff to walk an excessive distance to access files. Instead, position storage as close to them as possible.
- *Document indexing.* Make it as easy as possible to locate files.

These themes are expanded upon through the remainder of this section.

Report Purge

There may be a variety of good research reasons to maintain many of the month-end accounting reports for the current year. These include the ending aged accounts receivable and aged accounts payable reports, as well as the general ledger detail and ending trial balance reports. However, there is much less need for this information once the fiscal year has ended.

A good filing opportunity is to purge all of the month-end reports once the fiscal year has been completed, but to keep the year-end reports. A company may be presenting its year-end information for several years to come, and so may need to keep these supporting year-end documents on hand, especially if there is to be an audit.

Copy Elimination

In a few businesses, it is still a common procedure to print multiple copies of some documents, such as customer invoices, and keep several versions for internal filing. For example, one copy may be filed by customer name, while another copy is filed by invoice number. Since all businesses of any size have accounting software that can bring up on-line versions of almost any document, there is little point in printing and filing a document version just so that someone can manually access the same information. Consequently, no additional document copy should ever be printed and stored.

Individual Folder Creation Policy

The general folder in a filing system can become stuffed with an excessive number of miscellaneous records. This can make it difficult to properly file records into this folder, as well as to locate records within it. To keep the amount of records in the general folder at a manageable level, adopt a policy that an individual folder will be created once a certain number of records have piled up in the general folder that relate to a correspondent. For example, once the number of invoices issued to A.B. Smith & Sons exceeds five records, extract the records from the general folder and move them into an individual folder.

To make this policy work, establish a periodic date (perhaps quarterly) when all general folders are examined to see if record totals have exceeded the established corporate policy. This practice is more likely to be followed if the date selected is not in the middle of some other major activity that will consume the attention of the staff, such as the annual audit.

Record Pre-Sorting

It can be quite helpful to pre-sort a stack of documents before filing. This may involve just sorting within a letter of the alphabet or by topic, without attempting to achieve a more perfect level of sorting between individual documents. By doing so, a person engaged in filing will be able to move in one direction through the filing system while filing records approximately in sequence. This is a substantial improvement over a situation in which records have not been pre-sorted, which requires a filer to move back and forth through the filing area to file each unsorted record. For example, unsorted records might require a person to first file a document in a filing cabinet that houses all letter M records, then file a document in the A filing cabinet, and then switch to the Y filing cabinet. If the records had been pre-sorted, the person could have filed all A documents first, then moved to the B filing cabinet, and so forth.

Document Destruction Policy

In some businesses, documents may be retained until there is no more storage room, after which the oldest documents are thrown out to make room for the most recent arrivals. Alternatively, all documents may be eliminated after a short time, on the grounds that minimal records make it more difficult to find evidence against the company in court (!). In reality, the only approach that works is to consult with the company's legal counsel regarding the mandated time period over which documents are to be retained, and to follow those time periods religiously.

The controller can take the lean approach to this issue by adhering to a document destruction policy. The goal of the department should be to eliminate only those documents allowed by the document destruction policy, but to do so as soon as permitted by the policy. Thus, there should be at least an annual, if not a quarterly, comparison of the document destruction timelines to the documents that are being maintained in long-term storage. As soon as anything is eligible for destruction, do so by the method mandated in the policy.

Realistically, this is a minor issue from a lean perspective, since the amount of storage space being opened up through document destruction is relatively minor. The key issue is the reverse – to keep from incurring a legal liability by destroying documents too soon.

Off-Site Storage

Office space is quite expensive to own or rent. If a controller insists on storing multiple years of documents on site, this represents a waste of expensive office space. A better alternative by far is to shift older documents into the least expensive space available, which usually means off-site storage space. The location should have adequate fire protection, but certainly does not need all of the expensive amenities found in an office.

> **Tip:** The proper location for off-site storage should represent a combination of low cost, document safety, and also a reasonable distance from the offices where the accounting staff is located. After all, there will still be situations where archived documents must be reviewed, so the off-site location should not be at an inordinate distance.

Filing Cabinet Locations

A typical filing scenario is for all accounting documents to be stored in a row of filing cabinets in one part of the accounting area. When documents are consolidated in this fashion, travel times to and from the cabinets are only optimized for those people working close to the cabinets. Those working at the other end of the department will find that they are spending an inordinate amount of time walking back and forth between document storage and their offices.

A better approach is to replace a single large storage area with a number of smaller locations that are situated in the center of the areas where they are most needed. For example:

- Move all current supplier files into the accounts payable area
- Move the billing and collections staffs close together and park the current customer files in the middle of this group

- Move current payroll files into the payroll manager's office, and ensure that the office door is locked, to provide extra security for the files

Filing Carts

Even if filing cabinets are moved close to those employees most likely to use them, the staff must still stand up and walk to the cabinets, which means that there is still travel time to be rooted out of the system.

A possible solution is to provide the heavier users of files with mobile office carts. They can then shift any documents they need from fixed storage locations into the carts, and roll the carts to where they are working. If employees switch to different workstations during the day, they can just move the carts along with them.

> **Tip:** The only issue with office carts is that they can clutter up the work area, so only buy them in a size that can be readily rolled underneath a work surface to get them out of the way.

Longer Archiving Intervals

The standard practice at the end of a fiscal year is to move all files from the preceding year into long-term storage and prepare a set of new folders in which to store information for the new year. For example, customer billing files and supplier invoice files are routinely moved off-site in this manner. The problem with this approach is that the outgoing files may contain documents that are only a few weeks or months old (e.g., from the end of the last fiscal year) and which the clerical staff will almost certainly need to reference over the next few months, as the inevitable research questions arise. There are two ways to deal with this issue:

- Keep files on hand for both the old and new fiscal years in the same filing cabinets, so that the files are available for both. Then, after the need for the older files diminishes (probably in about 90 days), move the older files to archival storage. This approach has the advantage of not taking up too much additional on-site storage space, and should be sufficient for most research issues.
- Retain information on-site for two years, rather than one year. Then extract the oldest year of records from the files and move them to archival storage. This approach requires twice the amount of on-site storage space, but has the advantage of being able to address essentially all research issues. Any visits to archival storage should be extremely rare, which makes it possible to move the off-site storage area further away to take advantage of lower-cost storage space.

Storage Improvements

The accounting staff usually does quite a good job of labeling the current files that are located on-site. However, this discipline typically breaks down when the files are moved to long-term storage. The accounting staff has a disturbing habit of throwing files into boxes, palletizing the boxes, and sticking them on a distant shelf in the warehouse – and probably under a sprinkler head. Instead, consider the following storage improvements:

- *Consistent contents.* Do not jumble documents into a storage box. Instead, ensure that material is consistently filed, such as putting all bank records in one or a set of boxes. This may require the use of additional boxes.
- *Detailed content labeling.* Carefully identify everything in a box and state the contents clearly on the outside of the box.
- *Accessible storage.* Reserve a storage room in which storage racks are set up at no more than head height, and with readily accessible tables on which storage boxes can be opened.
- *Labels face outward.* Store all boxes in the storage racks so that the labeled end of each box is facing outward, with no additional boxes hidden behind them.
- *Functional storage layout.* Cluster together storage boxes containing similar document types (such as all supplier records), and in alphabetical order within these clusters.

Tip: Be sure to segregate permanent files (such as legal documents and property title documents) from those files that will eventually be destroyed. Keep the permanent files in an entirely separate location, in fireproof and locked cabinets.

Though these steps certainly take more time to complete, and may require additional storage boxes and storage space, the result should be vastly less research time to locate documents that have been placed in long-term storage.

Document Imaging

There may be situations where a business must deal with massive amounts of paperwork, or where documents cannot be stored near the accounting staff, or where several clerks may need access to the same document at the same time. A document imaging system can resolve these problems.

Document imaging involves scanning documents as they arrive at the company, assigning an index number to the images, and storing them in a high-volume storage device. Some higher-end accounting systems can link to these images, so that anyone researching a transaction in the on-line accounting records also has immediate access to the scanned images. The source documents are then sent to long-term storage. With document imaging in place, there is no need for any document storage in higher-cost office space. Also, many people can access the same image at the same time on their computer terminals. Thus, document imaging can be an excellent technology solution to the old problem of dealing with too much paper.

However, there are a number of issues with document imaging that make it an effective solution only in certain situations. First, there needs to be a system in place for scanning documents, which will require additional clerical help. Alternatively, there are suppliers to which paperwork can be routed, who will digitize documents on the company's behalf. Also, if documents are not properly indexed in the imaging system, they can be quite difficult to find. And third, the cost of the system's software and hardware can be excessive for a smaller business.

Document imaging is least practical where the accounting staff is relatively small, and is already centrally located with the relevant accounting documents nearby. Conversely, it may be an excellent solution if there are many documents, the department is large, and there is an ongoing need to access a large number of accounting documents.

Document Consolidation and Clarification

On rare occasions, a supplier or customer will change its name. While cross-referencing can be used in the filing system to trace back to documents filed under the original name, an alternative is to move all records under the new name. This approach is most effective when there are relatively few documents under the original name; it will result in fewer multi-location searches. If this approach is used, it will be necessary to create a cross-reference that leads from the old name to the new name.

It is quite easy for the number of records to completely overwhelm a folder. When this is the case, documents can be damaged and it is more likely that documents will not be sorted correctly. Both issues can make it more difficult to access information. To eliminate these issues, prepare additional folders for the same correspondent, and label them in chronological order. For example, a plethora of records for customer A.B. Smith could result in the following set of four consecutive folders:

1. A.B. Smith – Jan.-Mar.
2. A.B. Smith – Apr.-Jun.
3. A.B. Smith – Jul.-Sep.
4. A.B. Smith – Oct.-Dec.

The Tickler File

A tickler file is a chronological sorting of information that is intended to reminder a user when to take certain actions. The layout of a tickler file is a set of folders numbered for each date in the current month, followed by 12 folders that represent all of the months in a year. At the start of each month, notes are inserted into the daily folders to remind users of actions to take during certain days. Once the month has been completed, all notes are cleared from the daily folders, and replaced by notes from the next month's folder.

While a tickler file might appear to be nothing more than a manual reminder system, it can also temporarily store records. For example, a business license renewal reminder could be kept in a tickler file, as a reminder to renew the license as of a certain date. Once the reminder item is completed, the related record is moved from the tickler file to the main storage area.

Mis-Filing Solutions

There are ways to minimize the amount of record mis-filings. Consider the following approaches:

- *Color coding*. Use a specific color for each letter of the alphabet on all tabs. For example, every folder beginning with the letter "A" has a blue color. With this color coding in place, it will be immediately apparent if an "A" folder is filed anywhere else in the storage system.
- *Numeric coding*. When numbers are assigned to records instead of names or subjects, it is easier to find the records when they have been mis-filed, since it will be obvious when they are out of sequence.
- *Missing record tracking system*. Whenever a record goes missing, mark it down in a log, and routinely examine the log for patterns. It is quite possible that a procedure is not being followed, or errors can be traced back to a specific individual, in which case additional training can be used to minimize the ongoing rate of mis-filings.

There are also several techniques for locating missing records, which can be combined into a general search routine. They are:

1. *Look around the folder*. This means looking between the folders on either side of the correct folder, as well as underneath the folder. In the latter case, a record might have been inserted between two folders, and then slid underneath.
2. *Look within the folder*. Open the correct folder and search all the way through it, on the assumption that the record was not inserted in the correct chronological order.
3. *Look in the general folder*. If the person filing the record did not see an individual folder, the next logical place to file the record would be in the general folder for the relevant alphabet letter.
4. *Look for name transpositions*. A two-part name might have been filed under a transposed name. For example, the name of Quincy Jones might have been filed under Jones Quincy.
5. *Look under alternate indexing units*. The record might have been filed based on its second or third (or later) indexing unit, so look in those areas.
6. *Ask*. After the preceding approaches have been used, put out a general request to see if anyone has the record in their work area. If so, there needs to be a discussion about the proper usage of OUT indicators (see the Record Storage Supplies section).

Practices to Avoid

There are a few cases where a certain business practice runs counter to the operation of a lean accounting department. In the area of filing, we have identified the following practices that fall into this category:

- *Index numbers on archived boxes.* If a business has a large number of boxes in long-term storage, do not be tempted to identify each one solely with an index number that has no meaning. To locate a document, a person has to look up the contents of the box in the index record, and *then* locate the box. The trouble is that the index may be lost, located in a locked room or drawer, or require an extra walk to obtain. In short, it is usually better to just write the contents on the side of a storage box.
- *Document pruning prior to long-term storage.* It may be tempting to examine each file just before sending it to long-term storage, and prune out redundant or otherwise unnecessary documents. This is not necessary, since the cost of long-term storage is usually very inexpensive, and saving a few boxes and the cost of a few extra square feet of storage is not worthwhile. Furthermore, there is a risk of inadvertently throwing away key documents. Instead, just transfer all designated files to long-term storage in bulk.

Analysis of the Lean Filing Environment

The ultimate lean filing environment involves document imaging, since records are permanently available to anyone who has access to a computer. However, it is an expensive option, so a mix of the other recommendations in this section can be used to arrive at a suitably lean filing operation that is not so technologically advanced. In particular, we find that moving filing cabinets to employee locations is one of the better lean options, since it nearly eliminates employee travel times. Consider using the other suggestions if they are cost-effective.

Summary

We have noted several key issues in this chapter that can be used to create a lean filing environment. Of the greatest importance is questioning whether there should be *any* printed documents. In many computerized environments, it should be possible to keep the bulk of all documents on-line. Once this issue has been used to reduce the number of documents, the next point to consider is how to store the most necessary documents as close to the accounting staff as possible. The result is likely to be a highly dispersed storage system, instead of a single, monolithic storage area. Finally, all remaining documents that are only being retained for legal reasons should be expertly identified and tracked, so that they can be disposed of as soon as legally possible. By following these three steps, a controller can achieve a truly lean filing environment.

Chapter 15
Lean Controls and Procedures

Introduction

The preceding chapters of this book have focused on the extent to which an accounting department can streamline its operations, resulting in a much more efficient organization. However, these improvements can only be conducted in the context of the system of controls and documenting procedures that pervade the department. In this chapter, we describe the controls concept and how one can balance a number of factors to arrive at a set of controls that mitigate risk while avoiding an excessive level of inefficiency. We also discuss when procedures are needed, and when they can be skipped.

The Genesis of Accounting Controls

From the perspective of an overburdened management team, accounting controls are simply a form of bureaucracy that interferes with their running of the business; and in a small start-up firm, they may have a point. During the start-up phase, a company is so small that nearly all business transactions are visible to the owners, who may be able to maintain a reasonable degree of control simply because they are deeply involved in every aspect of the business. Adding any type of formal control system at this point is expensive in comparison to the relatively small number of business transactions being processed, so the owners are not thrilled about what they perceive to be a waste of time and money.

However, this situation changes when a company brings in a few employees, since the owners are no longer able to keep direct tabs on operations. At this point, controls are typically added wherever errors arise in the accounting systems. Thus, an inadvertent double payment of an invoice to a supplier will then trigger a set of controls to mitigate the risk of double payments. This is a reactive approach to accounting controls, since the owners are still primarily interested in expanding the business, not in adding "bureaucracy." In short, accounting controls in this stage of a company's life cycle are typically a hodgepodge of controls that were installed in reaction to prior problems.

If a business matures sufficiently, it will encounter an event that will trigger a review of its entire system of controls, probably resulting in an overhaul of the entire system. Examples of those events are:

- *Hire senior accounting management.* The company hires a controller or chief financial officer who has an auditing background, and who therefore has an interest in control systems.
- *Engage auditors.* The company is required by an investor or lender to have its financial statements audited, and the auditors generate a considerable

amount of advice regarding the inadequacy of the company's control systems.

- *Go public.* If the owners want to take the company public, it must have a strong system of controls, and an annual audit, *and* an audit committee – all of which result in a deep, multi-layered system of controls.

Thus, the system of controls tends to begin with a scattering of controls that were created in response to specific problems, and then becomes more structured over time as a business grows.

The Proper Balance of Control Systems

A person who has been trained in control systems will likely want to install every possible control, and will then feel satisfied that he or she has saved the company from an impending failure. Those on the receiving end of these controls have a different opinion of the situation, which is that controls slow down transactions, require more staff, and have the same general effect on a business as pouring sand into the gas tank of a car.

Because of these radically differing views of the utility of control systems, it is useful to adopt a set of controls that are based on the following points:

- *Risk – monetary.* If a control can prevent a large loss, such as one that could bankrupt a business, it makes sense to install the control, as long as the probability of the event is reasonably high. For example, having two people involved in every wire transfer transaction is a reasonable precaution, given the amount of funds that could be transferred out in a single wire transfer. Conversely, if a control can never save more than a few dollars (such as locking the office supply cabinet), it is entirely likely that the sheer annoyance caused by the control greatly outweighs any possible savings to be achieved from it.

- *Risk – financial statements.* A business must understand its performance, and it can only do so with reliable financial statements. Consequently, controls over recordkeeping should be among the most comprehensive in the company. However, this does not necessarily call for an oppressive amount of controls in those areas where the amounts involved are essentially immaterial to the financial statements.

- *Repetitiveness.* Only install comprehensive controls for those transactions that a business will engage in on a recurring basis. For example, if a company sells equipment to a foreign customer once a year, and wants to hedge the outstanding receivable, a once-a-year transaction does not require an elaborate control system (unless the receivable is for a large amount – see the preceding point about risk). Thus, it behooves a business to concentrate on a finely-tuned set of controls for the 20% of its processes that make up 80% of its business (the Pareto Principle). Of the remaining 80% of the company's processes, those items involving the most inherent risk should be the prime candidates for strong controls.

- *Offsetting controls.* It may be acceptable to have weak controls in one part of a business, as long as there are offsetting controls elsewhere. For example, it may not be necessary to have someone sign checks, as long as all purchases are initiated with an authorizing purchase order. This concept can be used to great effect if there is a good business reason to keep one business process running as smoothly as possible (i.e., without controls), with offsetting controls in a less noticeable part of the business.
- *Cost.* The cost of controls must be balanced against the expected reduction in risk. This is not a simple calculation to make, for it can be quite difficult to estimate the reduction of risk that will be achieved by implementing a control. One approach to quantifying risk is to multiply the risk percentage by the exposure to the business, which is known as the *expected loss*. See the following example.

Conversely, it is easy enough to measure the labor cost and other factors required to implement and maintain a control, so there is a tendency for businesses to focus on the up-front cost of a control and downplay the savings that may or may not arise from having the control. The result tends to be a control level that is lower than it should be.

EXAMPLE

High Noon Armaments operates a payroll system that pays employees on a semi-monthly basis. When there are a significant number of data errors in the payroll, High Noon's payroll manager requires that the payroll be run again, at a cost of $5,000.

The payroll manager is considering the installation of an automated data validation software package that is expected to reduce the payroll data error rate from 8% to 1%, at a software rental cost of $250 per payroll. The cost–benefit analysis is:

- *No data validation.* There is an 8% chance of incurring a $5,000 payroll reprocessing cost, which is an expected loss of $400 ($5,000 exposure × 8% risk) per payroll.
- *Data validation.* There is a 1% chance of incurring a $5,000 payroll reprocessing cost, which is an expected loss of $50 ($5,000 exposure × 1% risk) per payroll. There is also a charge of $250 per payroll for the software rental cost.

Thus, there is a reduction of $350 in the expected loss if the control is implemented, against which there is a control cost of $250. This results in a net gain of $100 per payroll by using the control. Changes in the estimated probabilities can have a significant impact on the outcome of this analysis.

The resulting system should be one where some failures will still occur, but either in such small amounts that they do not place the business at risk, or where the probability of occurrence is very low. It is difficult to maintain this balance between controls and operational effectiveness over time, seeing that a growing business is constantly in a state of flux, expanding some lines of business, curtailing others, and installing any number of new systems. It is the job of the accountant to watch the interaction of these processes with existing control systems, and know when it is an acceptable risk to pare back some controls, while introducing new ones elsewhere.

It is quite common to see a control system that lags behind the current state of its processes, usually due to inattention by the accounting staff. This means that some controls are so antiquated as to be essentially meaningless (while still annoying employees), while new systems are devoid of controls, and will only see new ones when a system failure occurs.

In summary, there is a balance between the system of controls and the efficient operation of a business that is difficult to manage. A good accountant will understand the needs of employees to keep operations efficient, and so should be willing to subsist in some areas on control systems that may appear rather skimpy, as long as the tradeoff is between a great improvement in efficiency and the risk of only modest losses that would have been prevented by controls.

The Nature of Risk

In the last section, we made reference to risk. What is risk, and how does it relate to controls? Risk is the probability that events will vary from expectations. Examples of risk are:

- That competitors will alter the business environment
- That new technology will alter the business environment
- That new legislation will alter the business environment
- That a product failure will lead to a product recall
- That a customer will enter bankruptcy
- That a key raw material will increase in price

Of these sample risks, the first three are caused by external factors and the last three by internal factors. Controls can be used to mitigate internal risks. For example, if there is a risk of product failure, controls can be designed to test the quality of components as they enter the production process, and of finished goods before they are shipped to customers. Similarly, the risk that a customer will enter bankruptcy can be mitigated to some extent by the imposition of strong credit controls.

No matter how thoroughly controls are integrated into an organization, it is impossible to use them to completely eliminate risk. Instead, there will always be some residual amount of risk that a business must accept. There is usually a tradeoff between imposing a really oppressive system of controls on a business in exchange for a lowered risk level, or a lighter system of controls that makes the business easier to manage, but at the cost of accepting a higher level of risk.

Common Fraud Risk Factors

There are a number of factors that make it more likely that fraud will occur or is occurring in a business. These fraud risk factors include:

Nature of Items

- *Size and value.* If items that can be stolen are of high value in proportion to their size (such as diamonds), it is less risky to remove them from the premises. This a particularly critical item if it is easy for employees to do so.
- *Ease of resale.* If there is a ready market for the resale of stolen goods (such as for most types of consumer electronics), this presents an increased temptation to engage in fraud.
- *Cash.* If there is a large amount of bills and coins on hand, or cash in bank accounts, there is a higher risk of fraud. At a local level, a large balance in a petty cash box presents a major temptation.

Nature of Control Environment

- *Separation of duties.* The risk of fraud declines dramatically if multiple employees are involved in different phases of a transaction, since fraud requires the collusion of at least two people. Thus, poorly-defined job descriptions and approval processes present a clear opportunity for fraud.
- *Safeguards.* When assets are physically protected, they are much less likely to be stolen. This can involve fencing around the inventory storage area, a locked bin for maintenance supplies and tools, security guard stations, an employee badge system, and similar solutions.
- *Documentation.* When there is no physical or electronic record of a transaction, employees can be reasonably assured of not being caught, and so are more inclined to engage in fraud. This is also the case if there is documentation, but the records can be easily modified.
- *Time off.* When a business requires its employees to take the full amount of allocated time off, this keeps them from continuing to hide ongoing cases of fraud, and so is a natural deterrent.
- *Related party transactions.* When there are numerous transactions with related parties, it is more likely that purchases and sales will be made at amounts that differ considerably from the market rate.
- *Complexity.* When the nature of a company's business involves very complex transactions, and especially ones involving estimates, it is easier for employees to manipulate the results of these transactions to report better results than is really the case.
- *Dominance.* When a single individual is in a position to dominate the decisions of the management team, and especially when the board of directors is weak, this individual is more likely to engage in unsuitable behavior.
- *Turnover.* When there is a high level of turnover among the management team and among employees in general, the institutional memory regarding

how transactions are processed is weakened, resulting in less attention to controls.

- *Auditing*. When there is no internal audit function, it is unlikely that incorrect or inappropriate transactions will be spotted or corrected.

Pressures

- *Level of dissatisfaction*. If the work force is unhappy with the company, they will be more inclined to engage in fraud. Examples of such situations are when a layoff is imminent, benefits have been reduced, bonuses have been eliminated, promotions have been voided, and so forth.
- *Expectations*. When there is pressure from outside investors to report certain financial results, or by management to meet certain performance targets (perhaps to earn bonuses), or to meet balance sheet goals to qualify for debt financing, there is a high risk of financial reporting fraud.
- *Guarantees*. When the owners or members of management have guaranteed company debt, there will be strong pressure to report certain financial results in order to avoid triggering the guarantees.

The presence of fraud risk factors may incline a company to implement a more comprehensive set of accounting controls, to guard against the possibility of fraud.

Control Principles

There are a number of principles to keep in mind when constructing a system of controls for a business. These principles are frequently the difference between a robust control system and one that appears adequate on paper, but which never seems to work in practice. The principles are:

- *Separation of duties*. The separation of duties involves assigning different parts of a process to different people, so that collusion would be required for someone to commit fraud. For example, one person opens the mail and records a list of the checks received, while a different person records them in the accounting system and a third person deposits the checks. By separating these tasks, it is much more difficult for someone to (for example) remove a check from the incoming mail, record a receivables credit in the accounting system to cover his tracks, and cash the check into his own account. Unfortunately, there is a major downside to the separation of duties, which is that shifting tasks among multiple people interferes with the efficiency of a process. Consequently, only use this control principle at the minimum level needed to establish the desired level of control – too much of it is not cost-effective.
- *Process integration*. Controls should be so thoroughly intertwined with business transactions that it is impossible for employees *not* to perform them as part of their daily activities. This level of integration substantially reduces the incidence of errors and the risk of fraud. An example of proper process

integration with a control is running all produced items past a fixed bar code scanning station on a conveyor belt, to ensure that all completed goods are recorded. The information is collected without the staff having to do anything. An example of minimal process integration that will likely result in frequent control problems is requiring employees to record this information by hand on a paper form.

- *Management support*. The management team must make it abundantly clear to employees that it thoroughly supports the system of controls. This does not mean that a general statement of ethics is included in the employee manual. Instead, it means that management takes the time to explain controls to employees, is highly visible in investigating control breaches, and takes sufficient remedial action to make it clear to the entire staff that controls are to be taken seriously. Management also does not override its own controls, nor does it set performance standards that are so difficult to attain that employees would be forced to circumvent controls in order to meet the standards.

- *Responsibility*. No control system will work unless people are made responsible for them. This means that someone should be assigned responsibility for every control, and that they receive regular updates on the status of those controls. It would also be useful if the status of their controls are noted in their compensation reviews, and have a direct impact on changes in their pay.

- *Conscientious application*. Employees cannot simply treat controls in a perfunctory manner. Instead, there should be a culture that encourages the close examination of control breaches to determine what went wrong, and how the system can be adjusted to reduce the risk that the same issue will occur again. This level of conscientious behavior must be encouraged by the management team through constant reinforcement of the message that the system of controls is important. It also requires the availability of communication channels through which employees can anonymously report suspected improprieties.

- *Systems knowledge*. It is impossible to expect employees to conscientiously inspect controls unless they already know how systems operate. This calls for the ongoing training of employees to ensure that they thoroughly understand all aspects of the systems with which they are involved. This requires not only an initial training session for new employees, but also reminder sessions that are timed to coincide with any changes in processes and related controls, as well as thorough documentation of the systems. A good level of systems knowledge may call for the use of procedures, training materials, and a core group of trainers.

- *Error reporting*. It is impossible to know if a control is functioning properly unless there is a system in place for reporting control breaches. This may be a report generated by a computer system, but it may also call for open communications channels with employees, customers, and suppliers to solicit any errors that have been found. In this latter case, error reporting is strongly supported by a management group that is clearly interested in spotting errors and correcting them in a way that does not cast blame on those reporting the information. In addition, errors should be communicated all the way up through the organization to the audit committee and board of directors, who can enforce the establishment of enhanced controls.

- *Staffing.* There must be an adequate number of employees on hand to operate controls. Otherwise, there will be great pressure to avoid manual controls, since they take too much time to complete. This is actually a profitability issue, since a business experiencing losses is more likely to cut back on staffing, which in turn impacts the control system.

- *Outlier analysis.* Most businesses create control systems to deal with problems they have seen in the past, or which have been experienced elsewhere in the industry. They rarely create controls designed to mitigate outlier issues – that is, problems that occur very infrequently. The sign of a great control system is one in which employees take the time to examine the control system from a high level, and in light of the current and future business environment, to see if there are any outlier events that present a risk of loss in sufficiently large amounts to warrant the addition of controls. This outlier analysis requires excellent knowledge of the industry and a perceptive view of the direction in which it is headed.

Of the principles just noted, management support is the most crucial. Without it, a system of controls is like a building with no supporting framework – the entire structure crashes to the ground if there is any pressure placed upon it at all. For example, the control system may appear to have proper separation of duties, but this makes no difference if the management team ignores these separations for transactions that it has an interest in ramming through the system.

The Failings of Internal Controls

A well-constructed system of internal controls can certainly be of assistance to a business, but controls suffer from several conceptual failings. They are:

- *Assured profitability.* No control system on the planet can assure a business of earning a profit. Controls may be able to detect or even avoid some losses, but if a business is inherently unprofitable, there is nothing that a control system can do to repair the situation. Profitability is, to a large extent, based on product quality, marketplace positioning, price points, and other factors that are not related to control systems.

- *Fair financial reporting.* A good control system can go a long ways toward the production of financial statements that fairly present the financial results and position of a business, but this is by no means guaranteed. There will always be outlier or low probability events that will evade the best control system, or there may be employees who conspire to evade the control system.

- *Judgment basis.* Manual controls rely upon the judgment of the people operating them. If a person engages in a control activity and makes the wrong judgment call (such as a bad decision to extend credit to a customer), then the control may have functioned but the outcome was still a failure. Thus, controls can fail if the judgment of the people operating them is poor.
- *Determined fraudulent behavior.* Controls are typically designed to catch fraudulent behavior by an individual who is acting alone. They are much less effective when the management team itself overrides controls, or when several employees collude to engage in fraud. In these cases, it is quite possible to skirt completely around the control system.

Thus, the owners, managers, and employees of a business should view its controls not as an absolute failsafe that will protect the business, but rather as something designed to *increase the likelihood* that operational goals will be achieved, its financial reports can be relied upon, and that it is complying with the relevant laws and regulations.

Special Case - Acquisitions

A particularly burdensome area from the perspective of controls is the acquisition. The controller of the acquiring company is usually responsible for determining the entire system of controls and underlying control principles at the acquired entity, and ensuring that the control environment is brought up to the standards of the acquiring entity as quickly as possible. There are a number of factors to consider in this situation:

- *Outside assistance.* The acquiring entity's accounting staff is fully occupied with integrating the operations of the two businesses, and certainly does not have time to spare for a review of controls. Accordingly, the controller should hire consultants to review the acquiree's control systems and recommend changes. This review should begin as part of the due diligence review prior to the acquisition, and continues through the subsequent integration process.
- *Principles review.* The fundamental principles outlined earlier in the Control Principles section still apply. This means that the acquiree's control system must be reviewed for separation of duties, process integration, management support, responsibility for controls, systems knowledge, and so on. A particular concern is that the acquirer might want to cut costs by reducing headcount at the acquiree, which may impact the principle that there must be adequate staffing to operate the system of controls.
- *Impact of change.* When there are large changes in an organization, as typically happens in an acquiree immediately following an acquisition, there can be equally major morale issues which usually have a negative impact on the system of controls. The controller should be aware of this problem, and

expect that there will be more control breaches in the near term as a result of it.

In addition to these concerns, the controller must consider whether a standardized set of controls should be installed throughout all company locations, or if variations will be allowed. If acquisitions are infrequent and the acquirees have business models differing from that of the acquirer, it may be easier to allow local variations on the basic system of control. However, if the parent company is buying a large number of similar businesses, it may make more sense to allow minimal variation, and instead impose the same basic control structure everywhere. The level of standardization has an impact on the variability of procedure documentation and training throughout the enterprise.

Special Case – Employee Turnover

A high level of employee turnover presents a particular problem for the control environment, for controls knowledge weakens with the departure of each successive group of employees. Eventually, employees no longer understand the full breadth of business systems, nor why controls are used. Instead, they are only aware of the particular controls for which they are responsible, and which they were instructed in as part of their abbreviated training. This problem is particularly pernicious when systems and controls are poorly documented, and when those with the most seniority (and presumed knowledge of operations) are the first to leave.

The likely result of a continuing series of employee departures is a gradual decline in the use of manual controls. Also, since employees do not know why controls are being used, they are less likely to be conscientious in pursuing any control breaches found. In addition, business processes will change over time, while controls will no longer change with them. The overall result is a control system that may appear on the surface to be reliable, but which in fact can no longer be relied upon.

The best way to resolve the control problems engendered by high employee turnover is to reduce the turnover. This may involve increased pay rates, improved benefits, less oppressive working conditions, and so forth. Though there is a cost associated with these improvements, they will hopefully be offset by the cost reductions that will occur as the control environment is strengthened.

Special Case – Rapid Growth

When a business grows at a high rate of speed, it encounters the same problems found with a high rate of employee turnover. The problem is that the knowledge of business processes and control systems is centered on the core group of original employees, and must be passed along rapidly to an ever-expanding group of employees. The risk in this situation is that controls knowledge will be so ephemeral among newer employees that a system of controls operated by new employees will be substantially less effective than the same system operated by longer-term employees.

The reduced effectiveness of a control system in this environment can be mitigated through the following actions:

- *System replication.* When there is a high rate of growth, there is no way to accommodate local variations on the basic control system, since each one must be separately documented. Instead, management must settle upon one control system, and replicate it throughout the business in a rigid manner. Such a system is much easier to replicate as the business continues to grow.
- *Written procedures.* When there are too many new employees to be properly trained in person, the fallback approach is to construct written procedures that are as thorough as possible. New employees can use these materials to learn more about controls, and they can also be used as training materials.
- *Training.* It is critically important to have a formal training program in a fast growth environment, since new employees can be rotated through it quickly, and they can all be taught exactly the same material. This allows for a considerable amount of uniformity, which is useful for replicating the same control system throughout a company.
- *Employee dispersion.* No matter how well new employees may be trained, they do not yet fully understand why the control system has been constructed in its present form. To lend credence to the current system, it may be necessary to disperse the original group of employees among the various company locations, where they can provide newer employees with a historical perspective on the system.

Even the recommendations noted here may not be sufficient. If it becomes apparent that the incidence of control breaches is increasing over time, it may be necessary to slow the rate of company growth until the experience level of the employees has increased sufficiently to operate systems in a competent manner. Thus, the level of control difficulties may determine the pace of further expansion.

Terminating Controls

Controls tend to slow down the flow of transactions within a business and result in extra costs, and so should only be used when there is a clear need for them. In addition, controls should only be retained for as long as the processes with which they are associated are unchanged. If a process is altered, the linked controls may no longer be needed, but are still retained because no one thought to remove them. The result is likely to be an excessive number of controls and a lower level of process efficiency than should be the case.

To avoid a burdensome number of controls, it is useful to periodically examine the current system of controls and see if any should be removed. This can be done in the following ways:

- *Review at process change.* Whenever there is a change to a process, incorporate into the process flow analysis a review of all controls built into the process. Doing so may point out that specific controls can be eliminated, or replaced by other controls that are more cost-effective.
- *Review on scheduled date.* Even if there have been no process changes, conduct a comprehensive controls review on a scheduled date, such as once a year. This review may pick up on minor process changes that have been implemented but not formally noted. This approach also allows for consideration of new, more technologically-advanced controls that were not available in previous years.

> **Tip:** Never review a control in isolation from the other controls in a process, since the entire set of controls may provide backup coverage for each other. Deleting one control may weaken a control issue elsewhere in the business process.

No matter which approach is used, it may also make sense to bring in a controls specialist to review existing systems and recommend which controls can be terminated. By doing so, the company gains the benefit of someone who has seen a broad range of controls in many other companies, and who therefore has more experience upon which to base recommendations for changes. The report of this consultant can also be used as justification for changes to the system of controls.

If controls are to be terminated, be sure to discuss the changes thoroughly with the controller and chief financial officer, as well as the company's audit committee. These people may feel that a control should be retained, despite the dictates of efficiency, in order to provide some additional risk reduction. In addition, the termination of controls should be brought to the attention of the company's auditors, who may need to alter their audit procedures to account for the missing controls.

The termination of a control should not be a special event. Instead, it is an ongoing part of the alterations that a company makes as it changes its business processes to meet the demands of the market.

The Nature of a Procedure

A procedure documents a business transaction. As such, it lists the specific steps required to complete a transaction, and is very useful for enforcing a high degree of uniformity in how those steps are completed. A procedure frequently incorporates one or more controls, which are designed to mitigate the risk of various types of losses. In some cases, an entire procedure is intended to *be* a control. Procedures may also be used to instruct new employees in how a company does business. Thus, a procedure has three purposes:

- To encourage uniformity in the completion of business transactions
- To enforce the use of controls
- To train employees

From the perspective of the management team, the first purpose (uniformity) is the most important, since it leads to greater efficiency. However, an auditor or risk manager may be more concerned with the second purpose (control), since they have a great interest in mitigating any number of risks to which a business is subjected. Further, the human resources staff has a great interest in the third purpose (training), since it is involved in training new employees. Thus, there are multiple constituencies within a business that have a major interest in the construction and maintenance of a set of procedures.

We will expand upon the nature of the procedure in the next section, where we address the specific issues that procedures can remedy.

The Need for Procedures

Procedures are needed to ensure that a company is capable of completing its objectives. For example, the primary purpose of a consumer products company is to place reliable and well-constructed products in the hands of its customers. In order to sell goods to those customers, it must be able to complete the following tasks consistently, time after time:

- Log in a customer order
- Pick the goods from stock
- Assemble them into a complete order that is ready for shipment by the promised date
- Reliably issue an accurate invoice to the customer

> **Related Podcast Episode:** Episode 174 of the Accounting Best Practices Podcast discusses undocumented processes. The episode is available at: **accounting-tools.com/podcasts** or **iTunes**

A procedure is needed to give structure to these activities. For example, one procedure could instruct the order entry staff regarding how to record order information from a customer into a sales order (which is used to process an order within a company), which errors may arise and how to deal with them, and where to send copies of the sales order.

It is certainly possible for very experienced employees to handle these tasks without a formal procedure, because they have been with the company long enough to have learned how to deal with most situations through experience. However, such an approach relies upon the verbal transfer of information to more junior employees, which is an unreliable approach that gradually leads to the use of many variations on a single procedure.

Imagine a situation where there are no formal procedures in a company that operates multiple retail stores. Each store develops its own methods for handling business transactions. Each one will have different control problems, different forms, different levels of efficiency, and different types of errors. Someone trying to review the operations of all the stores would be overwhelmed by the cacophony of different methods.

This example shows that procedures are of great value in providing structure to a business – they define how a business *does* things. In more detail, we need procedures because:

- *Best practices.* When a business routinely examines its operations with the intent of creating procedures, the documentation process often brings to light questionable or inefficient practices. If brought to the attention of management, there may be an opportunity to use best practices to upgrade the company's processes to a more efficient and effective level.
- *Efficiency.* It is much easier for the accounting staff to process business transactions and issue financial statements when there is a regimented approach to dealing with each type of transaction.
- *Errors.* It takes far more time to correct any transaction error than it takes to complete the transaction correctly the first time. Therefore, error avoidance is an excellent reason to use procedures.
- *Computer systems.* An accounting or enterprise-wide system typically works in conjunction with a set of procedures. If there is not a consistent set of procedures surrounding the system, employees may have difficulty entering information, and may not know the sequence of events needed to process transactions through the system.
- *Controls.* When it becomes evident that there is a control weakness in a company, the system of procedures can be adjusted to correct the problem.
- *Handoffs.* Many processes involve handing off work to someone in a different department. Any handoff involves a risk that work will not be transferred correctly, resulting in a transaction lapse that may ultimately impact a customer. A procedure states exactly how a handoff is to be completed, and so reduces the risk of a transaction lapse.
- *Governance.* In a business that has a top-down organizational structure, procedures are needed to ensure that the decisions made by management are carried out properly.
- *Roll out consistency.* It is vastly easier to roll out a business concept when every location uses exactly the same set of procedures.
- *Training.* Procedures can form the basis for employee training manuals that address the basic functions of a business.

The sheer volume of reasons presented here should make it clear that there is a resounding need for procedures. However, we do not need a set of procedures for *everything*, as discussed in the next section.

The Number of Procedures to Develop

Even a smaller business may have a large number of processes. How many of them really need to be documented in a formal procedure? If a business documents all of them, it may find that it has spent an inordinate amount of time and money on some procedures that are rarely used, and which must now be updated from time to time. To keep from making an excessive expenditure on procedure development, consider the following factors when deciding whether to create a procedure:

- *Auditor concern.* If the auditors have indicated that there are control problems in a particular area, it will be necessary to develop a procedure that incorporates any controls that they recommend. Otherwise, the issue will have an impact on the auditors' control assessment of the business, which may require them to employ additional audit procedures that increase the price of their audit. In short, an auditor finding essentially mandates the creation of a procedure.
- *Risk.* If there is no procedure, is there a risk that the company will suffer a monetary or reputational loss? If this loss is significant, a procedure is probably called for, even if the procedure will be rarely used. Conversely, a procedure may not be necessary if there is little underlying risk associated with it.
- *Transaction efficiency.* There may be multiple ways in which a business transaction can be completed, of which one is clearly more efficient. If so, create a procedure that directs employees to use the most efficient variation. If there is only one way to complete a transaction, there is less need for a procedure.
- *Transaction volume.* As a general rule, there should be a procedure for the 20% of all transactions that comprise 80% of the total transaction volume in which a business engages. These procedures cover most of the day-to-day activities of a business, and so can be of assistance in defining the jobs of new employees, as well as for ensuring that the most fundamental activities are followed in a prescribed manner.

The last point, transaction volume, is a key determinant of the need for a procedure. There are many low-volume activities where it simply makes no sense to engage in any documentation activities at all. Instead, allow employees to follow their best judgment in deciding how to complete a lesser activity.

Summary

There can be an enormous amount of risk associated with certain accounting transactions, while in other cases the risk of loss is insignificant. A critical judgment for the accountant is to discern the level of these risks, and install controls and procedures only where needed. When there is some uncertainty about whether to apply an additional control or procedure, it is best to adopt a conservative posture and implement the item, unless the amount of associated risk is quite low. By taking this approach, the accountant errs on the side of risk reduction, rather than creating a more lean system that is essentially designed to accept a higher level of risk.

Glossary

A

Account. A separate, detailed accounting record associated with a specific asset, liability, equity, revenue, expense, gain, or loss item.

Account reconciliation. The investigation and verification of the items stored in an account, sometimes based on information contained in a similar account maintained by a third party.

Accounting period. The span of time covered by a set of financial statements. For internal financial reporting, an accounting period is generally considered to be one month.

Accounts receivable aging report. A report that lists unpaid customer invoices and unused credit memos by date ranges. This report is the primary tool used by collections personnel to determine which invoices are overdue for payment.

ACH debit. A bank transaction that allows the payee to initiate a debit of the payer's bank account, with the funds shifting into the payee's bank account.

Activity-based costing. A cost allocation system that compiles costs and assigns them to activities based on relevant activity drivers. The cost of these activities is then charged to cost objects based on their usage of the activities. The intent is to arrive at a relevant allocation of costs.

Adjusting entry. A journal entry that is used at the end of an accounting period to adjust the balances in various general ledger accounts to meet the requirements of accounting standards.

Allocation base. The basis upon which an entity allocates overhead costs. It takes the form of a quantity, such as machine hours used, kilowatt hours consumed, or square footage occupied.

Asset class. Assets of a similar nature and use that are grouped together. Examples of asset classes are land, buildings, machinery, furniture and fixtures, and office equipment.

B

Backflushing. The automatic reduction of inventory levels based on the amount of goods that have been produced.

Bad debt. An invoice not paid by a customer, and therefore written off.

Bank reconciliation. A comparison between the cash position recorded on an entity's books and the position noted on the records of its bank, usually resulting in some changes to the book balance to account for transactions that are recorded on the bank's records but not the entity's, such as bank fees and interest income.

Base unit. The unit of measure used to measure a fixed asset. It is essentially the corporate definition of what constitutes a fixed asset.

Bill of materials. The record of the standard amount of materials used to construct a product. It can include raw materials, sub-assemblies, and supplies.

Block budget. A budget in which funds are allocated to an entire department or other functional area, and managers are given authority to expend the funds as they see fit.

Budget. A set of interlinking plans that quantitatively describe an entity's projected future operations. It is used as a yardstick against which to measure actual operating results, for the allocation of funding, and as a plan for future operations.

C

Capital budgeting. A series of steps followed to justify the decision to purchase an asset, usually including an analysis of the costs, related benefits, and impact on capacity levels of the prospective purchase.

Capitalization limit. The amount paid for an asset, above which an entity records it as a fixed asset. If the entity pays less than the capitalization limit for an asset, it charges the asset to expense in the period incurred.

Chart of accounts. A listing of all accounts used in the general ledger, usually sorted in order of account number. The account numbering system is used by accounting software to aggregate information into an entity's financial statements.

Commission. A fee paid to a salesperson in exchange for his or her services in facilitating or completing a sale transaction. The commission may be structured as a flat fee, or as a percentage of the revenue, gross margin, or profit generated by a sale.

Constraint. A process or factor that prevents a system from attaining a higher level of output.

Cost pool. A grouping of individual costs, typically by department or service center. Cost allocations are then made from the cost pool.

Credit application. A standard form sent to customers, on which they enter information needed by a company's credit department to determine the amount of credit to grant customers.

Credit insurance. A guarantee by a third party against non-payment of an invoice by a customer.

Credit memo. A contraction of the term "credit memorandum," which is a document issued by the seller of goods or services to the buyer, reducing the amount that the buyer owes to the seller under the terms of an earlier invoice.

Customer purchase order. A document that a customer may submit to the receiving company, in which it authorizes the purchase of specific items or services.

Cycle counting. The process of counting a small proportion of total inventory on a daily basis. A key aspect of cycle counting is to investigate and correct the reasons for any errors found, rather than merely adjusting the inventory records when an error is found.

D

Deduction. An amount that an employer withholds from the earnings of an employee. Examples of deductions are for payments into a pension plan, or for the employee-paid share of medical insurance, or for child support garnishments.

Depreciation. The gradual charging to expense of a fixed asset's cost over its expected useful life.

Derecognition. The process of removing a transaction from the accounting records of an entity. For a fixed asset, this is the removal of the asset and any accumulated depreciation from the accounting records, as well as the recognition of any associated gain or loss.

Direct cost. A cost that can be clearly associated with specific activities or products.

Drop shipping. The practice of having suppliers ship directly to a company's customers, bypassing the company itself.

E

Earnings per share. A company's net income divided by the weighted-average number of shares outstanding. This calculation is subject to a number of additional factors involving preferred shares, convertible instruments, and dividends.

Evaluated receipts. A system of paying suppliers based on a combination of goods or services received and the authorizing purchase order. There is no need for a supplier invoice.

Expense report. A form completed by an employee, with attached receipts, stating the expenses that he or she paid on behalf of the company. A business uses this report as the basis for reimbursement payments to employees.

F

Financial statements. A collection of reports about an organization's financial condition, which typically include the income statement, balance sheet, and statement of cash flows.

Finished goods inventory. Goods that have been completed by the manufacturing process, or purchased in a completed form, but which have not yet been sold to customers.

Fiscal year. The twelve-month period over which an entity reports on the activities that appear in its annual financial statements.

Fixed asset. An expenditure that generates economic benefits over a long period of time. It is also known as property, plant, and equipment.

G

General ledger. The master set of accounts that summarize all transactions occurring within an entity.

I

Income tax. A government tax on the taxable profit earned by an individual or corporation.

Invoice. A document submitted to a customer, identifying a transaction for which the customer owes payment to the issuer.

J

Job costing. The accumulation of the cost of materials, labor, and overhead for a specific job.

Journal entry. A formal accounting entry used to record a business transaction. The entry itemizes accounts that are debited and credited, and should include some description of the reason for the entry.

K

Kanban. A physical or electronic notification that authorizes the production and delivery of a specific component.

L

Labor routing. The record of the standard amount of labor used to construct a product.

Letter of credit. A document issued by a bank, guaranteeing that a scheduled payment from a buyer will be received by the seller in the correct amount and on the designated date. If the buyer cannot pay, the bank will do so.

Line item budgeting. A budget in which there is a budgeted amount for every line item in the chart of accounts.

Lockbox. A mail box operated by a bank, to which the customers of a company send their payments. The bank deposits all payments received into the company's bank account, and posts scanned images of all payments on a secure website, which the company can access.

M

Magnetic ink character recognition. A character recognition technology using toner with iron oxide to print the bank routing number and account number on a check. The characters are read by automated scanning equipment to process check payments.

Mail float. The time required for a payment to travel from the payer to the payee through the postal system.

Master purchase order. An agreement between a company and its supplier, under which the company commits to a certain purchase quantity within a designated period of time, usually in exchange for reduced pricing.

N

Negative approval. An approval technique where authorizers only notify the accounts payable department if they do not approve of the payment of a supplier invoice.

Not sufficient funds check. A check issued for which there are not sufficient funds in the issuer's bank account.

P

Payroll cycle. The length of time between payrolls. Thus, if an employer pays employees once a month, the payroll cycle is one month.

Payroll register. A summarization of the payments made to each employee in a payroll, including gross pay, deductions, and net pay.

Periodic inventory system. An inventory system under which the ending inventory balance is only updated with a physical inventory count.

Perpetual inventory system. The continual updating of an entity's inventory records to account for additions to or subtractions from stock, caused by such activities as raw material purchases and product sales.

Physical inventory count. The formal process of counting a large block of inventory items, usually involving a shut-down of the storage area for the duration of the count.

Positive pay. An anti-fraud measure whereby a company issuing checks notifies its bank of all checks it has issued. The bank then compares this information to checks being presented for payment, and refuses to accept any checks for which it has not received prior notification from the company.

Procurement card. A credit card used to make small-dollar purchases for a business.

Purchase order. A document authorizing the purchase of goods from a supplier.

R

Raw materials inventory. The total cost of all component parts currently in stock that have not yet been used in work-in-process or finished goods production.

Receipt. A document used as evidence of an expenditure. Examples of receipts are hotel bills and air travel invoices.

Remittance advice. An attachment to a check payment, detailing the contents of the payment.

Remote deposit capture. The use of a scanning device to create a legal, scanned image of both sides of a check, which is then uploaded to a bank as a valid deposit.

Return merchandise authorization. An authorization granted by a seller for a buyer to return goods to it.

Rolling forecast. A forecast of key revenue, expense, and cash flow information that is updated frequently.

S

Salary. A fixed amount paid to an employee for services performed, irrespective of the actual hours worked during a time period.

Sales order. An internal document used to specify the details of a customer order. It may be derived from a customer purchase order or some less-formal type of communication.

Sales tax. A tax imposed by the government of a city, county, or state on the retail price of a product or service.

Salvage value. The estimated amount that would be currently obtained upon the disposal of a fixed asset at the end of its estimated useful life.

Shipping log. A summary of shipments issued by the shipping department, usually organized by day.

Skip tracing. The process of locating the address at which a person or business can be found.

Step cost. A cost that does not change steadily, but rather at discrete points. It is fixed within certain boundaries, outside of which it will change.

Straight-line depreciation. The recognition of depreciation expense evenly over the estimated useful life of an asset.

Stop payment. A designation placed on a check by the issuing bank, so that it will not be accepted if presented for payment.

T

Target costing. The process of designing a product to meet a predetermined price point, product margin, and feature set.

Three-way matching. The comparison of a supplier invoice and related purchase order and receiving document by the accounts payable staff prior to payment.

Throughput. Revenues minus all totally variable expenses.

Timecard. A standard form on which an employee records time worked, or on which a time clock stamps an individual's start and stop times.

U

Useful life. The estimated lifespan of a depreciable fixed asset, during which it can be expected to contribute to company operations.

Glossary

W

Wage. An amount paid to an employee that is based on time worked or units produced.

Withholding. The portion of an employee's wages that an employer holds back and then forwards to the government as payment for the taxes owed by the employee.

Work-in-process inventory. Inventory that has been partially converted through the production process, but for which additional work must be completed before it can be recorded as finished goods inventory.

Work order. An internal document that authorizes the construction of a product or provision of a service.

Index